LEADING SELF-DIRECTED WORK TEAMS

LEADING SELF-DIRECTED WORK TEAMS

A Guide to Developing New Team Leadership Skills

REVISED and EXPANDED

KIMBALL FISHER

Cofounder of The Fisher Group, Inc.

McGraw-Hill

New York   San Francisco   Washington, D.C.   Auckland   Bogotá
Caracas   Lisbon   London   Madrid   Mexico City   Milan
Montreal   New Delhi   San Juan   Singapore
Sidney   Tokyo   Toronto

Mcgraw-Hill

A Division of The **McGraw·Hill** Companies

Copyright © 2000 by Kimball Fisher. All rights reserved. Printed in the United States of America. Except as permitted under the United States Copyright Act of 1976, no part of this publication may be reproduced or distributed in any form or by any means, or stored in a data base or retrieval system, without the prior written permission of the publisher.

1 2 3 4 5 6 7 8 9 0   DOC/DOC   9 0 9 8 7 6 5 4 3 2 1 0 9

ISBN 0-07-134924-3

The sponsoring editor this book was Richard Narramore, the editing supervisor was Stephanie S. Landis, the editing liaison was Patricia V. Amoroso, and the production supervisor was Elizabeth J. Strange. It was set in Janson Text by North Market Street Graphics.

Printed and bound by R. R. Donnelley & Sons Company.

 This book is printed on recycled, acid-free paper containing a minimum of 50% recycled de-inked fiber.

McGraw-Hill books are available at special quantity discounts to use as premiums and sales promotions, or for use in corporate training programs. For more information, please write to the Director of Special Sales, McGraw-Hill, 11 West 19th Street, New York, NY 10011. Or contact your local bookstore.

I rededicate this book to Reenie,
My wife, my colleague, and my best friend

"Don't mourn what you aren't, celebrate what you are."
—Mareen Fisher

Contents

Foreword xxi

Acknowledgments xxiii

Introduction xxvii

PART I

A NEW KIND OF LEADER FOR A NEW KIND OF BUSINESS ENVIRONMENT

Chapter 1: Bosses Who Don't Boss 3

Empowerment Is the Second Industrial Revolution 4

SDWTs Pose a Challenge to Traditional Management 4

P&G Declares SDWTs a Trade Secret 5

Jack's Problem 6

The Changing Workplace 6

Team Leaders Don't Supervise 7

All Traditional Managers Are Supervisors 8

Operations, Management, and Culture Team Leaders 8

Summary 9

Chapter 2: Self-Directed Work Teams:
   What Are They and Where Did They
   Come From? 11

Why Are Organizations Changing? 13

How Are Organizations Changing? 13

People Are the Competitive Advantage 14

Defining Empowerment 15

Defining Self-Directed Work Teams   16
SDWT Watchouts   18
SDWTs Outperform Traditional Operations   19
The Origin of Self-Directed Work Teams   20
   Scientific Management: Strengths and Weaknesses   20
   Socio-Technical Systems   21
   From Manufacturing to Service and Public School SDWTs   22
Summary   22

Chapter 3: Team Empowerment: Passing Fad or the Future of Work Design? 25

SDWTs Have Been Here for Decades   25
SDWTs Work   26
When SDWTs Don't Work   26
SDWTs and Business Results   27
Examples of Company Results   28
Research Verifies Improved Results   30
SDWTs Are the Probable Future   35
Summary   36

Chapter 4: The Classic Supervisor Is an Endangered Species 39

The Supervisory Role Is Evolving   40
Why Empowerment Practices Will Continue   41
An Idea Whose Time Has Come   41
   Different Business Environments Require Different
      Organizations   42
   Time-to-Market Pressures   43
   Reduce Design Time   44
   Cost Drivers   44
   Learning from Success   45
   Reduced Defense Spending   45
   New Social Complexity   46
   Changing Workforce Expectations   46
   Adapting to Change   47
Technology to Support Empowerment   47
   Team Decision-Making and Problem-Solving Technologies   48
   Team Information Systems   48

Information Gathering 50

Information Is Power 51

Technological Substitutions for Hierarchy 51

Technology Helps but Is Not the Whole Answer 52

Worker Participation Is Inevitable **53**

The World of Democratic Reform 53

Democratic Reform in the Workplace 54

Summary **55**

Chapter 5: A Rocky Road: The Transition from Supervisor to Team Leader 57

Typical Transition Problems **59**

**It Is Difficult for Supervisors at Every Management
Level to Become Team Leaders** **61**

**Changing to SDWTs Is Harder for Team Leaders
than Team Members** **61**

Four Reasons the Transition Is So Difficult **62**

Dealing with the Perceived Loss of Power or Status **63**

Position Status 64

Dysfunctional Status Symbols 64

Unclear Roles Cause Unnecessary Transition Difficulties **64**

The Wingwalker Problem 65

Job Security Concerns Frustrate Supervisory Change **66**

Every Team Needs a Coach 66

What Happens When There Are Too Many Supervisors? 67

The Double Standard **68**

Successful Team Leader Transition at Kodak **69**

Summary **70**

PART II

BUILDING THE FOUNDATION FOR CHANGE

Chapter 6: The Kodak 13 Room Story: Empowering Team Leaders 73

Background **74**

Management Practices Reflected the Military Background
of the Supervisors 75

An Environment of Trust Is Created 76

The Change Process Begins with Education   **76**

Operators Become Interested in the Study Group   76

The Supervisor Group Is Empowered to Make
Unitwide Decisions   77

The Organization Is Structured into SDWTs   78

Team Meetings and Training Are Critical   78

13 Room Is Declared a Business   78

Results   **79**

Summary   **79**

Chapter 7: Overcoming Common Transition Difficulties: Four Learnings from the 13 Room   81

Create an Expanded Role for Team Leaders   **82**

Avoiding the Wingwalker Problem   82

Using Symbols to Reinforce the Changing Team Leader
Responsibilities   83

Develop a Self-Directed Management Team   **83**

Applying SDWT Principles to Team Leaders   83

The Importance of Example and Feedback   84

Manage by Shared Vision and Principles   **84**

Develop Capability   **85**

Building Team Leader Capability   85

Building Team Member Capability   86

Training   86

The Importance of Ongoing Learning   86

Summary   **87**

PART III

THE POWER OF VALUES AND ASSUMPTIONS

Chapter 8: The Visible and Invisible Elements of Team Leadership   91

Problems with Focusing Only on Actions   **92**

Situational Leadership Does Not Help Much Either   **92**

The Role Is More than a Style of Managing   **93**

A Model for Discussing the Things You Cannot See   93

Summary   95

Chapter 9: Theory X Assumptions and Control Paradigm Thinking: You Can't Get There from Here   97

Our Thinking Affects Our Behavior   98

The Invisible Team Leadership Elements in Action   99

Demonstrated Values Are More Important
than Stated Values   100

Theory X and Theory Y Revisited   101

Theory X in Action   102

We Get What We Expect   102

Theory X Assumptions Can Be Anywhere
in the Organization   103

How Theory X Assumptions Become
Self-Fulfilling Prophecies   103

Try Some Different Assumptions On for Size   104

Work Paradigms   104

Paradigm Paralysis   105

People Who Don't Have the SDWT Paradigm Don't
Understand SDWTs   105

Control and Commitment Management Paradigms   106

The Pervasive Influence of the Control Paradigm   107

The Language and Structure of Control   108

Results Versus Control   109

SDWTs Require the Commitment Paradigm   110

Summary   111

PART IV

THE ROLE OF THE TEAM LEADER

Chapter 10: The Supervisor Versus the Team Leader: Sheep Herders and Shepherds   115

Sheep Herding Versus Shepherding Management   117

Sheep Herders Drive Subordinate Flocks   118

Shepherds Lead and Develop   118

Problems with Sheep Herding   118

Shepherds Live in Traditional Organizations Too   119

Summary   120

Chapter 11: The Role of the Team Leader   121

Team Leader "Job Description"   122

The Boundary Manager   123

SDWTs Are Open Systems   124

SDWTs Manage Inside the Boundary   126

Team Leaders Manage the Boundary   126

Boundary Management Is a Nontraditional Role   127

Supervisors "Taste the Sausage"   127

Supervisors Work *In* the System, Team Leaders Work
On the System   129

Organization Design   129

Infrastructure Building   130

Substitutes for Hierarchy   131

Cross-Organization Collaboration   131

Seven Competencies of Boundary Managers   131

Summary   135

Chapter 12: Essential Competencies for Team Leaders: Leader, Results Catalyst, and Facilitator   137

Acting Like a Leader   138

Leaders as Change Agents   138

Vision: Gotta Have One   138

How Have Leaders Influenced You?   140

Nested Vision   141

Shared Vision   141

A Joint Visioning Process Example   142

The Results Catalyst   144

Managing by Principle Rather than by Policy   144

Break Some Rules   145

Using Operating Guidelines   146

Facilitating Skills 146

How Do You Facilitate? 147

Training 148

Career Development 149

Summary 149

Chapter 13: The Barrier Buster, Business Analyzer, Coach, and Living Example 151

Eliminating Barriers to High Performance 152

Quality of Work Life Concerns 152

Eliminate Unnecessary Policies 152

Analyzing Business 153

Empowerment Without Business Information Is a Sham 154

We Need Better Knowledge Management Systems 155

What Kind of Information Do SDWTs Need? 155

Institutionalized Methods for Joint Business Analysis 156

Customer Advocacy 157

Team Leaders Develop Customer Empathy 158

Misusing Customer Advocacy 158

Coaching Teams 159

Socratic Coaching 160

High Expectations 161

Performance Appraisals Are a Lousy Way to Coach 161

Being a Living Example 161

Team Leaders Aren't Above the Law 162

Summary 163

Chapter 14: The Myth of the Marshmallow Manager 165

Team Leaders Are Neither Permissive Nor Passive 166

Marshmallow Managers 167

Why Team Leadership Sometimes Looks Passive 167

The Role Can Look Confusing to Outsiders 168

Team Leaders Aren't Marshmallows 168

Setting Boundary Conditions   169

Good Boundary Conditions Clarify   170

The Natural Consequences of Being Unresponsive
   to Boundary Conditions   171

Summary   171

Chapter 15: The Five Stages
of Implementing Empowerment   173

The Cycle of SDWT Maturity   174

The Five Stages of SDWT Implementation   176

Challenges During the Five Stages   177

Stage One: Investigation Challenges
   (Challenge = Understanding It)   177

Stage Two: Preparation Challenges
   (Challenge = Accepting It)   178

Stage Three: Implementation Challenges
   (Challenge = Making It Work)   179

Stage Four: Transition Challenges
   (Challenge = Keeping At It)   180

Stage Five: Maturation Challenges
   (Challenge = Keeping It Continuously Improving)   181

Leadership Tasks During the Maturation Process   181

Summary   182

Chapter 16: Leadership Roles During
the Early Stages of Team Maturity   183

Investigation Roles   184

Create Bridges to Span the Chasm Between Old
   and New Cultures   185

Demonstrate Support for the Change   186

Create a Common Vocabulary to Facilitate
   Communication and Learning   186

Couple Team Design to Business Changes   187

Preparation Roles   188

Create a Common Vision to Facilitate Change   188

Share Business Information and Line Up Resources   189

Make Technology and Operating Principle Changes   190

Implementation Roles   **190**

Begin Appropriate Training and Development   191

Summary   **191**

Chapter 17: Leadership Roles During the Later Stages of Team Maturity   193

Transition Roles   **194**

Managing Skepticism   194

Protecting the New Team   194

Maturation Roles   **196**

Facilitating Continuous Improvement   197

Summary   **198**

PART IV

THE TEAM LEADER WORKOUT

Chapter 18: Three Days in the Life of a Team Leader   201

Summary   **213**

Chapter 19: A Weekly Activity Guide for Team Leaders   215

Short Runs   **216**

Communication Skills   216

Communication Topics   217

Team Meetings   **217**

Meetings as a Substitute for Hierarchy   218

Longer Runs   **220**

The Speed Workout   **222**

Running the Marathon   **222**

Summary   **224**

PART V

COMMON PROBLEMS
AND UNCOMMON SOLUTIONS

Chapter 20: When Team Members Resist
the Change to a Self-Directed
Work Team   227
Change Model   **228**
Clarity   **229**
Using Simulations to Clarify the New Role   230
Explain the New Team Member Competencies   230
SDWT Role Descriptions Differ Significantly
from Traditional Job Descriptions   232
SDWT Members Make Up Their Own "To Do" Lists   232
Felt Need   **233**
People Will Not Change Until They Feel They
Need to Change   234
Present a Case for Change   234
Support   **235**
Make Employment (Not Job) Assurances   235
Pay and Other Reinforcements Need to Be in Sync
with SDWTs   236
Organization Structures Need to Be Aligned with SDWTs   236
Financial Reports, Training, and Other Tools Need
to Be Consistent   237
Self-Awareness   **238**
Peer Feedback   238
Summary   **239**

Chapter 21: Helping Supervisors Become
Team Leaders   241
Change Model Affects Team Leaders   **242**
Clarity   **243**
Involve Supervisors in Defining the Team Leader Role   243
Not Involving Supervisors Creates a Self-Fulfilling Prophecy 244
Supervisors Need to See How Team Leaders Act   244
Felt Need   **245**
Different Supervisors Require Different Approaches   246
Trailblazers, Pilots, and Intellectuals   247
Late Bloomers and Traditionalists   247

Support 247

Get Rewards and Recognition Systems in Sync with the
New Role 248

Peer Networks Provide a Different Kind of Support 249

Use Empowerment Schedules to Provide Transition Help 249

Self-Awareness 250

Self-Aware Team Leaders Admit Mistakes Openly 251

Summary 252

Chapter 22: Managing Upward: When You Don't Have the Support of Senior Management 253

Orderly Top-Down Change Is More Fiction than Fact 254

SDWTs Start with Champions in the Middle
of the Operation 254

Change Influencers Versus Change Drivers 255

How Do Change Influencers Act? 255

Vision, Opportunity, and Tenacity 256

Change Influencers Are Politically Astute 257

Case Study 257

Vision 258

Opportunity 258

Tenacity 258

What If the New Boss Is Unsupportive of SDWTs? 259

Being Results Oriented Versus Control Oriented 259

Dare Greatly 260

Working with Resistance from the Senior Levels 261

Commit to the Success of the Leader 261

Make the Deal to Share Feedback 262

No Surprises 262

Make Heroes 263

Summary 263

Chapter 23: Creating Accountability Systems for Teams 265

If Everyone Is Responsible, Then No One Is Responsible 266

Social Loafing 266

Accountability Systems Shouldn't Be Used to Punish   **267**

Accountability Systems   **268**

Task Accountability   268

A Task Accountability System in a Consulting Firm   268

Results Accountability   270

The Star Point System   270

A Star Point System at Cummins Engine   271

Goals and Measures Are Essential   **272**

Summary   **272**

Chapter 24: When the Problem Is the Organization: Redesigning for Teams   273

Why Redesign?   **274**

Organization Redesign   **275**

Redesign Methods   **276**

The STS Redesign Approach   277

The Conference Method   278

The Hybrid Method   279

The Learning Lattice Organization   **280**

Summary   **283**

Chapter 25: Overcoming the Special Challenges of Leading Knowledge Workers   285

Shifting from Physical to Mental Labor   **286**

The Industrial Legacy   **287**

Different Work Requires Different Forms of Organization   287

Knowledge Work in Factories   288

Responsibilities for Knowledge Management   **289**

Knowledge Transfer   290

Knowledge Management at Andersen Consulting   290

Low-Tech Solutions   291

Learning in Public   **293**

Summary   **293**

Chapter 26: Leading Virtual Teams:
How to Work with Teams
That Are Geographically Dispersed   295

Characteristics of Virtual Teams   296
Virtual Teams on the Rise   297
Common Challenges for Virtual Teams   298
    Multiplexing Problems   298
    Working with Home-Office–Based Team Members   298
Use Operating Guidelines   299
Use Goals   301
Virtual Collocation   301
Virtual Team Start-Ups   302
Summary   303

PART VI

TEAM LEADER EVALUATION TOOLS

Chapter 27: The Team Leader Litmus
Test: Do I Fit as a Team Leader?   307

Chapter 28: Assessing Team Leader
Effectiveness Sampler   313

Chapter 29: The Team Leader Survival
Guide   317

Things to Remember   317
Things to Do   319
Summary   321

Endnotes   323
Index   333

Foreword

EMPOWERMENT AND TEAMS have taken the world by storm. Managers have found that remaining competitive means tapping into the vast, underutilized resource of knowledge within their workforces. Furthermore, customer responsiveness requires greater integration across functional groups. Cross-functional teams have thus become commonplace as organizations strive for reduced product-to-market times and continuous improvement throughout the value chain. But making teams function effectively has remained an elusive dream for many organizations.

Modern business culture, to a great extent built on individualism and a diversity of interests, runs counter to teams. Teamwork requires pulling a group of diverse individuals together to work toward a common goal. Some managers take the term self-management literally and expect teamwork to happen somehow by magic. But teamwork does not just emerge. It requires strong leadership throughout the entire organization.

Managers at several new plant start-ups believed they could run their operations without supervisors or first-level managers, only to find they needed to add back that level of management as their operations failed to perform. A manager at one plant where first-level supervisors were eliminated noted that things ran fairly smoothly four out of five days a week but that the plant could really use supervision on that fifth day. However, the manager was afraid to reinstitute a leadership role because he did not know how to keep team leaders from reverting back to acting as traditional supervisors.

For years, organizational consultants have used the terms *coach*, *trainer, facilitator,* and *resource* to describe the leadership role. *Coach* and *trainer* are at least fairly familiar words, but *facilitator* and *resource* often sound like terms from another world. They are ambiguous. Worse yet, the role evolves as teams mature. Making sense out of this new environment is far from easy. Much confusion still exists as to what the role of team leadership is all about.

Kimball Fisher helps to elevate us out of the jargon with real-world examples and tips to make the transition. He has seen what works and what doesn't from firsthand observation—both as a team leader in a successful self-directed team operation and as a consultant helping organizations transform themselves from traditional to empowered work systems. He is thus able to provide a roadmap showing how organizations can create an environment that promotes the development of team leaders.

But as Kimball rightly stresses, it is insufficient to merely develop leaders at the first level of management. Leadership must occur at every level of the organization, including the top executive suite. And as difficult as the task of changing to team leadership may seem at the first level of management, at the middle management and executive levels it is even harder. Fortunately, Kimball provides a vision for how to make the journey.

Janice Klein
Gloucester, MA

Jan Klein has taught operations management at the Harvard Business School and MIT's Sloan School of Management. Over the past decade, she has been studying the changing role of managers and supervisors in organizations.

Acknowledgments

N<small>O AUTHOR CREATES</small> something utterly original. Even the most "innovative" management writers I know often simply repackage the thinking of others or add an unusual insight or snappy vocabulary to an established body of knowledge. This book, in particular, is clearly an example of a collaborative effort rather than being an exclusive product of my own creation. In even the most original parts of this book, for example, I write some reflections on my own experience that I came to understand better only with the help of other team leaders, workers, consultants, teachers, artists, and cab drivers. In other parts of the book I am even more indebted to a rich intellectual and experiential heritage, which I catalog in those chapters.

This book has also clearly been influenced by conversations with some of the great thinkers in this field, including Jan Klein, Pam Posey, Cal Pava, Alan Wilkins, Jack Sherwood, Marv Weisbord, Fred and Merrilyn Emery, Lou Davis, Bill Dyer, and Gene Dalton. I hope a little bit of those scholars who have passed on since our discussions lives on in this work. The writings of these pragmatic philosophers, along with those of Eric Trist, Richard Walton, William Westley, Dave Hanna, Ed Lawler, Len Schlesinger, and Albert Cherns, underpin much of my thinking, although any possible misinterpretation of their work contained herein is solely my responsibility.

I actually started writing this book in 1983, when I was working as an internal consultant at the Procter & Gamble soap plant in Chicago. At that time I distributed a short white paper to selected P&G managers partly to communicate some ideas that I thought might be helpful to the people transitioning from supervisory to team leader roles. But I mainly wrote the paper to create an excuse to force myself to write down some of the things I had learned while working in the innovative Lima plant. Bits and pieces of what would later grow into this book have been surfacing ever since.

Parts of Chapters 1, 5, 17, 18, and 19, for example, appeared in The University of Michigan's *Human Resource Management* journal under the title "Management Roles in the Implementation of Participative Management Systems." Sections of what later became Chapters 5, 8, 10 and 11 were modified from an article in *Organizational Dynamics* entitled "Managing in the High-Commitment Workplace."

The case study on Kodak appeared originally as a chapter titled "Creating a High-Performance Management Team: Eastman Kodak's 13 Room" in *The Manager as Trainer, Coach and Leader.* This is one of a series of excellent books published by the Work in America Institute on the topic. Edited excerpts from the original appear as Chapters 6 and 7, with some bits from the original in Chapters 1 and 2 as well. Although I am listed as a coauthor of this case, my authorship was more of a courtesy than a reality. Steve Rayner and I worked on the research and interviews together and we formulated the primary learnings and basic message of the case as a team. But credit for the writing of this excellent piece belongs solely to Steve. I have used large excerpts from the original with Steve's permission.

Parts of Chapter 24 come from "Vision, opportunity and tenacity: Three informal processes that influence formal transformation," which was coauthored with Steve Rayner and Bill Belgard. Chapters 12, 21, and 22 and part of Chapter 5 also were originally commissioned by the Work in American Institute, though they have never been published before. Parts of Chapters 26, 27, and 28 were adapted from *The Distributed Mind: Achieving High Performance Through the Collective Intelligence of Knowledge Work Teams,* which was coauthored with Mareen Duncan Fisher.

I would like to thank those mentioned above for permitting me to include these materials in the book. Thanks also to the folks at The Fisher Group, Inc. for allowing me to reproduce copyrighted models and tools. Pieces of the book are also excerpted from a Fisher Group training program called *Leadership Skills* and are used by permission. They add significantly to this revision of *Leading Self-Directed Work Teams.*

I would especially like to thank those who helped with specific feed-back about the book and my thinking. Marv Weisbord gave me needed encouragement and suggestions on craftsmanship. Jan Klein and I discussed several iterations of the book and she helped to improve the flow and strengthen the message considerably. Special thanks to Alan Wilkins and Pam Posey for their endurance, caring, and tenacity. Alan gave me numerous helpful critiques and showed me how to buttress some weaknesses in logic that appeared in earlier drafts. Pam read the book 3 times and sent me more than 40 pages of detailed notes ranging from recommendations on voice and grammar to constructive criticism on fundamental themes and postulates. Steven Rayner and William Belgard offered important insights and suggestions on much of the earlier version of the book. Thanks too to Stephanie Ford and Kelly Cziep at the Fisher Group for their work and suggestions on the revision.

In particular I would like to express appreciation to Mareen Fisher, my dear wife and business partner, to whom I rededicate this book. During the years that I have been learning about the role of the team leader, she has been my personal confidante, coach, and consultant. And this book has her touch on every page. She displayed both the patience required to offer continuous suggestions for improvement and the compassion not to make fun of my two-finger typing method on the Macintosh, which allowed me to progress on this manuscript with the blinding speed of a Northwest garden slug. She has made this a better book and me a better team leader.

K.K.F.

Introduction

The State of the Art of Team Leadership: What We've Learned Since the First Edition

This is a different way of life, it is not a quick fix. There is no program or formula. We have been working for 12 years and we're still working on it. We thought it was like a jigsaw puzzle and someday we would find the last piece, but there is no last piece.

—Ross Silberstein, *former vice president of Sherwin-Williams Company*

WHEN MCGRAW-HILL INVITED me to do an updated and expanded version of *Leading Self-Directed Work Teams*, I was both flattered and a little disturbed. Flattered because the book has been received well enough by business readers to justify this special edition, but disturbed to think that the book already needed updating. After all, self-directed work teams (SDWTs) have been around for decades and the values underpinning these organizations are at least as old as the world's first democracies.

It has only been six years since the publication of the first edition, and it doesn't seem right that significant change can occur in that seemingly short period of time. But in the business world, six years is a lifetime. Whole new technologies have been born and buried since the book was first published, companies have risen to prominence and slipped back into obscurity, and products in many industries have already been through two or three life cycles. I think it makes sense to review what we have learned during this period.

How Have Teams Changed Since the First Edition?

There are a number of things that have changed. For example, in the last few years numerous studies have finally vindicated the effectiveness of the team concept. For both good and ill, self-directed work teams have become *much* more common than they were when the book was first published. (People now tend to favor terms such as *high-performance work systems*, a change I applaud for reasons to be reviewed in detail throughout the book.) What once was an aberration is more often the norm. The business leader who never uses teams is rare. Not that self-directed work teams have suddenly emerged as the dominant organization structure; they haven't. And I believe there are still places where they aren't the most appropriate choice. But there has been dynamic growth in the application of teams. This is good news for those who are serious about empowering leadership. What we once observed primarily in the factories of progressive companies is now commonly applied in a wide variety of businesses, schools, hospitals, and governments. With this wider application of these ideas has come a variety of important learnings.

What We Have Learned About Leading Teams

Here are five things we have learned since the wider application of teams:

I. Teams Are Here to Stay

While it is true that numerous organizations have scuttled their attempts to use self-directed work teams, the vast majority of operations that have implemented the system continue to use and improve it. Logan Aluminum, for example, continues to upgrade and improve its high-performance system rather than abandon it for a traditional operation that is much easier to manage. Procter & Gamble has expanded the Lima facility from the 200-person operation that existed when I worked there as a production manager nearly 20 years ago to an 800-person operation at the time of this writing—all while several other P&G plants were downsizing. Weyerhaeuser corporation spent the last three years training general managers, human resources managers, and union officers to create high-performance work systems out of traditional organizations. When the Mayo Clinic wanted to improve its already world-class medical service, it implemented self-directed work teams of doctors. Insurance companies, financial service organizations, oil refineries, special operations in the U.S. military, middle schools, prisons, e-commerce operations, and hundreds of other organizations now use self-directed work teams. Why? Because these teams normally outperform the alternative. As one Weyerhaeuser executive noted, that company's high-performance work systems consistently display "dramatic improvement in safety, product quality, and productivity compared with our facilities without such systems."

2. SDWTs Need to Be Implemented Properly to Be Successful

We have clearly learned that there are right ways and wrong ways to implement teams. The wrong ways include attempts to empower ill-prepared employees to do management work they don't know how to do. No matter how well intended, empowerment without support such as training or good information systems is doomed to fail. And teams need a certain amount of infrastructure to survive. Creating a team-based operation that still maintains an individual-focused pay system, for example, is a waste of time and money. Similarly, claiming that you want to create self-directed work teams while maintaining the management-dominated governance systems of traditional operations is worse than poor implementation technique: it is self-defeating hypocrisy. High-performance work teams will eventually succumb to traditional work policies and practices that are left unchanged in the organizational host.

As mentioned in the quote that opens this Introduction, a high-performance work system is a new culture, not a quick fix. In the last few years several good companies have made bad mistakes, assuming that implementation only required retitling their work groups "teams" while maintaining the core work paradigms of a traditional work system. Simply naming a traditional organization a self-directed work team does no more to make it one than calling a pig an eagle enables the pig to fly.

3. People on Teams Must Be Accountable for Organizational Improvements

Organizations that have created self-directed work teams as some type of paternalistic social experiment in industrial democracy have almost always been disappointed in the business results. Teams are a means to an end and not an end in themselves. Most successful operations even shy away from the title *self-directed*, favoring terms that emphasize the purpose of the teams (to get good results) rather than the process used to obtain the results. For example, although Sun Microsystems (you may know them as the people who put the dot in .com) doesn't currently use high-performance work systems for day-to-day natural work groups, high-performance work systems are employed for special project teams where people spend the bulk of their time. Sun has found that these teams have to be commissioned properly. Anyone can start a special project team, but they must find a champion (a management sponsor who will bankroll the project) and they must create a team charter, using a format found on the company intranet.

Sun and others have found that when the teams have a clear business-oriented purpose such as reducing costs or development time, and the metrics to measure their progress, they are more likely to be successful. These teams also need good performance management just like any other work system. One of the great misunderstandings of the last few years is that *self-directed* somehow means *non-directed*. It doesn't. In these teams people take their primary direction from customers, charters, and goals and from observing the work itself, rather than from a manager who is more removed than they are from day-to-day operations.

4. Teams Need Alternative Systems to Hierarchy to Be Effective

Although this is related to earlier learnings, it deserves some special discussion. In many ways hierarchy and bureaucracy have taken an undeservedly bad rap in the last few years. In an attempt to rid themselves of any vestige of these organizational structures, some operations have gone too far. While I am certainly not someone who wants to sing the praises of hierarchy, I have learned over the last few years that ripping it out of an organization without substituting alternatives that provide the direction and coordination once provided by autocratic work structures creates a dangerous vacuum. Without substitutions such as accountability systems, goals, measures, information technology, and employee governance councils, organizations devolve into chaos.

5. Leadership Is the Key Variable to Team Success

It will come as no surprise to most business leaders that the key to team success is leadership. I'll review some data and stories to reinforce this critical learning throughout the book. Suffice it to say that we now know three important things about team leaders and team effectiveness. One is that the thing that differentiates successful team implementations from unsuccessful ones is leadership support. Without clear sponsorship from key leaders, the culture of high performance never really takes root.

We also know that once teams are established, leadership effectiveness is the most important variable in their ongoing operational effectiveness. Teams without the benefit of a good coach are not as successful as those who have one. As evidence of this, consider the example of companies like Rohm and Haas, P&G, and Tennessee Eastman, all of which have added back into their organizations team leader resources that were originally stripped away during redesign. In a time period where even traditional organizations are cutting out levels of management for cost savings purposes, adding managers definitely goes against the grain. Please don't misunderstand: the number of formal leaders employed in high-performance work systems is generally less than the number of managers used in traditional work systems for the same number of employees. But, although the last few years have clearly taught us that not as many managers are needed, teams do need an appropriate amount of formal leadership support. Without this support, team member skill development suffers, interface problems with other teams often go unresolved, and teams may be starved of necessary resources.

The third thing we know about leading teams is that there are certain skills and behaviors that successful team leaders employ. The leadership behaviors are, of course, not the autocratic or benevolent dictator behaviors that may have been lauded in the past. Recent research, for example, suggests that there are certain leadership characteristics such as conscientiousness (things like follow-through and thoroughness) and integrity (things like telling the truth and doing what you say you'll do) that have a positive correlation with organization results. We also know that leaders who master empowering behaviors such as facilitating, barrier busting, and Socratic coaching inspire the type of discretionary effort of team members that creates competitive advantage.

All teams need a coach. But what does a coach do? That is why I wrote this book in the first place. And it is why I wanted to update and expand this edition now.

How Is This Edition Different from the Earlier Book?

In this updated version of *Leading Self-Directed Work Teams* I add more recent examples and share what I am learning about team applications in knowledge work organizations. I also add new research about teams and team leadership competencies and review the interesting dilemmas associated with leading virtual teams. With another six years of experience under our belts, the consultants I work with have also encouraged me to modify the original competencies associated with the team leader role so that they reflect our most recent learning.

While the bulk of the book will remain true to the original work, the stories will be more current, the application broader, and the suggestions more specific to contemporary teams. Some material has been cut to streamline the book. New material has been added. It is time to revisit the concepts in this book, if for no other reason than to provide an opportunity to share some more stories about the amazing organizations that use these teams to harness the creativity and responsiveness of an empowered workforce.

Fortunately, more information about leading teams has become available since this book was first released. But leaders are still asking for more practical help. The questions I want to discuss are some of the same ones that I struggled with as a new leader at P&G: What are team leaders? How are they different from supervisors? What is required to be successful in this role? What does it take to change from a supervisor to a team leader? How does this apply to real organizations?

Understanding the leadership roles in a high-performance work environment has been a passion of mine since I was introduced to the ideas of socio-technical work systems in graduate school. As I have made friends with some of the great thinkers and practitioners in this field, and most importantly, as I have worked side by side with the men and women who labor in self-directed work teams across the U.S., Canada, Africa, Asia, and Western Europe, I have been touched by the dedication and relentless tenacity of people who are consumed by this work. I hope this book will be a vehicle to share with you some of the things my friends have taught me about managing workplaces characterized by dignity, purpose, and competitive advantage.

LEADING SELF-DIRECTED WORK TEAMS

PART
I

A New Kind of Leader for a New Kind of Business Environment

CHAPTER

Bosses Who Don't Boss

"The teams at Goodyear are now telling the boss how to run things. And I must say, I'm not doing a half-bad job because of it."

Stanley Gault, *chairman of Goodyear**

E MPOWERMENT HAS CLEARLY become the latest in a long litany of vogue practices that have ebbed and flowed over corporations like the changing of the tide. Today it is estimated that virtually all major corporations in North America and Western Europe are using various forms of empowerment somewhere in their organizations. Many even utilize an advanced form of empowerment called *self-directed work teams* (SDWTs)—now more commonly termed *high-performance work systems.*

The companies that take this seriously are convinced that employee empowerment is more than just another management fad. Why? Because real empowerment upends traditional organizational structures, policies, and practices and forces operations to question the traditional methods of management that have dominated corporations for

---

* All quotes will use the titles of the individual at the time the statement was made. I expect the titles, of course, to change over time.

the last hundred years. Many experts believe it is potentially as profound a change in contemporary organizations as the first industrial revolution was in the eighteenth and nineteenth centuries.

Empowerment Is the Second Industrial Revolution

The first industrial revolution took people off of their family farms and put them into corporations organized into narrow jobs with bosses to supervise their work. Conversely, the second industrial revolution makes companies act more like the family farms did—the farm workers now run the day-to-day operation with only minimal supervision. They assume numerous management tasks themselves and are organized into flexible teams instead of into rigid functional departments with narrow job descriptions.

Support for the empowerment transformation has come from a wide cross section of managers, employees, union executives, and professionals in a number of organizations ranging from steel mills to hospitals, from government offices to coal mines. It is not, of course, universally supported. But even managers like John Welch, chairman of General Electric, preach empowerment. Although highly respected for his ability to get results, Welch was once known as "Neutron Jack" for his autocratic style, manifested in dictates like the one that laid off 100,000 GE employees in the 1980s. Like a corporate neutron bomb, the action left all the buildings intact but eliminated the people. This isn't the profile of someone you might expect to tout the benefits of worker participation. But Jack Welch is now talking about a very different way to wage business warfare. "The idea of liberation and empowerment for our work force," he says, "is not enlightenment—it's a competitive necessity."

SDWTs Pose a Challenge to Traditional Management

SDWTs pose some very special challenges for managers at every level in an organization. I know they did for me. I worked as a production manager in what was arguably the most advanced high-performance organization in Procter & Gamble. But when I first went to the plant I was uncomfortable and unclear about managing a self-directed work force. It seemed like a contradiction in terms. How do you manage a

self-managed team? Did they really need me? Was there any job security for me as a team leader? Was the purpose of these operations to
eliminate management?

It soon became clear to me that management did, in fact, have a crucial role to play in the SDWTs. But it was not the role I was used to
playing. Before I went to P&G, a brief stint as a manager with another
organization had convinced me that traditional practices were the best
way to manage. I soon found out, however, that many of the classic
management practices I had mastered in my previous job were entirely
inconsistent with SDWT requirements. Many of the supervisory
responsibilities I had had in the other organization, for example, were
handled here by the team members themselves. And, despite my early
skepticism about "turning the prison over to the inmates," it seemed to
be producing extraordinary results.

P&G Declares SDWTs a Trade Secret

The soap plant where I worked is located in Lima, Ohio. It was started
up in the 1960s as one of the first and most successful SDWT experiments in the U.S. and has continued into the new millennium to be a
model organization. It tested the then little-practiced theories of a small
group of British, U.S., and Australian social scientists. How well did it
work? The results of the experiment were so good that P&G declared
them trade secrets with all the same restrictions and security precau-
tions associated with product formulations and marketing plans. Only
in the last few years has the understandably tight-lipped company
engaged in more open discussion of its SDWT experience.

The P&G Downy Fabric Softener team averaged 99.9 percent
within quality limits, held numerous safety records, and could make,
pack, and ship cases of product to our California Downy factory less
expensively than what it cost the California factory to get it out to their
own loading dock. Perhaps even more remarkable than the types of
results the Lima plant was getting was the fact that, by the time I had
arrived, this SDWT "experiment" had already been operating very successfully for over a dozen years. This clearly was not a momentary flash
in the pan. It was turning out sustainable improvements then and has
continued to do so for nearly four decades. And my experience convinced me that high-performance work systems required a nontradi-

tional approach to management. What happens when traditional managers don't change? Consider the following:

Jack's Problem

Jack (not his real name) was a veteran middle-level manager in a major consumer products company. He was well respected and had a very senior position. His facility had recently been gutted and all new equipment had been installed successfully. The technology changeover was also being used as a platform for implementing empowerment. Although it was surrounded by a 50-year-old facility using traditional management practices, this business unit had been selected as the organization's first attempt to redesign a department into a fully functional high-performance work system. Employee teams would form nearly self-sustainable business units, in which workers would act more like partners than subordinates. Not many months after the equipment was operational, however, the work team part of the project was failing badly. Tempers flared, grievances were filed, and trust was eroding rapidly. Jack had heard in conversations with the supervisors reporting to him that they thought he was to blame for the sluggishness of the empowerment effort. The consultant had given him frank feedback about how his autocratic style was impeding the team effort, along with very specific suggestions about how to change his behavior to be more participative.

Jack had honestly tried. His intentions had been good, his concern for results was unquestionable, and he had taken what he thought were the necessary actions to create the work culture change that his superiors wanted. Within a short period of time, however, he was moved out of his position. To add insult to injury, his new replacement succeeded in getting the self-directed work teams to function properly in a short period of time. The replacement rebuilt employee trust by listening to team members' concerns and making some modifications to the work design process to accommodate them.

The Changing Workplace

Jack's career was ruined when he was branded an "old-style" manager incapable of managing successfully in a facility using empowered work teams. His later assignments were a series of lateral arabesques that eventually took him so far away from corporate center stage that he couldn't even *see* the spotlight he used to occupy as a key manager. Jack's story is true.* And until managers and supervisors can be better prepared for the changes occurring in organizations today, Jack won't be the last needless casualty of the changing workplace.

Thousands of managers and supervisors like Jack have seen their worlds suddenly turned upside down. Tens of thousands of others will face the same situation in the years to come. Once at the power pinnacle of the work floor or office, these newly named team leaders are now required to support rather than direct employees. They bear a variety of titles such as *resource, facilitator,* or *advisor.* Their new job descriptions use words like *lead, coach,* and *train* to replace the traditional hierarchical standbys like *plan, organize, direct,* and *control.* But for the majority of management this new role brings a host of new and sometimes uncomfortable demands. This is especially true in the organizations using self-directed work teams. As their name implies, self-directed work teams require a fundamentally different and seemingly contradictory kind of leadership: bosses who don't boss.

Team Leaders Don't Supervise

In later chapters we will be using the terms *supervisor* and *team leader* in an unusual way. Let me explain what I mean by the title *supervisor.* In my previous management assignment I had learned that a significant, though often unwritten, part of the traditional manager's responsibility was to "supervise subordinates." This is a euphemism for bossing. No one really sat down and told me this, but that was what nearly all the successful managers did. You don't have to be mean or even very forceful to supervise. You just have to control subordinates. Supervisors can do this by telling people what to do and then by making sure they do it properly. More subtle control methods include maintaining the right to authorize the decisions of subordinates or limit the information or resources available to them. Whatever the means used, the end is the

---

* Most of the references and quotes from clients and associates come from personal interaction and interviews. Some of these people will not be identified by name for various reasons. As these statements have not been published elsewhere, I will typically not include a note for a reference such as this throughout the rest of the book.

same. Supervisors create organizations where employees are driven by management, not by customers, and where conformity becomes more important than creativity.

All Traditional Managers Are Supervisors

Whether supervising welders as a night shift crew boss or regional sales managers as a corporate vice president of sales and marketing, the traditional manager *supervises*. That is, the manager is charged with controlling his or her subordinates. Supervisors, managers, and executives have typically been given separate titles depending on the numbers of employees over whom they have stewardship. But classic corporations, built on the turn-of-the-century notion of chain of command, have long required that a significant portion of the responsibilities of management at the bottom, middle, *and* top be supervisory in nature. In that way all levels are the same. For purposes of this book, the title *supervisor* therefore refers not just to the first level of management but to all traditional managers who are charged with supervising a group of subordinates.

Supervisors at all levels have to change to being team leaders, or else they will impede the empowerment efforts.

Operations, Management, and Culture Team Leaders

Just as all traditional managers are supervisors, *team leaders* are all managers who support self-directed work teams at every level of an organization. SDWTs are now used not only on the work floor, but on the top floor of corporate headquarters buildings as well.

Although most general responsibilities are the same for all team leaders, there are some responsibilities that differ from one type of team leader to another. For purposes of our discussion, when it is important to differentiate between team leaders, I will use the following titles:

- Those who lead teams of individual contributors will be called *operations team leaders*, because they interface directly with those who perform the core work of the organization. In traditional operations these are the people who would have been called *supervisors, lead people,* or *foremen.*

- Mid-level managers who lead teams of team leaders will be called *management team leaders,* because they lead other leaders.
- The most executive level of leaders will be called *culture team leaders,* because they have the ultimate responsibility for organization-wide empowerment and cultural change.

These distinctions are particularly helpful in the discussion of roles and responsibilities during the transition of an organization from traditional work systems to increased levels of empowerment.

Summary

Empowerment is in vogue for the new millennium. However, managers at every level of the workplace are required to change from being supervisors to being team leaders if empowerment is really going to work. High-performance work systems, in particular, require a fundamentally different role for managers who have traditionally been responsible for supervising subordinates, regardless of their management level in the operation.

I know from my own experience that changing the management role isn't easy. Traditional organizational forms and management perspectives have been so pervasive that, like the air we breathe, they are invisible to most of us. Unfortunately, it is hard to change something that seems so normal that you don't even see it anymore. And it isn't until we start choking that we really understand how much we depended on the stuff that has been withdrawn. Nowhere are the changes effected by empowerment—the so-called second industrial revolution—more evident than in high-performance work teams.

To help us better understand these unique organizations, as well as the values and business conditions that created them, the next chapter explores the characteristics and historical roots of the self-directed work team.

CHAPTER 2

Self-Directed Work Teams: What Are They and Where Did They Come From?

"The great revolution of modern times has been the revolution of equality. The idea that all people should be equal in their condition has undermined the old structures of authority, hierarchy and deference. . . . But when rights are given to every citizen and the sovereignty of all is established, the problem of leadership takes a new form, becomes more exacting than ever before. It is easy to issue commands and enforce them by the rope and the stake, the concentration camp and the gulag. It is much

harder to use argument and achievement to overcome opposition and win consent."

Arthur M. Schlesinger Jr., *historian and former advisor to Presidents Kennedy and Johnson*

CONSIDER THE ANCIENT Latin proverb *Tempora mutantur, nos et mutamur in illis,* which can be roughly translated as, "The times are changed and we are changed with them." From the beginning of recorded history we have known that change in both ourselves and in our institutions is inevitable. Expanding on this theme, Bob Dylan (a more current philosopher) sang, "the times, they are a-changing" about a dynamic time in American history that led to significant cultural change in the country. The times Dylan sang about were the 1960s and 1970s, when many of the activities that would lead to the development of self-directed work teams took root.

What led up to the interest in empowerment? Simple economics. Traditional organizations had difficulty competing with more agile adversaries. Says John Stepp, former undersecretary of the U.S. Department of Labor, about the typical organization:

There are too many rigidities that have slowed us down and hampered our effectiveness. We see top-down decision making. We see overly prescribed tasks and narrow job definitions. We see long, drawn-out labor contracts and negotiations that more closely resemble cease-fire agreements among combatants than a rational agreement for organizing work and work relationships. Our industrial relations system is hampered by too many restrictions; too many inhibiting work practices, work rules, and personnel policies.

Why Are Organizations Changing?

Traditional organizations were rapidly becoming uncompetitive. What had been a strength for decades—the organizational stability and control created by traditional management practices—was rapidly becoming a millstone around the necks of many corporations. Something had to be done. By the 90s many businesses felt the pressure to transform themselves from the hierarchical and bureaucratic organizations that had been popular and effective since the early 1900s. But what should they change to? Businesses weren't alone in this: public organizations were experiencing their own problems.

For example, even during good economic times, many government agencies came under heated attack for waste and inefficiencies caused by what many frustrated citizens believed was bureaucracy at its worst. In the U.S. the Republican Party created a "Contract with America" to simplify government and the Democratic White House leadership initiated a campaign for "Reinventing Government" for similar reasons. Whether the changes made were significant is certainly debatable; but public pressure for reform continues into the new millennium. Government organizations in Asia fared even more poorly as pressures from poor economic conditions created significant demand for more responsive government. European governments faced their own challenges associated with economic unification.

How Are Organizations Changing?

Different organizations responded to these pressures in different ways. Some took desperate measures, closing down operations and laying off thousands of white- and blue-collar workers in an attempt to stanch the blood-colored ink on their income statements. Survivors in these operations found themselves in reengineered "lean and mean" organizations with decreased resources and increased responsibilities. Those who were laid off often started their own small companies, aided by new technologies like the Internet that allowed them to compete without large corporate overheads. This in turn created more disenchanted employees and more competition that further increased the pressures on businesses to survive.

Other organizations began to move in a more measured manner to alternative practices, which promised to bring more flexibility and responsiveness to the turbulent business environment. Corporate programs in areas such as just-in-time inventory management, Materials Resources Planning, Employee Involvement, Total Quality Management, Enterprise Resource Planning, large-scale data management systems, and a whole host of other initiatives became popular. Some organizations bet the farm on new whiz-bang technologies and product designs. Service organizations recommitted themselves to scrutinizing cost-effectiveness and refocusing their operations on providing service excellence. Large, successful companies like Hewlett-Packard and Microsoft actually began to split themselves into smaller organizations to recapture the drive and focus of the more nimble operations they had been when they started. Much good came from these activities. For example, almost everybody incorporated quality management perspectives into their operations, with an emphasis placed on customer focus, open information sharing, and continuous improvement.

People Are the Competitive Advantage

But the bottom line of all of this activity didn't surprise perceptive leaders. Many of the government reforms, much of the reengineering and refocusing efforts, and even many of the employee involvement, quality, and resource planning efforts failed to produce long-lasting benefits.

But the organizations that experimented with empowerment initiatives, particularly those that began to use high-performance work systems, had a different experience. They learned that people, not programs, are the answer to increased competitiveness in a changing work environment. Reports Norman E. Garrity, executive vice president of Corning, "We found that if you don't pay attention to the people aspects, such as empowering workers to make decisions, you could only get 50 percent of the potential benefits of restructuring." And in companies like Corning, which have the active support of leaders, the new work culture change appears to be working. Says Robert A. Hubble, a production worker in the Corning plant in Blackburg, Virginia: "Everybody that works here is competitive. We're willing to work long hours. We want to be multiskilled and learn how we can make the product better so we can be the best in quality and service to the customer. And if we do that, this plant will be around a long time." These skills and attitudes pay off. Blacksburg turned a $2 million profit in its first eight months of production, instead of losing $2.3 million as projected for the start-up.

Empowerment is also paying off in service organizations that are reforming themselves into nontraditional, empowered operations. "It's no longer coming to work and slugging data into a terminal," says Mary Vandehay, a member of an insurance rep team at Aid Association for Lutherans. "We have to work with each other. We can't pass problems up the line to managers. We have to be honest and up-front with our co-workers."

The kind of attitude expressed by team members like Hubble and Vandehay may be the difference between the winners and the losers in the competitive marketplace. Tools, technologies, and projects are necessary but insufficient; they don't matter if people don't want to use them to full advantage. And almost everybody has access to the same tooling, technology, and funding nowadays. Competitive advantage comes from fully utilizing the *discretionary effort* of the workforce, not from buying the latest gadget or using the latest management fad. Voluntary effort comes from employee commitment, and commitment comes from empowerment. It is simple human nature. Why? In the words of Doug King, human resources manager at Weyerhaeuser, "It's hard to resist your own ideas."

It is becoming increasingly clear that organizational responses like new product and service development, cross-functional projects, and technology deployment require a flexible and empowered workforce. Put more succinctly, without significant levels of empowerment, projects and programs won't deliver the promised results. Speed, quality, productivity, and new products and services come from people, not from tools. And the stakes are high. In a competitive work environment only the winners survive.

Defining Empowerment

What is empowerment? It is a function of four important variables: authority, resources, information, and accountability. You might remember these variables by using the memory word ARIA, which is composed of the first letter of each variable. The beauty of the opera solo of the same name depends on whether the music is written, performed, and accompanied well. Similarly, the empowerment melody works only when all the variables are in complete harmony. To feel empowered, people need formal authority and all of the resources (like the budget, equipment, time, and training) necessary to do something with the new authority. They also need timely, accurate information to make good decisions. And they need a personal sense of accountability for the work. This definition of empowerment can be expressed as follows:

$$\text{Empowerment} = f(\textbf{A}\text{uthority}, \textbf{R}\text{esources}, \textbf{I}\text{nformation},$$
$$\textbf{A}\text{ccountability})$$
$$\text{Empowerment} = \textbf{0} \text{ if } \textbf{A}\text{uthority or } \textbf{R}\text{esources or } \textbf{I}\text{nformation}$$
$$\text{or } \textbf{A}\text{ccountability} = \textbf{0}$$

In this formula we can see that empowerment is a function of the four variables and that if any of the variables in this equation go to zero then there is no empowerment. This explains why some empowerment initiatives are a sham. Authority without information and resources, for example, is only permission. Telling team members that they should go ahead and make decisions or solve problems without providing them access to accurate business information and without providing them the skills training, budget, and time to accomplish the task is a prescription for volatile failure. Not sharing accountability is paternalistic and condescending. It sends the message that the empowerment isn't real. Only when all four elements are present do people feel responsible and act responsibly.

Defining Self-Directed Work Teams

Empowerment gives people greater control over their own destiny. And there are varying degrees of empowerment. It is not something you either have or don't have. Visualize empowerment as a continuum of employee involvement with lower empowerment techniques like selected employee input on projects on one end, ongoing employee task forces in the middle, and higher empowerment processes like SDWTs on the other end (See Figure 2.1). Jack Sherwood, a prominent STS

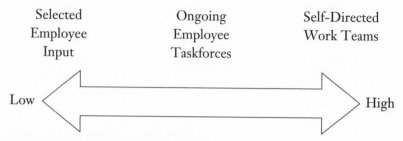

Selected	Ongoing	Self-Directed
Employee	Employee	Work Teams
Input	Taskforces	

Low ⟸⟹ High

Figure 2.1 The empowerment continuum.
Adapted from the work of John Sherwood.

consultant, introduced this idea to us at Tektronix in 1983. We found it a simple and effective way to describe empowerment choices to people.

Self-directed teams are the most advanced form of empowerment. Whether it is called employee involvement, a socio-technical system, a high-performance system, partnership, semiautonomous work teams, or any of the multitude of names referring to organizations based on SDWT concepts, parts of companies like Corning, Procter & Gamble, Esso, TRW, Aid Association for Lutherans, Chevron, Monsanto, Microsoft, Digital Equipment Corporation, Sherwin-Williams, Honeywell, Weyerhaeuser, Shell, and a host of others have been using the technique aggressively.

What are self-directed teams? Let's use a slightly modified version of the definition employed by the Association for Quality and Participation for its study on the subject (which I will reference in the next chapter):

> **Self-directed team (noun): A group of employees who have day-to-day responsibility for managing themselves and the work they do with a minimum of direct supervision. Members of self-directed teams typically handle job assignments, plan and schedule work, make production- and/or service-related decisions, and take action on problems.**

Where traditional work groups typically are organized into separate specialized jobs with rather narrow responsibilities, self-directed teams are made up of members who are jointly responsible for whole work processes, with each individual performing multiple tasks. Whereas a traditional organization might be divided into groups of functional specialists, for example, SDWTs are usually responsible for delivery of an entire service or product, or they might be responsible for a geographic or customer base. This is done to create (wherever possible) small self-sustaining businesses that can be jointly managed by the organizational membership. At P&G Lima, for example, we were divided into product organizations. The team members made decisions about who would perform which task rather than having individuals separated into jobs like operators, mechanics, and tradespeople. Everyone had the same title, "technician," and everyone had a shared responsibility for the success of the team. These are common elements of SDWTs. For other key differences between self-directed work teams and traditional organizations, see Table 2.1.

SDWT Watchouts

A caveat is in order when defining SDWTs. It is critically important that we recognize an enormous trap associated with overemphasizing the structure (self-directed work teams) more than the process of empowerment. For the sake of clarity and simplicity, this book, for example, spends a lot of time and attention on SDWTs as the unit of discussion. Inappropriate focus on the teams in the workplace, however, can cause some serious problems.

Two problems in particular result from focusing too much on the teams themselves. First, we can begin to believe that the teams are an

Table 2.1   SDWTs Versus Traditional Organizations

Self-Directed Work Teams	Traditional Organizations
Customer-driven	Management-driven
Multiskilled work force	Workforce of isolated specialists
Few job descriptions	Many job descriptions
Information shared widely	Information limited
Few levels of management	Many levels of management
Whole-business focus	Function/department focus
Shared goals	Segregated goals
Seemingly chaotic	Seemingly organized
Purpose achievement emphasis	Problem-solving emphasis
High worker commitment	High management commitment
Continuous improvements	Incremental improvements
Self-controlled	Management-controlled
Values/principles-based	Policy/procedure-based

end in themselves instead of the means to an end. SDWTs are a method of improving results, not a substitution for them. This all-too-common inversion of means and ends has caused some organizations to lose sight of their organizational purpose and to focus instead on the care and feeding of the structures ("Sorry, our poor customer service is caused by the fact that everyone is in a team meeting right now"). This is obviously a bad mistake.

Second, overemphasizing the self-directedness of the teams can lead people down the wrong path. In fact, the name *self-directed work team* itself can be misleading. Some believe that it connotes an absence of management personnel (which is inaccurate). SDWTs mean a change in the role of management, not the elimination of supervisors and managers. Others assume that the name implies that the team has complete latitude to do whatever it wants (which is equally inaccurate). All teams operate within appropriate boundary conditions. Probably a more accurate term is *work-centered teams* or *high-performance work systems*. Simply stated, these operations are ones in which skilled, well-informed people take direction from the work itself rather than from management. More on this later in the book.

SDWTs Outperform Traditional Operations

Whatever you call them, if all else is equal, these work cultures are often credited with outperforming their traditional counterparts. At a conference about these unique workplaces, Charles Eberle, a former vice president of Procter & Gamble, said:

> At P & G there are well over two decades of comparisons of results—*side by side*—between enlightened work systems and those I call traditional. It is absolutely clear that the new work systems work better—*a lot better*—for example, with 30 to 50 percent lower manufacturing costs. Not only are the tangible, measurable, bottom line indicators such as cost, quality, customer service and reliability better, but also the harder-to-measure attributes such as quickness, decisiveness, toughness, and just plain resourcefulness of these organizations. Importantly, the people in these organizations are far more self-reliant and less dependent upon hierarchy and control systems than in the traditional organization.

The excitement caused by these kinds of reports has accelerated the development of self-directed work teams. To better understand this emerging role of the team leader and to determine whether self-directed teams are here to stay, let's briefly consider the history of these unique work cultures.

The Origin of Self-Directed Work Teams

Most attribute the origins of self-directed work team concepts to the early work of an Englishman named Eric Trist. In the 1950s Trist coauthored a paper in which the term *socio-technical system* first appeared. In this and other papers that were to follow, Trist challenged many of the fundamental assumptions of "scientific management," an idea developed by Frederick Taylor at the turn of the century and perfected by Henry Ford in the U.S. automobile factories of the 1930s. At that time, scientific management appeared to be the answer to the problems caused by the dependence of rapidly growing industries on a largely unskilled and ill-educated workforce. Breaking down job responsibilities into small, specialized increments meant that workers could become proficient more rapidly and that a sense of order and predictability could be imposed on the emerging chaos of industrialization. This, coupled with having decision making and problem solving become the sole provenance of foremen and supervisors, facilitated the movement away from the little shops of independent craftsmen that characterized industry of the period and toward mass production and standardized factory work.

Scientific Management: Strengths and Weaknesses

Scientific management brought with it a number of advantages that current critics often fail to remember, including improvements in the quality and efficiency of work processes. It helped workers with little experience and education become fairly productive quickly. In fact, it often actually improved the work life of the employee who had previously been subjected to deathtrap mining operations, exploitative sweatshops, and capricious shop owner management. Although it facilitated industrialization, scientific management also had some very serious negative side effects. It separated the workers from the results of their work. It stripped them of an opportunity to understand the whole work process, participate in a variety of tasks, and do the planning, evaluating, and improving of work processes. Perhaps most detrimentally, it prevented them from understanding the customers who used their products and services. These were all normal aspects of working in a small workshop or family farm. Consequently, workers became focused over time on the things scientific management left them to worry about. Typically this was limited to concerns about job security and job rights instead of concerns about work efficiency and customers. These job concerns, ironically, often became counterproductive to both the good of the enterprise and the individual.

Socio-Technical Systems

After discovering a remarkably productive coal mining team in postwar England, Trist suggested an alternative to scientific management. He said that through the formation of work teams that had complete responsibility for an entire operation, the interface between people (the social system) and their tools (the technical system) could be more fully optimized. This, Trist further postulated, would lead to job performance that was more rewarding and productive for the increasingly experienced workforce.

About a decade later, these ideas took root in the United States. In the 1960s and early 1970s, experiments with what were called "semi-autonomous work teams" or "technician" operations started in Procter & Gamble plants in Ohio and Georgia, a Cummins Engine facility in Jamestown, New York, and a General Foods plant in Topeka, Kansas. In these organizations academicians joined ranks with practitioners to create self-directed work teams that demonstrated remarkable competitive and social advantages over scientific management. Since that time numerous other organizations have followed suit by creating or redesigning workplaces in which teams of employees get involved in operational decisions and in many of the traditional supervisory responsibilities of managing the day-to-day business. In these organizations the traditional barriers to maximum employee contribution, such as narrow job descriptions, restrictive functional distinctions, lack of ongoing business information, and hierarchically geared compensation and status systems, are minimized.

From Manufacturing to Service and Public School SDWTs

What started in a few manufacturing plants has also spread into the service sector in organizations like Shenandoah Life Insurance and American Transtech, a company broken off from the AT&T monolith during the divestiture. These teams have even spilled over into public organizations and utilities like the financial arm of Seattle Metro, schools like those in the Dade County, Florida "school-based management" program, hospital and research organizations like the Mayo clinic, and tourist and recreation facilities such as the San Diego Zoo.

Impressed with its own results with SDWTs, for example, Champion Paper established a partnership with interested middle schools in communities where Champion has mills. These schools use consultants funded by Champion to create SDWTs of teachers. The teams of four core teachers are now responsible for most of the daily curriculum of a common set of students, allowing the teachers to modify the traditional one-hour classes to spend more or less time on subjects according to student needs. This also allows the three other teachers to cover for one of their peers who might need some personal development time.

The teachers meet in daily team meetings to do planning and discuss the specific needs of individual kids who often fall through the cracks in traditional junior high schools where teachers don't have time to get together to compare notes about how children perform in different classes. Using teams in middle schools has reduced teacher burnout, increased teaching effectiveness, and focused the classes on the real needs of the students. In addition to improving education, it just may provide some of the answers to the frightening rise of violence in schools where classes are driven by curriculum rather than learning.

Is worker empowerment another of the countless flavor-of-the-month business fads we see from time to time? No. For reasons to be discussed in the next chapter, empowered work systems like the SDWT are the next inevitable step on the ladder of workplace evolution.

Summary

Once-cherished rules for the organizing and managing of people are becoming obsolete in today's rapidly changing world. Numerous organizations in a wide array of public and private sectors have started using

SDWTs in an attempt to respond to the demand for increased flexibility and responsiveness. Some operations have made mistakes by not understanding that empowerment requires authority, resources, information, and accountability ($\mathbf{E} = f(\mathbf{A,R,I,A})$). Others have misapplied SDWTs by focusing too much attention on the structure and not enough on the purpose of the operation. But overall, those who have used SDWTs have been rewarded with significant organizational improvements. The first published writing about these remarkable workplaces is generally attributed to Eric Trist and other members of the Tavistock Institute in postwar England. These unique workplaces have fundamentally changed the role of the supervisor at every level of the organization. And it looks like SDWTs—a commonsense idea that has probably been practiced by some people since the beginning of organizational history—are here to stay. A question asked by many team members and team leaders alike is, "What took so long?"

Team Empowerment: Passing Fad or the Future of Work Design?

"No matter what your business, these teams are the wave of the future."

Jerry Junkins, *CEO of Texas Instruments*

HIGH-PERFORMANCE WORK SYSTEMS are rapidly becoming the norm in many organizations. Although not all operations will find these organizations appropriate, self-directed work teams will not be a short-lived fad for two reasons: (1) they have been around a long time, and (2) they get results.

SDWTs Have Been Here for Decades

Unlike fads, which tend to be popular for a few years and then fade away into obscurity, self-directed work teams have been around for decades. Many corporations like Cummins Engine, Procter & Gamble, and General Foods have actively used these teams since at least the early 1960s and arguably earlier. Several companies have also reported that they originally used SDWTs at the start-ups of their organizations or new ventures. As they grew, the start-ups usually moved away from the self-directed work teams to the management philosophies and structures in vogue for organizations of their size and type. Many are now trying to get back to their roots.

SDWTs Work

The second and more powerful reason that self-directed work teams are here to stay is that (all else being equal) they get better results than their traditional counterparts. In a review of organizations that had transitioned from traditional work systems to SDWTs in seven countries, John Cotter, a prominent socio-technical system consultant, found that:

> Ninety-three percent reported improved productivity.
> Eighty-six percent reported decreased operating costs.
> Eighty-six percent reported improved quality.
> Seventy percent reported better employee attitudes.

Reports from organizations within Cummins, Xerox, Tektronix, Mead, TRW, James River, P&G, Boeing, General Electric, Esso, Ford, and other corporations confirm these findings and indicate that SDWTs frequently outperform comparable traditional operations. Unlike a number of other corporate initiatives that have promised fire but delivered mostly smoke, SDWTs often improve many of the key organizational measures by 30 to 50 percent.

When SDWTs Don't Work

SDWTs don't always get sterling results, of course. Although I am not aware of any studies to confirm this, SDWT consultants normally suggest that empowerment has about a 50 percent success rate. That is, for every 100 companies that begin this work, about half fail to get the desired improvements. Why? The single biggest reason is a lack of management commitment to the whole change process. A study published by Mercer Management consultants confirms that "top management commitment and support" is the single highest "lever of high performance" work systems. Absent this support, many operations are starved of the resources and attention necessary to create cultural transformation. Impatience for results or an unwillingness to make the necessary personal management changes have foiled many attempts to create sustainable SDWTs. A related shortfall is the organizational unwillingness to provide the necessary budget and time for training to help team leaders and team members acquire new skills.

But sometimes, even when SDWT implementation and support are flawless, failure can occur. No organizational design or management style can guarantee success. The airline People's Express, for example, was well publicized for using self-directed work teams effectively—just prior to its failure. Caught in a whipsaw between rapid growth and a questionable market, the airline went bust. Similarly, both DEC and P&G have shut down SDWT organizations. Although these operations in the eastern U.S. and Europe were more cost and quality effective than traditional facilities, they were not good enough to compensate for major declines in the market or for distribution advantages of other locations, respectively. SDWTs are not a substitute for sound business basics. If you have a product or service no one wants to buy, teams won't necessarily help. Nor will they help if you are in the wrong business or if you don't have the right technology. They can only give you a better chance to be successful by more efficiently leveraging the human potential across the whole of the organization.

SDWTs and Business Results

While leveraging human potential can't guarantee anything, it does provide enormous benefits. Many organizations in the consumer products, aerospace, and paper industries are actively using SDWTs because they believe the teams provide a significant competitive advantage. David Swanson, a P&G senior vice president, confirmed this in a closed meeting at Harvard. He stated that the P&G SDWT plants were "30–40 percent more productive than their traditional counterparts and significantly more able to adapt quickly to the changing needs of the business." Adds Ted L. Marsten, Cummins Engine vice president, "this is the most cost-effective way to run plants . . . the people felt a lot better . . . and we got a much higher quality product." GM has actually used references to its teams in its Saturn automobile ads, apparently assuming that the advantages in quality, service, and/or cost-effectiveness will be obvious even to the consumers who may be completely unfamiliar with different organizational alternatives.

These teams aren't just for the megacorporations either. Johnsonville Foods, a sausage manufacturer in Sheboygan, Wisconsin, claims that its productivity has improved 50 percent since the company started using teams. Nor is the SDWT revolution limited to manufacturing companies. Federal Express claims that a team of clerks found and solved a billing problem that was costing the company $2.1 million per year. Insurance companies like Aetna and Shenandoah Life Insurance have reduced costs and improved service through empowered teams. And American Transtech office teams can process twice as many forms as they could under the traditional work system.

Examples of Company Results

Consider some additional examples. *Boeing's* management notes that the faster-than-normal FAA certification and multiple aircraft improvements on the 777 were due to high-performance work systems. As a result, the 777 is more manufacturable, serviceable, and cost effective. For example, a service door that would normally be located aft of the cockpit was to be eliminated by structural engineers to reduce weight. It was retained when maintenance technicians (who would not normally be on a new product development team) argued successfully that eliminating the door would make servicing certain equipment nearly impossible. Making this change while the aircraft was still in the design phase probably saved the company hundreds of thousands of dollars over retrofitting existing planes.

Corning has witnessed numerous hard number benefits of high-performance work systems. The Administrative Center, for example, has 135 employees and is divided into 17 self-directed teams. The initial goal was to save $2 million in costs over a 5-year time frame; the company actually ended up saving in excess of $3 million. In the medical claims area, for example, turnaround times were improved from 16 days to 10 days. Customer service and employee flexibility improved measurably. Other Corning groups have had similar results. The corporate I.S. group saved $500,000 because of the team concept.

NBTel, a Canadian telecommunications giant, has had similar bottom-line improvements with service teams. After less than a year, one team's revenues increased 20 percent, compared to 10 percent in the rest of the region. Long-distance sales plans improved 65 percent over the rest of the regions. Troubles decreased by over 30 percent and repeat customer trouble decreased by over 40 percent. Inventory was cut in half and overtime decreased by 30 percent.

AT&T reports that in the case of a critical new product, the team approach was essential in reducing time to market: "As a result of the new team approach, AT&T cut development time from two years to just one year," notes an article about the effort. "Also, cost was lowered and quality improved." Organizational improvements associated with speed are likely to become critical as we move further into the new millennium. Software giant Bill Gates has claimed that organizational forms and technology that help us do work more quickly will be the major competitive advantage of the future.

Amdahl credits teams with major business improvements over traditional approaches. The service operation for the large computer and server manufacturer saw cost savings in the first year after implementation of about $3.75 million. Overtime was reduced by 55 percent in the Atlantic area, "and we attribute that decrease to the teams being responsible for scheduling along with the responsibility to determine profit and loss," the company reports. "Significantly, revenue per employee has also increased by 26 percent since 1994."

"The senior people really feel that the teams have added to our sales efficiency," say leaders at *Toyota* marketing. "For example, in the launch area (before we went to teams) we had three or four situations where the launch wasn't as successful as we had hoped. We took a long look at our organization and saw that we were too divided. The coordination and lateral relations weren't strong enough to support a product launch. Now when we launch a product with the Series Teams, we do a much better job of it. . . . The Series Teams have reached a whole new level of performance, and they're here to stay."

Welch's showed an interesting contrast between teams and traditional operations in the same facility. The team was the only department in the Lawton, Michigan plant to reach all of its department goals for fiscal year 1996. This shipment team shipped 637,559 cases of product in 1 week and handled a total of 924,125 cases—all-time record numbers for the Lawton facility.

At the *Mayo Clinic*, self-directed physician teams are used in parts of the hospital. When a patient is first diagnosed, an appropriate mix of doctors is temporarily assembled to serve as the patient's team. The clinic believes this has resulted in per person costs that are 15 to 22 percent below the national average.

Weyerhaeuser, a large forest products company, has had high-performance operations in some of its organizations for many years. Executives state that these teams exhibit "dramatic improvement in safety, product quality, and productivity compared with our facilities without such systems."

At *Microsoft*, technical recruiting teams outperformed traditional staffing organizations. Results? "We have increased productivity well over 50% during the last year. We were able to hire twice as many people. We basically blew every metric we had out of the water. Self-directed teams have really empowered people to do things they were never able to do before. In terms of diversity (age, ethnicity, etc.) our hiring metrics all increased well over 50%," reports the team leader.

For more examples, see the illustrative SDWT results in Table 3.1.

Research Verifies Improved Results

In a 1993 U.S. Department of Labor Study entitled "High Performance Work Practices and Firm Performance," the trend for improved performance in team-based operations (what the department called "innovative work systems") became increasingly clear. Twenty separate university studies showed a positive correlation between effective team practices and organization performance:

- In steel industry finishing lines, innovative work systems ran at 98 percent of schedule, versus 88 percent for the traditional plants.
- In the automobile industry, innovative plants produced vehicles at a rate of 1 every 22 hours with 0.5 defects per vehicle versus 1 every 30 hours with 0.8 defects per vehicle for the traditional plants.

Table 3.1   Examples of SDWT Results

Organization	Results	Source
P&G Manufacturing	• 30–50% lower manufacturing costs	Eberle
Federal Express	• Cut service glitches (incorrect bills and lost packages) by 13% in 1 year	Dumaine, p. 54
Shenandoah Life Insurance	• Case handling time went from 27 to 2 days • Service complaints "practically eliminated"	Hoerr and Pollock, p. 70
Sherwin-Williams (Richmond)	• Costs 45% lower • Returned goods down 75%	Fisher
Tektronix Portables	• Moved from least profitable to most profitable division within 2 years	Fisher
Rohm and Haas (Knoxville)	• Productivity up 60%	Hoerr and Pollock, p. 75
Tavistock coal mine	• Output 25% higher with lower costs than on a comparison face • Accidents, sickness, and absenteeism cut 50%	Trist, p. 16
Westinghouse (Airdrie)	• Reduced cycle time from 17 weeks to 1 week	Sherwood, p. 16
AT&T Credit Corp.	• Teams process 800 lease applications per day vs. 400 per day under old system • Growing at 40–50% compound annual rate	Hoerr and Zellner, p. 59
General Electric (Salisbury)	• Productivity improved 250%	Hoerr and Zellner, p. 58
Cummins Engine (Jamestown)	• Production cost savings allowed 25% price reduction on new engine	Fisher

(Continued)

Table 3.1 (*Continued*)

Organization	Results	Source
Xerox	• Teams at least 30% more productive than conventional operations	Hoerr and Pollock, p. 75
	• 75% fewer worker hours lost to scrap, 42% fewer defects per worker, and 17% higher productivity	Cutcher-Gershenfeld
Bestfoods (Little Rock)	• Highest-quality products at lowest costs of any Bestfoods plant	Productivity, p. 1
Volvo (Kalmar)	• Production costs 25% less than at Volvo's conventional plants	Hoerr and Pollock, p. 74
Ford (Hermosillo)	• Lower defect rate in first year of operation than most Japanese automakers	Sherwood, p. 5
Hewlett-Packard (Santa Clara)	• Improved customer responsiveness, business results, and speed of problem solving	Casement
Northern Telecom (Harrisburg)	• Profits doubled	Zenger
General Mills	• Productivity 40% higher than at traditional factories	Dumaine, p. 55
Honeywell (Chandler)	• Output increased 280% • Quality went from 82% to 99.5%	Sherwood, p. 16
American Transtech	• Reduced cost and processing time by 50%	Sherwood, p. 16
Port of Seattle	• Average project cost reduced by 11% (more than $850,000 saved in first year)	Fisher
Apple Computer (Fountain)	• New plant start-up completed in record-setting time	Kinni

(*Continued*)

Table 3.1   (*Continued*)

Organization	Results	Source
Aid Association for Lutherans	• Raised productivity by 20% and cut case processing time by 75%	Clipp, p. 21

Sources:

Casement, C., "Santa Clara Division: Implementing High Performance Work Teams" (Internally published paper, Hewlett-Packard Company Strategic Change Services, December 1, 1997).

Clipp, F. Paul, "Focusing Self-Managing Work Teams," *Quality Digest*, April 1990, pp. 20–22, 24–29.

Cutcher-Gershenfeld, J. "The Impact on Economic Performance of a Transformation in Workplace Relations," *Industrial and Labor Relations Review*, January 1991.

Dumaine, Brian, "Who Needs a Boss?" *Fortune*, May 7, 1990.

Eberle, Charles, "Competitiveness, Commitment and Leadership," a speech about P&G, *Ecology of Work Conference*, June 24, 1987.

Fisher, Kimball, Personal interviews, 1990–1999.

Hoerr, John and Michael Pollock, "Management Discovers the Human Side of Automation," *Business Week*, September 29, 1986.

Hoerr, John and Wendy Zellner, "The Payoff from Teamwork," *Business Week*, July 10, 1989.

Kinni, T., "Apple Grows Self-Directed Work Teams," *Quality Digest*, April 1993.

Productivity, "An American Miracle that Works," November 1982, pp. 1–5.

Sherwood, John, "Creating Work Cultures with Competitive Advantage," *Organizational Dynamics*, Fall 1988.

Trist, Eric, "The Evolution of Socio-technical Systems: A Conceptual Framework and an Action Research Program," *Ontario Ministry of Labour and Ontario Quality of Working Life Centre*, June 1981.

Zenger, John, Presentation at American Society of Training and Development (ASTD) Annual Conference, 1991.

- Among 700 firms from all major industries studied, those using most of the innovative practices have higher shareholder return and gross return on capital.
- In the Forbes 500, there is higher growth in profits, sales, and earnings per share over the five-year study period in innovative operations than in traditional operations.
- Among 6000 work groups in 34 firms studied, cooperation and involvement are positively correlated with future profitability.

Consider these additional findings:

- A study of several hundred firms by a Georgetown University researcher showed that 70 percent of the organizations using high-performance practices experienced a positive impact on productivity.
- A study of Fortune 1000 companies by Edward Lawler and colleagues at the Center for Effective Organizations at the University of Southern California showed that among companies increasing responsibilities in the business process, 60 percent reported productivity increases and 70 percent reported quality improvements.
- A long-term review of 131 field studies comparing 44 practices (structural, human resources, and technological) with productivity showed that changes in work practices (job design and teamwork) were "strongly related to increased productivity"— generally associated with 30 percent to 40 percent performance improvements.

The summary of the study concluded: ". . . existing evidence suggests that innovative work practices are positively related to both productivity and firm performance. The adoption of such practices could prove crucial to the future competitiveness of the United States economy."

There's more. A 1995 Rutgers University study found that within a year after team implementation the average company can expect $27,044 more in sales per employee, $3,814 more in profits per employee, and $18,641 more in market value per employee. A study of 179 large companies reported by Mercer Management Consulting in April of 1996 notes that about 20 percent of Fortune 1000 companies are profitable growing companies (growing at 25 percent annually for past 5 years and growing faster relative to others in their industry on both profit and revenue), but about 50 percent of the Fortune 1000 companies that employ best team practices are profitable growing companies. A Texas Tech University study compiled by Barry Macy is a meta-analysis of 1800 North American field sites from 1961 to 1991, including a 7-year study of 131 organization redesign efforts. According to the June 1998 summary, "A holistic and integrated organization design across all four categories of action-levers can yield a 3–7% financial improvement in results per year." The financial improvement index per year for traditional organizations is 103.8 percent; for team-based redesigns (brownfields) it is 106.8 percent and for new team-based operations (greenfields) it is 110.1 percent. Finally, a recent study by the Center for Effective Organizations indicates a strong positive correlation between employee involvement practices and results. Companies in the 1996 survey reported a positive or very positive impact on productivity (85 percent), quality of products/services (85 percent), customer service (83 percent), competitiveness (66 percent), profitability (66 percent), and employee satisfaction (78 percent).

It simply has become difficult to argue that team-based organizations aren't more effective than traditional organizations. Compelling evidence exists to the contrary.

SDWTs Are the Probable Future

Will the SDWT become the predominant organizational structure of tomorrow? A *Business Week* cover story suggested that the concept "appears to be the wave of the future," while a report in *Fortune* magazine boldly proclaims it *is* the wave of the future. But whether they completely displace traditional work systems or not, self-directed work teams are clearly growing. In a study done in 1988 by the Center for Effective Organizations at the University of Southern California, for example, researchers found that 67 percent of the organizations surveyed that said they were using empowerment techniques were also using SDWTs somewhere in their organizations. In a related 1990 study by *Industry Week*, the Association of Quality and Participation (AQP), and Development Dimensions International, a remarkable 83 percent of the companies experimenting with SDWTs at that time said they planned a considerable increase in the use of these teams by 1995.

The bottom line is this:

1. It seems that almost everybody is using some form of empowerment.
2. Most of the organizations using empowerment will eventually experiment with SDWTs in parts of their organizations.
3. Once they use SDWTs somewhere, most corporations say they want to expand them into other parts of their operations.

Everybody wants to keep up with the Joneses—especially when the Joneses can deliver the same products and services faster, with higher quality, and with lower cost. After P&G used the teams on the soap side of the company effectively, Colgate became interested and involved. Improvements on the pulp and paper side of the company were not unnoticed by competitors (now SDWT devotees) James River, Crown Z, Champion, Weyerhaeuser, and others. Why isn't everybody doing it yet?

For most firms, the lack of movement comes either from a lack of information or from resistance to the concept. It is too early to tell whether the vast majority of managers will be able to make the personal changes necessary for such universal transformation from traditional to SDWT operations. These SDWT organizational practices are often in direct contradiction to the management philosophies and styles that catapulted powerful supervisors into their current positions of control and responsibility at every level of the corporation. Nor is it clear that front-line employees will be able to change from the comfortable and pervasive work practices of the past. John Myers, human resources vice president for Shenandoah Life, suggests that "bureaucratic organizations become habit-forming, just like cigarettes." The supervisors and supervisees alike often just can't bring themselves to change. A number of contemporary organizations are still on the fence watching the SDWT parade go by. Some of them may wait too long.

SDWTs are clearly on the rise, not because they are more humane and not because altruistic managers find SDWTs morally compelling. To paraphrase Winston Churchill, SDWTs are the worst form of organization except for all the others. They are frustrating and messy and chaotic. But they work. They get results. Some organizations are excitedly leading the charge, others are moving cautiously, while still others are being dragged into an SDWT future by customers, competitors, or technologies. But they will go. Because as long as somebody can figure out how to improve results using SDWTs, others will have to figure out how to keep up with them.

Summary

Many supervisors at every level of an operation can see that the handwriting on the wall for their organizations reads: *self-directed work teams*.

SDWTs are not just another passing fad. There have been successful examples of these operations around for decades. In the last few years in particular, numerous organizations have used teams to improve results by 30 to 50 percent. SDWTs have clearly now matured from a small handful of applications to well into the thousands. Other current social and technical trends (discussed in the next chapter) clearly suggest that these operations are more consistent with contemporary organizational and social realities. If these trends continue, it is unlikely that a supervisor who fills multiple assignments during his or her career will not have a chance to act as a team leader in a high-performance work system. For many whose companies are making stronger commitments to these teams, the days of traditional supervision are already gone.

The Classic Supervisor Is an Endangered Species

"It can be argued that the traditional supervisor is an anachronism and an impediment to productivity."

Peter F. Drucker, *consultant and author*

IN A SURVEY at Monsanto's Krummrich plant in Sauget, Illinois, supervisors were asked if they believed that the traditional supervisory function would continue into the foreseeable future. Eighty percent replied that self-directed work teams were inevitable and that significant changes in their responsibilities would rapidly render the traditional role for supervisors obsolete. Other managers have echoed this prediction for their own companies as well. I remember the apprehension we felt as management in P&G's Chicago soap plant, for example, when in 1983 we received a memo from a senior officer of the company suggesting the eventual closure of facilities that did not make the transition to self-directed work teams with the necessitated change in the supervisory role. Says Bob Condella, Director of the Administrative Center at Corning, "Corning and American Industry are moving to empowerment. It is a competitive edge." What is the implication of this for traditional supervision? "We are absolutely looking for different qualities in leaders today."

Are these examples isolated instances, or are they harbingers of the future of management? Are traditional supervisors the dinosaurs of workplace evolution, destined to be placed in museums of natural history rather than in living organizations?

The Supervisory Role Is Evolving

We already see a broad-based organizational evolution toward highly empowered work teams and away from the traditional hierarchical and bureaucratic organizations of the past. We may be witnessing, in fact, the single most significant change in the role of management since the first industrial revolution created the job of professional supervision.

These changes will greatly reduce the need for traditional supervisory jobs because the teams will perform most of those supervisory responsibilities themselves. Peter Drucker, a consultant who has had an uncanny ability to anticipate future management trends, has predicted the demise of the traditional supervisor for some time. Edwards Deming, the father of the quality movement, also suggested that traditional management practices are not only obsolete but actually detrimental to the contemporary workforce. Known more for his clarity of thinking than his tact, Deming said: "Our prevailing system of management has destroyed our people."

Is the traditional supervisor an endangered species? Yes. Does this mean the people who are supervisors are no longer needed? No. But their role must evolve into something else. If the role of supervision stays static in the changing workplace, it will cease to add appreciable value to the organization. This is true, of course, for all levels of traditional supervision in the organizations attempting self-directed work. And understanding and gaining competency in these evolving team leadership responsibilities is becoming more important in corporations, schools, and public organizations for a number of reasons.

Why Empowerment Practices Will Continue

We have already reviewed why SDWTs are not just another management fad because of their remarkable (and sustainable) competitiveness. But there are at least three other reasons why the practices of empowerment will displace traditional supervisory practices at all levels of organizations:

1. Empowerment is an idea whose time has come.
2. Technology now makes empowerment practical.
3. Basic human needs make worker participation inevitable.

An Idea Whose Time Has Come

Empowerment tends to be most effective in precisely the kind of environments many organizations find themselves in today. Although these work systems are not a new idea, they are an idea whose time has come.

Many people argue that SDWTs are not as useful in settings where the work is highly mundane and repetitious and where consistency is more important than innovation. Nor, they say, do teams provide much benefit where performing the work requires little interdependence, where technologies are forgiving, and where single experts are best qualified to make independent decisions. SDWTs aren't for organizations in which stability is more important than flexibility, they say. But even if we accept these arguments, there are fewer and fewer of these kinds of organizations around anymore. And although there is some merit to these arguments, I do know of successful examples of SDWTs in each of the disputed categories. Lots of organizations, for example, use the teams to get rid of unnecessary mundane and repetitious work. By rotating from job to job, each team member gets a chance to learn a number of skills and avoid the boredom that comes from performing the same task ad nauseum. In fact, in many companies, managers who believe that SDWTs aren't appropriate for them because of the reasons just cited are simply dragging their feet while competitors in their own industries are already using high-performance work systems.

Different Business Environments Require Different Organizations

Complex work assignments usually require the input and buy-in of multiple people. The watchwords of responsiveness, quality, customer orientation, speed, productivity, and quality of work life have become more important than the previous unspoken workplace mottoes of control and regulation. Many people are finding that, even though they may have come from an organizational setting where empowered work teams may not have been as useful in the past, changes are being caused by customer demands, employee expectations, competition, government intervention, public pressure, environmentalism, technology, or any other of a host of possible reasons. They find themselves in a new world where empowered teams make a lot more sense than they did before. These new realities require organizations to evolve and roles to change, as illustrated in Figure 4.1. Look at some examples that range over the last several years.

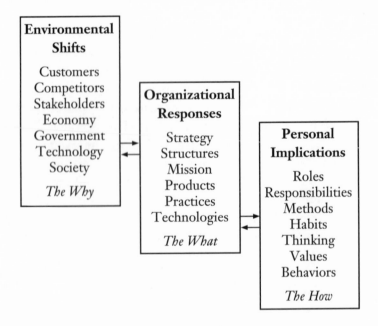

Figure 4.1   Responding to change.
Used with permission of The Fisher Group, Inc.

Time-to-Market Pressures

One division of Tektronix faced significant challenges from portable oscilloscope competitors who were quicker to the market and less expensive. For certain Tek divisions, market demands for development speed and manufacturing flexibility required a change to self-directed work teams. Traditional work systems simply would not have allowed the innovation—and, more importantly, the speed—required.

Historically, Tek design engineers had taken about five years to develop a new product technology. As long as they could keep a product family in the marketplace for about 10 years, this was not a problem. But increased competition from numerous well-financed and technologically advanced organizations changed the rules forever. Major product technologies were becoming obsolete in two years instead of ten. The technologies that new engineers learned in school were, in fact, often obsolete 12 months after graduation. Product development simply had to be done much more quickly. Designers no longer had time to waste in lengthy management reviews. Budget approval and tooling purchase couldn't wait for hierarchical red tape. There certainly wasn't time or money for major product and process rework once designs were finalized. Being first or second to the market (with a quality product) was important for capturing early market share with a longer revenue stream.

Once a new technology was introduced by Tek or by one of its able global competitors, there were fewer than 800 days to recoup the investment and make a profit. Looked at in this light, every day of lost opportunity caused by bureaucratic slowdowns was costing the company thousands of dollars.

Design teams of engineers and assemblers were empowered to make design decisions within certain boundary conditions. Approval-type activities were minimized and manufacturing team members were included early in the design process to lessen the downstream redesign work. Empowered manufacturing workers put a customer hotline on the floor to enable employees to respond to customer questions directly, and they put their workstations on wheels to allow for frequent reconfiguration of the workplace to correspond to ever changing process improvements. Most of the changes were instituted in real time by the empowered product SDWTs of manufacturing, marketing, finance, and engineering employees, who often couldn't afford to wait for management approval. The results? Several design teams brought new test and measurement products to market in half the time previously required. The need to redesign existing product lines to make them more manufacturable has decreased significantly.

Reduce Design Time

Boeing 777 design teams are another example of empowered teams being used to improve the speed and quality of product delivery. The teams are cross-functional groups of engineers, assemblers, and finance and marketing people. Decisions are made in real time without the traditional wasted periods while one department waits for the reactions or approval of another. Rotating leadership of the teams depends on the phase of the project. The early leadership of the teams came from design engineers because the primary product of the early phases is a good design for the new airplane. But in the production phases, the leadership shifted to manufacturing team members. Significant results occurred from what was then the largest industrial project of its type in the world, as mentioned in Chapter 3.

Cost Drivers

Stan Zelleck, plant manager of the Corning plant in Oneonta, New York, described some of Corning's reasons for moving to work cells (that company's version of SDWTs). In an employee meeting Zelleck walked up to the newsprint pad and began writing down the names of three competitors in the biotech and medical research plastic labware industry. He then wrote a comparison of financial data obtained from annual reports for the Corning plant and the competitors. The demonstration showed the difference in gross production costs for a large company like Corning and for small companies like some of the competitors.

While competitiveness has always been important, the new business challenges created by the global marketplace, small but well-capitalized competitors, and significantly higher customer expectations can't be met in the Oneonta plant with traditional bureaucratic solutions. They are too slow, too rigid, and too costly. With pressures from insurance companies to lower medical costs and from colleges to lower research costs, only dramatically increased productivity and rapid, ongoing process improvement can help Corning be competitive. The plant couldn't compete if everybody did one separate job in the traditional way. It couldn't afford equipment downtime while operators waited for engineers to fix the equipment. It couldn't afford the expensive material waste caused by not empowering workers to make real-time improvements to their processes. Corning had to offset the lower wage costs and lower overhead costs of its competitors by acting differently.

Cost pressures are affecting a number of similar operations. Says Jimmy Bilodeau, a plant manager with Apple Computer, "We have to show that we can still make quality, cost-competitive products at U.S. labor rates. That's what we intend to prove here with our teams. We can compete globally by using empowerment."

Learning from Success

In the late 1990s Weyerhaeuser embarked on a multiple-year project to transform numerous sawmills, pulp mills, box plants, and knowledge work organizations composed of corporate staff people into high-performance work systems. Why? Among other reasons, the forest products giant had purchased some pulp mills from Procter & Gamble that had been using self-directed work teams for some time. Like the handful of high-performance facilities already in place at Weyerhaeuser, these operations were impressive. Interested in the responsiveness, flexibility, positive employee relationships, and business results of these operations, Weyerhaeuser decided to improve work systems throughout the company.

Reduced Defense Spending

At companies like Lockheed Martin and Texas Instruments, one of the driving factors for empowered project teams is the dramatic change in defense spending. The end of the Cold War has affected millions of defense jobs across the globe. Only the most effective organizations— those that capitalize on the full potential of their human and technical resources—will survive. Executives know that this kind of effectiveness cannot be mandated by management but must be generated willingly by the workforce, which is empowered to take action on process improvements to lower costs and to improve speed, quality, and responsiveness.

New Social Complexity

Many other elements in the current business environment drive organizations toward high-performance work systems. There are more competitors. We are in the midst of a technology and information explosion. There are heightened environmental concerns. Both public utilities like Iowa Public Service and corporations like Monsanto, for example, are looking for ways to cover the cost of conformance to stricter pollution laws through work redesign improvements by teams.

Current complexities are affecting noncommercial enterprises as well. What is teaching school like today? Consider the speed with which important education information changes now. How would you like to teach social studies when even the people who make maps can't keep up with all the country name and border changes of modern society? For the last several years there have been periods of only a brief few months when even the latest world globes were accurate. Can traditional centralized curriculum committees plan classes and purchase texts anymore, or do SDWTs of teachers have to make these calls in real time? Consider this. Steve Posner, a former USC professor, has a monthly periodical for high school students called *Fast Times*. The periodical has a distribution of more than 19,000 schools with a readership of more than a million students. Its purpose? To supplement social science texts, which can't keep up with the changes in today's world. Texts can't be printed fast enough to be relevant, let alone accurate, in today's quick-paced world. Even the periodical format is becoming too slow. Schools without Internet connections are now at a serious educational disadvantage. To keep school materials updated, they must normally be downloaded from the Internet rather than purchased from a bookstore.

Changing Workforce Expectations

Some organizations are finding that they need SDWTs to recruit topnotch talent. Highly trained technical people nowadays want more than money; they want influence and high quality of work life too. This is affecting a number of operations. In parts of the United States, for example, the baby boom workers are gone. For R.R. Donnelley & Sons in the Los Angeles area, the reason for empowerment is attracting and retaining skilled talent, workers who are no longer willing to accept the quality of work life of a traditional printing operation. Teachers are increasingly unwilling to endure the rigorous demands of teaching and extracurricular schedules without more say on how school and professional development days should be spent.

There are other human reasons, of course, for moving away from traditional operations. The general manager of the financial division of the Seattle Metro public transportation organization, Tracey Petersen, is supporting the SDWT concept because she believes it is now a moral imperative. Today's workforce has higher expectations for involvement and is better educated and more capable than ever before. This human potential is often vastly underutilized in traditional organizations, which treat workers as hands and backs instead of whole human beings with minds and hearts.* "They deserve better," says Petersen. "I have come to believe that I have a moral responsibility to manage the workforce in a way that allows them more influence over their work life. It's the right thing to do for our staff and it has given us better results for our customers."

Adapting to Change

For these and other reasons, SDWTs are a timely idea in the modern work environment. In fact, some operations are using the teams primarily for their proven flexibility and adaptability to almost any change. While we don't know what specific changes will be in store for us, the last decades have taught us that we can depend on constant change. The nature of the future—the "constant whitewater" described by Professor Peter Vaill and others—is such that more and more organizations find self-directed work teams newly appropriate for their evolving needs.

Technology to Support Empowerment

The second major reason why these nontraditional work organizations and work roles will become more prominent in the future is team facil-

---

* Jack Sherwood has often used this terminology when working with clients.

itating technology. Now, with e-mail, videoconferencing from personal computers, faxes, the Internet, company intranets, and telephone networking alternatives, there are cost-effective technological options that allow the increased utilization of meaningful work team involvement. Groupware software packages facilitate team involvement as well. These packages include decision support systems (automated Delphi and nominal group techniques, etc.) and systems to support collaboration (shared authoring processes, shared project management software, virtual meeting support, bulletin boards, etc.). Most importantly, business information systems now make timely cost, quality, and project status information available to all team members without regard to rank or level.

It is difficult to overstate the impact of this on the workplace. Technology can now provide some substitutions for the information passing and coordination role of the traditional hierarchy. This allows teams to be directed by the work and information rather than by managers. Each of these facilitating factors deserves some elaboration.

Team Decision-Making and Problem-Solving Technologies

In a front-page story in the *Seattle Times* a few years ago a reporter noted that Boeing had begun replacing "imperious, turf-minded supervisors with self-regulating, cross-discipline teams" in various parts of the corporation. The story described the 777 design teams of 8 to 10 designers, production experts, customer support personnel, and finance specialists. "The idea," the paper reported, "is to have each team consider the aircraft as a whole and to empower each team to act quickly on ideas, free from the chain-of-command second-guessing." To do this has required a technology that until recently was not cost-effective. "Computer modeling," the story continued, ". . . is a linchpin tool. The teams have the capability, via a computer screen, to design and match up parts for the entire aircraft, minimizing the need for expensive mockups" and time-consuming management authorization "to see if parts fit and alterations work." These technologies have enabled the teams to make decisions and solve problems that would have required a traditional supervisor before. Since this observation just a few years ago, similar technologies to facilitate empowerment and lessen the need for supervision have exploded into the workplace.

There are software packages that facilitate team staffing decisions by compiling complete work and education histories of employees everywhere in the search area. Motorola uses computer polling to allow groups to do assessments and display results in real time as charts and graphs. Teams can use virtual whiteboards to display and copy their meeting notes. Voice recognition systems will soon simplify computer systems further by reducing the training required to operate these software packages.

Other human technologies like the search conference and large-group information and decision-making processes are used widely by companies like Ford, Corning, Weyerhaeuser, and others to enable groups of 200 people or more to participate in real-time decision making. My partners and I participated in a process at a Chevron refinery where groups of 500 employees met to share information and make decisions. Many companies have also used both synchronous and asynchronous voting technologies to make decisions or gather data affecting and involving large groups. Corporations can pass along information about a business decision to employees using the company intranet and/or e-mail, and then get representatives together in a conference and have them vote or gather data at terminals spread throughout the meeting room. The information is displayed in real time in front of the room. Many Microsoft products now allow multiple-user input and review.

There are countless additional examples of technology aiding empowerment. NASA and others are working on small personal communicators that will have all the functionality of modern personal computers in a box the size of a computer mouse. These or other wearable computers now under development will eventually make it possible for team members to be in constant communication with each other.

Team Information Systems

All of these technologies, if used properly, provide processes that can focus teams and define legitimate opportunities for action. Effective utilization of these and other decision-making and problem-solving technologies depends, of course, on the quality of the data used. Thankfully there are also technologies to aid teams with information gathering, sharing, and evaluation. This eliminates much of the ineptness that often characterizes the ineffective groups that are "unbur-dened" by timely and relevant facts and data. Those are the kinds of groups we have ridiculed in the past. (Question: What is a camel? Answer: A horse designed by a committee.)

In the past, organizations that wanted to include team members in decisions had a difficult time getting so many people good information in a timely way. But group information sharing is no longer the logisti-cal problem it once was. My colleagues Steve Rayner and Mareen Fisher and I were duly impressed, for example, when we visited an NEC factory in Toyama, Japan to see the work area filled with terminals that could be accessed by anyone on the floor at any time. These terminals were linked to a file server containing information on goal achieve-ment, cost, quality, waste sources, machine efficiencies, and specific project indicators, which was updated every forty minutes. Armed with this kind of timely data, people can become significantly involved in the management of the business in ways that were not practical before the introduction of these technologies. In the U.S., several companies are developing similar systems.

At the Elkton, Maryland, Air Products and Chemicals Polymers chemical plant, any employee on site can access real-time information on new orders, production status, quality, schedules, and a variety of other production information. As I look back on these systems now, I am amazed at how far the technology has come. Certain Hewlett-Packard employees now have data about their production lines updated and dis-tributed every 20 minutes. Cummins employees view real-time produc-tion and order completion information on large screens distributed throughout the factory. The technology explosion won't stop until every-one knows everything anytime they want. The downside to this technol-ogy, of course, is dealing with information overload. Data mining—the ability to dig into data to sort out the really important information from the nice-to-know information—will be the biggest information challenge for teams in the future.

Information Gathering

Other technologies also make information gathering for teams much more practical. Communication from customers, vendors, and other people in the company can be done in a way that is more accurate, more understandable to the team, and more human than memos or supervisory monologues. Members of one organization design team from Northern Telecom, for example, took a film crew with them as they searched the world for cutting-edge organizational alternatives in Canada, the United States, Japan, and Korea. The video was a much more powerful way for the representatives to communicate their findings than a lecture from a supervisor or human resources professional would have been. New computerized training programs have menus or story-driven activities that allow the team member to access world-class technical experts at the touch of a button without going through any time-consuming management channels.

Information Is Power

These technologies have facilitated empowerment because ultimately information *is* power. Information is the power to foresee trends, to solve or avoid problems, and to make good decisions. Participation without information is a sham. But with good information (as well as legitimate authority and resources to act on that information), people can effectively get involved as partners in their organizations. Information not only supports involvement, it *causes* involvement. I have seen numerous examples of team members who have been drawn into improving a long-standing work process, for example, simply because they learned that there was a better way or because they found out for the first time how much money the process cost. I have seen people at all levels of organizations—*even though it sometimes meant personal inconvenience*—decide to do things differently when confronted with the facts.

Technological Substitutions for Hierarchy

These same technologies can often complete some of the traditional tasks of supervision. Control equipment in factories, for example, can provide operators with up-to-the-minute information that previously had to be communicated by the boss. Computers in service operations can help professionals synthesize and prioritize information in a way that was possible before only by depending on the supervisor. Federal Express drivers carry palm-sized computers that give them pickup and delivery addresses for overnight packages. These digital readouts substitute for supervisor-determined job assignments—which, by the way, would be too slow.

Other technologies are allowing substitutions for the oversight and coordinating functions of a traditional hierarchy as well. For example, T. J. Rodgers, CEO of Cypress Semiconductor, has a system that allows him to review the goals of all 1500 employees in 4 hours. He does this weekly, then telephones and chats with people. He doesn't call to supervise but to offer the help his position and clout allow. This substitutes for layers of expensive bureaucracy to align teams toward common goals and to minimize overlapping efforts in different parts of the operation. Bill Gates takes e-mail from any employee at any time. This allows a flattening of the hierarchy and give Gates direct access to information such as customer complaints, new product ideas, and employee concerns that would have been filtered out by middle management in a traditional operation.

Technology Helps but Is Not the Whole Answer

As always, technology by itself is not the answer. In their book *Teams and Technology*, authors Donald Mankin, Susan Cohen, and Tora Bikson argue that advances in information technology cannot unleash the full potential of collaborative work unless complementary changes are made in work flow, team structure, supervisory styles, and work cultures. But if teams apply and customize the technologies appropriately, the technology can become a tremendous tool for real empowerment, which until recently was unavailable.

AT&T, IBM, and others, for example, put many of their salespeople into virtual offices. The virtual office concept means that sales professionals work almost exclusively out of their cars and homes without common offices, clustered desks, or weekly staff meetings on site. Only a few years ago this organization design would have required a hierarchical approach to management. Someone (presumably the boss) would have to approve decisions, solve problems, and maintain consistency and control across the sales force. With modern technology, however, there are other alternatives to a single boss coordinating everything. Cellular phones, portable faxes, and computer networks allow the rapid transmittal of information from one salesperson to others. Teleconferencing makes meetings and real-time group decisions possible for people who are located all over the globe. While this setup will certainly still have its special challenges, as mentioned in Chapter 26, virtual office members can be self-directed work teams. That would have been nearly impossible in even the recent past.

Worker Participation Is Inevitable

The third and perhaps the strongest reason of all to question the long-term viability of the traditional supervisory role is that some form of worker participation is inevitable. Look at the remarkable world events of the last few decades. Forever etched in the minds of the observers of communism and authoritarian governments is a nearly incomprehensible television picture: the mobs tearing down the Berlin wall with crowbars and fists as the guards look on passively. Many of us thought that event would not occur in our lifetimes. And that was only one of the remarkable developments of these last few important years. We saw Boris Yeltsin calling successfully for the Soviet people to stand up against the military leaders who kidnapped Mikhail Gorbachev in a coup attempt designed to stave off impending republican reform. We saw the limp body of an executed oppressive East European dictator, and the bravery of the single demonstrator attempting to block an approaching tank column in Tienanmen square. In countries in Eastern Europe, Asia, Africa, and South America, democratic reformers have replaced totalitarian predecessors (with varying degrees of success). The former U.S.S.R. has been dissolved.

The World of Democratic Reform

Think about the amazing political collage of these last few years. Popular revolutions either toppled long-standing and seemingly unmovable autocratic governments or focused world attention on the population's demands for significant democratic reform. Why? Because the human spirit longs to be free. Repression is less tolerated in the modern world of human rights advocates supported by a world press. For all its weaknesses, people still want democracy. Some have been willing to die for it.

In a world that celebrates a rich diversity of cultural heritage, I find it interesting that virtually all cultures have stories or religious texts that are remarkably similar to what the Judeo-Christian cultures know as the Golden Rule: to treat others as you want to be treated. Most people eschew even the subtle forms of human subjugation of one class of people by another. People will continue to seek equality, influence, and freedom.

Democratic Reform in the Workplace

This freedom will be demanded increasingly, not only from political systems but from organizational systems as well. The autocratic practices of traditional organizations will simply be rendered obsolete as people demand the right to be included in the governance of their work lives, just as the students and citizens of the world are demanding the right to influence politics. Modern-day revolutionary heroes in the mold of Thomas Jefferson are alive and well in today's workplace. And they are still saying the same thing. Consider the following only slightly modified version of a famous revolutionary document:

> **We hold these truths to be self-evident, that all people are created equal, that they are endowed by their Creator with certain unalienable Rights, that among these are Life, Liberty and the pursuit of Happiness. That to secure these rights Management is instituted among People at work, deriving its just powers from the consent of the managed. That whenever any Form of Management becomes destructive of these ends, it is the Right of the People to alter or to abolish it, and to institute new Management, laying its foundation on such principles and organizing its powers in such form, as to them shall seem most likely to effect their Safety and Happiness.**

Worker participation is a manifestation of people's desire for democracy in the workplace. This trend will naturally follow the democratization of other political systems. SDWTs are typically the natural extension of this movement. Although they are not democracies in the strict sense of the term, they do allow the kind of influence on the workplace that has normally been unavailable in traditionally managed operations.

Summary

Because companies are replacing traditional organizations with self-directed work teams, a number of supervisors at all levels of organizations are in the middle of a major evolution of their work roles and responsibilities. This trend is not an aberration but instead a harbinger of the future. Why?

1. Empowerment is an idea whose time has come. Recent time-to-market pressures, cost drivers, social complexities, reduced defense spending, demographic changes, and regular unpredictable change are a few of the reasons why SDWTs are newly appropriate for today's workplace. Traditional workplaces just can't handle these situations as well.
2. Technology now makes empowerment practical.
3. Basic human needs make worker participation inevitable.

For many team leaders newly submerged in SDWTs, however, the transition is considerably more difficult than they expected. Managers newly introduced to team management often face the predictable kinds of dilemmas that are highlighted in the next chapter.

A Rocky Road: The Transition from Supervisor to Team Leader

"Working through the corporation for 40 years under the autocratic system was a lot easier, particularly when you want something done quickly and you are convinced you know the right way to do it. It is a lot easier to say, 'Okay, boys, we're going to Chicago tomorrow,' rather than sit down and say, 'All right, first of all, do we want to go out of town? And where do we want to go—east or west? And if we're going west, which of seven cities do we go to?' And we finally narrow it down and go to Cedar Rapids, Iowa, and I really didn't want to go

there. I spend a lot of time working at participative management. But I have to be honest and say that I think we get better decisions out of it."

Roger Smith, *former CEO of General Motors*

CHANGING INTO A team leader is difficult. Not everybody makes it. Fred Eintracht, a manager who pioneered SDWTs at Texas Instruments, puts it this way: "Self-managed work teams are not for the faint of heart." Consider a few of the predictable problems people encounter when they are changing from the role of traditional manager (supervisor) to that of leader of an empowered work team:

The programmers Bob supervised at the insurance company had gone through a major organizational change to become a self-directing team. When he asked for clarification about his role, however, people would usually tell him what not to do: "Don't control" or "Don't direct people anymore." Or sometimes he would be told to "lead instead of manage" or to "be a coach instead of a boss." Was he supposed to just turn over all of his responsibilities to the team? Was there a job for him here anymore? What value did he add?

Carlos, a rookie operations team leader in a progressive manufacturing plant in the southwest United States, was confused and frustrated by a recent workshop he attended. Titled "The Role of Team Leaders," the workshop made him feel that there was a right and a wrong style of management for self-directed work teams. The right style described by the instructors felt unnatural and awkward to Carlos. Was he supposed to act like he was somebody else? He wondered if his decision to come to this plant had been a mistake.

Mary was a management team leader for a division of an electronics company that was changing to work systems based on a high level of employee commitment and participation. She saw the teams struggling with important issues about which she had extremely strong opinions. But should she say something to them at the possible risk of "taking over" and shutting down their emerging sense of involvement?

Typical Transition Problems

Bob, Carlos, and Mary are experiencing the painful but predictable transition problems associated with the change from being a supervisor to being a team leader. Some people make the switch almost effortlessly. Says Terri Volpe, a controller who became a team leader of an SDWT of finance and accounting professionals at Tektronix:

> **For me it was major relief. It was finally the opportunity to do business the way I thought business ought to be done. Instead of hanging around the office every day checking to make sure that everybody was doing what I told them, people go off and do their jobs . . . and come up with some better results than what I originally thought they were going to go after.**

But this sense of relief is not a common sentiment for people who struggle with the personal change required. One team leader from Shell Canada, for example, described his feeling during the transition from traditional to team leader practices as being like having one foot on the dock and one foot on a boat. You're not sure whether to stay on the dock (which represents the stable, predictable management methods of the past) or whether to jump on the speedboat revving up to head off in a new direction (the uncertain and fast-moving future). In some ways it comes down to taking a leap of faith.

Paul Whitesides, the staff psychologist for the Highline School District near Seattle, Washington, says this is a very personal change for team leaders to make. He compares it to moving a cemetery. "You have to move one body at a time," he says. Changing traditional approaches to management requires far more than changing technique. For many of us it requires a fundamental reassessment of the hierarchical paradigm on which organizations have been based since the turn of the century. How do you know when you had made the switch successfully? One Tektronix operations team leader says it is harder than most people think. Many who claim they have always acted this way are fooling themselves. "If you think you are already there," the team leader says, "you haven't even started." She adds that there is hope, however. "If you think you have a long way to go, then you're already on the way."

To further complicate matters, we have often developed our traditional approaches to management because it was required of us by the same organization that now wants us to change. Says Rick Nicholson, a former human resources executive with Weyerhaeuser:

> **... One of the most difficult changes to make when implementing high performance systems is for the "manager" to become the "leader." ... they have been promoted, recognized, and rewarded for their controlling skills, not their delegation, coaching and facilitation skills.**

Supervisors feel a little schizophrenic as they watch the leaders who built the system that created the need for traditional management practices in the first place (and who were often seen as the personification of those practices) turn around and call for a change.

There is considerable evidence that making the change from traditional supervisor to team leader can be very unpleasant. Prominent researchers like Rosabeth Moss Kanter, for example, have highlighted some of the typical concerns associated with this change; while they were at Harvard, professors Walton, Schlesinger, and Klein also catalogued the difficulty in numerous articles with titles like, "Why Supervisors Resist Employee Involvement," "Work Restructuring and the Supervisor: Some Role Difficulties," and "Do Supervisors Thrive in Participative Work Systems?"

It Is Difficult for Supervisors at Every Management Level to Become Team Leaders

First-level supervisors are not alone. Senior-level and mid-level supervisors have also experienced some considerable difficulty in these transitional settings. At Honeywell, R. J. Boyle, a vice president, reported that supervisors in upper management expressed discouragement when early attempts at empowerment created numerous task forces that were clearly "out of control." Roger Smith, former CEO of General Motors, says it was easier just to tell people what to do than to manage his own team of direct reports as a leader/coach. Mid-level management supervisors confess frustration with their ever increasing loss of control over work processes; senior staff supervisors dislike the premature challenge to their expertise made by others who take on responsibilities previously held only by the supervisors as functional experts. It just flat *ain't easy* for many supervisors to become team leaders regardless of their position in the organization. In fact, it is harder for management to make the change to SDWTs than for anybody else.

Changing to SDWTs Is Harder for Team Leaders than Team Members

Based on research by the experts just mentioned, as well as my own experience with these transitions, the graph in Figure 5.1 depicts the contrast in the ease of transition to self-directed work teams between non-managers and managers. While the difficulty may not be manifested until later in the implementation process, it is almost always significantly more difficult for supervisors to make these changes than it is for the rest of the workforce.

Unfortunately, to avoid these transition problems, some companies have given up and walked away from self-directed work team philosophies partway through the implementation process. Thinking that the medicine is worse than the illness, they have prematurely aborted the empowerment process before it has had a chance to show a return on the financial and human investment already made. Some have abandoned the effort because they were more interested in maintaining management control than in taking the uncomfortable personal risks

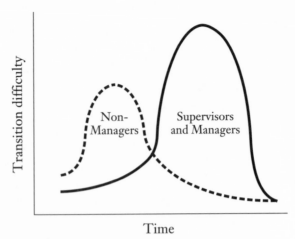

Figure 5.1 The relative difficulty of changing to self-directed work systems.
Used with permission of The Fisher Group, Inc.

required to get improved results from empowerment. Others, like Jack's company mentioned in Chapter 1, have eliminated or steamrolled over some supervisors to try to make the implementation work without them. Obviously, none of these options is the best way to resolve these difficult but predictable transition issues. When organizations are committed to the change process, they will take the time to work through the difficulties with supervisors in a way that makes the most sense for their set of circumstances. It doesn't make the transition easy, but it does make it possible.

Four Reasons the Transition Is So Difficult

Some supervisors are frustrated with the change to the team leader role because they have a fundamental, gut-level disagreement with this direction. They feel it is an abrogation of management rights and responsibilities that will lead their company on the sure path to chaos and destruction. Generally speaking, however, very few supervisors continue to have this disagreement once they really understand SDWT leadership. The four most common reasons for supervisor transition difficulty are:

1. The change to SDWTs is frequently seen as a net loss of power or status for management.
2. The team leader role hasn't been well defined for most supervisors.
3. Some supervisors are concerned about losing their jobs due to SDWTs.
4. In what may be called a double standard syndrome, many supervisors are expected to manage in a way that is very different from the way they are managed themselves.

Each of these issues deserves elaboration.

Dealing with the Perceived Loss of Power or Status

The first reason that supervisors at every level of the organization resist the change to team leadership roles is that they see it as giving up something. Two senior-level supervisors I worked with at one large company, for example, had this difficulty. Both were asked to relinquish certain executive perquisites to create an egalitarian climate more conducive to SDWTs. One of the supervisors hesitated to part with his preferred parking space and the other refused to give up a spacious office. When I asked them about their concerns, both said that they had worked long and hard to get where they were. They felt they deserved the little extras commensurate with their positions. I don't think that in either case was the parking space or office the real concern. It was the power, the prestige, or the status that these things symbolized.

"I miss the prestige, I can't say I don't," says Miles Majure, who was a second-level manager with Duke Power in Huntersville, North Carolina. He helps to coach new teams now and likes the fact that the workers are happier than before. But he still has that sense that he has come down in the world. That is not an uncommon perception. Our society often judges us by the work titles and responsibilities we have. People understand and respect *supervisor, manager,* or *vice president. Team leader* they don't. It isn't common enough yet to have earned its own appropriate level of recognition.

Position Status

Once, in a training class, as we were talking about the role of the team leader, a burly middle-level supervisor from Shell Canada interrupted the discussion. "What am I going to tell my mother?" he asked. At first I thought he was joking. Then he continued. "How am I going to explain to my family and friends that I am not a director anymore? How can I tell them that I don't run this business?" He was genuinely concerned that his change in responsibilities and job title would be seen as a demotion by the people he cared about.

Dysfunctional Status Symbols

Some people might think these are trivial concerns. They are not. Some companies are now holding sessions for the families of former supervisors to help them understand the importance of the new roles and reduce the anguish of the transitioning leader. Even if these responses sound petty, I would suggest that many of us feel the same way even if we don't admit it openly. We all want to be recognized, rewarded, and important. But we can't let these normal desires interfere with workplace effectiveness.

Substituting the dysfunctional status symbols common to hierarchical organizations with more functional ways to meet these personal needs is very important. Some companies, for example, have team leaders mentor other people. These assignments help the organization by facilitating the transfer of skills and knowledge to a broader base of the population while also recognizing teachers for their expertise. Other organizations have made former supervisors into consultants or have given team managers key roles in important technical or business projects with high visibility.

Unclear Roles Cause Unnecessary Transition Difficulties

Most of supervisors' concerns about a loss of power or status are resolved when organizations create appropriate team leader roles and then make these roles clear. The feeling of disempowerment is often based on a misunderstanding (or an organizational misapplication) of the SDWT concept that engenders the belief that empowerment is a win-lose game. Workers win and supervisors lose.

Much of the concern expressed by traditional supervisors at all levels of the organization, as illustrated in the stories of Bob, Carlos, and Mary, can be alleviated through ongoing discussions that clarify the new role of team leader (assuming, of course, that the role has been appropriately designed). The proof then is in the pudding. The organization must back up these discussions by reinforcing them through the reward and information systems. Successful organizations aid the team leaders in defining and becoming skilled in the new roles. Unfortunately, this is often not done very well. A lack of organizational support and role clarity condemns the typical supervisor to what is becoming known as the "wingwalker problem."

The Wingwalker Problem

The predicament of many supervisors can be compared to that of the wingwalkers in the barnstorming days of early aviation. Like the wingwalkers, supervisors at all levels are asked to figuratively change positions on a moving biplane when they start using any significant form of empowerment. There is an important rule known by all wingwalkers, however, that is very useful for people in similarly turbulent situations: *Never let go with one hand before you grab hold with the other one.* All experienced wingwalkers know this to be a useful rule.

But this rule is often broken during the transition process. Supervisors like Bob are told what to let go of (e.g., "Do not control or direct anymore") rather than what to grab hold of. That is not good enough. The result is as devastating to the organization as it is to the wingwalker. The most common response is to hold on more tightly as the "wind velocity" of business demands increases (thereby struggling even harder to hold on to the comfortable but no longer appropriate role). Other supervisors simply let go and abdicate responsibility to ill-prepared team members.

To use another analogy, being told what not to do is like trying to teach someone to ride a bike by telling him or her how not to do it. The results are almost always disastrous as the new bike rider keeps thinking, "Don't lose your balance and fall down." What usually happens?

We do exactly the thing we are trying so hard to avoid. Supervisors at all levels need to have a clear understanding of the team leader role and how it differs from that of classical management. Moreover, we need to understand that this new role will change over time as the teams mature. Without this understanding, supervisors are left in the dark with unrealistic expectations for their teams and each other. This is a very serious problem, and the bulk of the next two chapters will deal with a better approach to this role clarification process.

Job Security Concerns Frustrate Supervisory Change

The third reason for frustration among supervisors in transition is that they often perceive self-directed work teams as organizations without a real role for them. For some it is a basic job security issue. Look at what we call these organizational structures. *Self-directed* or *self-managed* work teams sound suspiciously like organizations that do not need supervisors anymore. This notion is reinforced when companies like Dana Corporation publicly announce the reduction of management levels from 14 to 6 due to moving responsibilities down into the organization. General Mills claims that much of the productivity improvements it has realized from SDWTs come from the elimination of middle management.

Other companies, like Tektronix and Monsanto, have offered early retirement incentives to encourage management downsizing, and then engaged in efforts to create self-directed work teams because there were not enough supervisors to manage in the traditional way. All of this is, obviously, a matter of concern for supervisors.

Every Team Needs a Coach

While it is true that fewer policing and directing tasks are required in these organizations, there is a corresponding need in SDWT operations for an increase in group facilitation, skill development activities, and information processing. These work systems require a formal leadership role. Although organizations (both SDWT and traditional operations) are eliminating supervision positions, this doesn't necessarily mean an elimination of people. In fact, some organizations have discovered that they have taken out managers to the peril of the operation.

Tom Clark, a senior manager at Tennessee Eastman, notes that while self-directed work teams can be successful in sustaining their operations without management (Tennessee Eastman has had some examples of teams operating without managers), these ". . . Teams haven't improved their operation without the help of a team leader." Clark's conclusion? We need team leaders. These are not supervisors who direct and control people, of course, but team leaders who teach and support them. In the Procter & Gamble plant where I worked as a team leader, a level of management that had been eliminated earlier was added back several months later. Was this a failure of the self-directed work team design? Certainly not. Our assumption about the elimination of management from the teams was naive. Every team needs a coach. Successful organizations normally change supervisory jobs into team leadership positions. They don't just strip the resources from the operation.

What Happens When There Are Too Many Supervisors?

Some organizations find during the transition that they have too many supervisors. Originally staffed for traditional operations, which required multiple levels of supervision, these organizations find they have more supervisors than new team leader positions. What do they do? Some operations have laid these supervisors off. This is extremely unwise for several reasons. First, the unnecessary loss of the supervisors' expertise to the operation can be deadly to less mature teams. Second, management support is critical to the success of these implementations. We simply cannot expect support from managers who suspect that they will lose their jobs as a result of SDWTs. What are some alternatives?

- When the Rohm and Haas Louisville, Kentucky plant changed over to self-directing work teams several years ago, there were fewer team leader positions available than people who had been supervisors. To deal with this problem, the company made a number of supervisors into training coordinators who were responsible for managing the endless education requirements of the team. Interestingly, after several years of using high-performance work systems, Rohm and Haas, like P&G, found that it needed to add back some of the resources that had originally been stripped from the teams. The "temporary team coordinator" role was formalized rather than being eliminated as originally planned. Although the plant still operates with fewer managers than before, Rohm and Haas found that the teams needed the formal leadership support.

- While most companies don't replace retiring supervisors in this situation, one company *hired back* some of the supervisors who took early retirement as part-time trainers.
- At another company supervisors agreed to provide 18 months of technical advice to the teams. At the end of that time the company agreed to place the supervisors into other positions.
- In still another company 25 supervisors participated in designing an SDWT system with only 10 team leader positions. Those who weren't selected for the jobs were guaranteed their existing salary package if they became team members, or they had the option to transfer.
- Many organizations find meaningful work for supervisors in special assignments.

Other companies have used other solutions. Although there are no perfect solutions to these difficult business realities, these approaches minimized what could have been not only a serious disenfranchisement of the displaced supervisors, but also a great trauma to the survivors. Instead, these approaches institutionalized a process for skill, interpersonal, and business development in the facilities and gave these supervisors a personal vehicle for providing their teaching and mentoring resources to the team members.

The Double Standard

The fourth common transition problem comes from the all-too-frequent perception that there is a double standard for treating team leaders and team members. The way some organizations implement self-directed work teams reinforces the notion that self-direction is only for the work team and not for the leaders. It is seen as something that "the top tells the middle to do with the bottom." Empowerment should work everywhere in the organization and not just for nonmanagement teams. If these participative systems are to endure, they will have appropriate inclusion and roles for everyone.

Unfortunately, many organizations have introduced self-directed work team practices in a way that has greatly threatened supervisors—the most critical players in assuring the overall success of the SDWT effort. These shortfalls have created frustration and resistance, which are unnecessary when compared to what some organizations have encountered during the transition process.

Successful Team Leader Transition at Kodak

There are, fortunately, some good examples of successful transitions from the supervisor to the team leader role. Several team leaders at Kodak, for example, made what workers called "big changes." Most of the supervisors had three things going against them, if one were inclined to believe these frequently repeated (but often inaccurate) stereotypes. First, they had military management backgrounds. ("When I say jump, you say how high.") Second, they worked in a company with a reputation for management techniques that were contrary to many of the SDWT concepts. ("It might work in some new companies in California, but it will never work here.") Third, they had held traditional supervisory roles for a number of years. ("You can't teach old dogs new tricks.") Despite these three strikes, and although they had had reputations as successful autocratic supervisors, these managers had changed over several months to be very good examples of SDWT team leaders. This same story has been repeated in other companies by supervisors at other levels as well.

What was different for this group of supervisors? They managed their change process to assure the maximum possibility of success. They started a weekly study group, for example, to review the dozen books they had been reading as a group. These sessions ended up providing a lot of learning, helping the supervisors to understand the changing nature of the Kodak business environment and to clarify the leadership role required to be successful in the future. Through their reading, the supervisors discovered that a number of different companies were facing challenges that could no longer be met successfully with a traditional approach to supervision. Consequently, through their discussions about the challenges facing their own business with strong competitive pressure from Fuji film, the supervisors decided together that they needed to change the way they managed.

The supervisor team then made a number of changes. Traditional supervisory functions were assumed by the work teams as the teams were trained to accept them. Their job assignments then expanded to incorporate work tasks that before had only been done by higher-level managers. Performance appraisals were changed to support the new responsibilities of team leaders. Perhaps most importantly, the new leaders were led, empowered, and supported through the transition by a manager who modeled appropriate team leader behaviors. Much of the clarity they received about the new role came from watching their "boss" act that way himself. Rather than tell them, for example, that they needed to be sensitive to team input, he opened an early study group by requesting feedback on his own performance. Though the team was initially cautious about giving the boss honest feedback, it gradually became a norm inside and outside of the study group. And once they saw it done, it was much easier to go out and do the same thing with their own teams.

Summary

Changing from a supervisor into a team leader is a difficult process. In fact, it is much more difficult for supervisors at all levels of the operation to change to SDWTs than it is for anyone else. Many supervisors have problems during the transition because (1) it is seen as a loss of power or status, (2) the new role is unclear, (3) they fear losing their jobs, or (4) this role isn't modeled by the leaders of their own management teams. Despite what the name might imply, however, self-directed work teams do need team leaders. While these role changes are usually difficult, examples like that of the team leaders at Kodak show that they can be made very successfully.

A more detailed look at the 13 Room department at Kodak in the next two chapters will begin to clarify some of the key transition learnings to consider during the change from supervisory to team leader roles.

Building the Foundation for Change

The Kodak 13 Room Story: Empowering Team Leaders

"The signal benefit the great leaders confer is to embolden the rest of us to live according to our own best selves, to be active, insistent, and resolute in affirming our own sense of things . . . And they attest to the wisdom and power that may lie within the most unlikely of us . . . Great Leaders, in short, justify themselves by emancipating and empowering their followers."

Arthur M. Schlesinger Jr., *historian and former advisor to Presidents Kennedy and Johnson*

My colleague Steve Rayner and I were commissioned by the Work in America Institute to write a case about a successful SDWT of team leaders at Kodak. We discovered what we think you will agree is a remarkable story. Following are excerpts from that case, which was written primarily by Steve.

HOUSED ON THE grounds of Eastman Kodak's enormous industrial complex in Rochester, New York, is a manufacturing department known as 13 Room. Here color film for the consumer and professional markets is manufactured. Eastman Kodak's 13 Room offers a dramatic example of how to introduce self-directed work team management in a manner that draws strength from the management team rather than alienating it.

Background

The process of producing color film is very complex. Some 3000 potential variances have been identified through the process flow—any one of which can result in an unacceptable final product. To add to the difficulty of manufacturing, many of the steps done by the 13 Room employees are still performed manually. The critical step of formulating the chemicals, for example, is still done entirely by hand in a manner similar to the method devised by George Eastman decades ago.

After completion of a successful project with Eastman Kodak's International Operations, Ralph Olney became manager of 13 Room. The organization he inherited consisted of nearly 200 operators, supervisors, and managers. Within the corporation the operation was seen as a solid and consistent performer.

During his project with International, Olney had had the opportunity to broaden his perspectives of not only the film business, but of industry in general. He had witnessed dramatic competitive changes in a variety of markets and could see the traumatic impact they were having on many corporations. As Olney was reflecting on his new position and what he hoped to achieve, he began to recognize that a new management approach would be required, one that unleashed the energy and creativity of the workforce by developing workers' capabilities. He needed a team of managers who were selflessly committed to transferring their knowledge and expertise to those who worked with them.

Management Practices Reflected the Military Background of the Supervisors

Historically, nearly 80 percent of the supervisors in the various film production departments at Kodak had backgrounds that included military service. As a result, many of the management practices seemed to reflect a military model. Typically the supervisor was the technical expert and gave directives that specified exactly what was to be done and how to do it. Orders were generally followed by subordinates without comment or question. The hierarchy was clearly defined.

Olney recognized that this perspective had some predictable consequences. First, supervisors tended to be so directly involved in the running of the work area that it was not uncommon for them to be on 24-hour call. If a process problem arose, regardless of the hour (day or night), it was likely that they would be called to fix it. Second, operators had come to believe that the correct way to address a problem was to call the supervisor or some other technical expert for the solution. Generally, operators had been given little opportunity to take on expanded responsibilities and were sometimes punished when they did. Although 13 Room was unique in many respects, it was not immune to the impact of a work culture that had tended to reward tight, autocratic supervision, along with minimum operator development and involvement. As one operator described it:

> You were literally told what to do and how to do it. You never got any information about the business or even how the unit was performing. You were completely in the dark. And if you didn't follow up on a demand you'd been given and the foremen found out about it, the comment back would be "You don't need a badge to leave here."

An Environment of Trust Is Created

Olney's first words to his reports were, "Let's figure out a way to work ourselves out of our jobs." The comment was taken seriously by the majority of his staff. Olney quickly created an unusual environment of trust because he had worked with several of the supervisors before. As one staff member recalled:

> When Olney said that, I thought "Sure, why not?" It never occurred to me to be concerned with job security or anything like that—I trusted Ralph [Olney]. I figured if I really could work myself out of my job there would be something better ahead.

The Change Process Begins with Education

The process of introducing self-directed work team management in 13 Room began with the formation of a study group. The group consisted of Olney and his five reports. Starting in June 1987, they met one or two days every month to discuss one of the dozen books that they had jointly decided were the essentials in understanding high-performance work systems. During their discussions they would note specific concepts, learnings, or models that were directly applicable to their operation. These observations from the readings later became the foundation for the vision, the operating principles, and many of the strategies that were specified in the 13 Room business plan. The study group continued through November.

Operators Become Interested in the Study Group

One of the interesting and unexpected benefits of the study group was the response of the operators. As one team leader recalls:

> People would ask, "Where've you been?" and I'd tell them about the study group sessions and what I was learning from the books we were reading. The next thing I knew people were asking to read my copy after I was done. Then copies started appearing in the work area that people had gone out and bought on their own. Everybody was thirsting for knowledge.

The Supervisor Group Is Empowered to Make Unitwide Decisions

Based on their learnings from the various readings, the staff decided to identify and eliminate the bottlenecks that were currently having a detrimental impact on the operation. The foremost bottleneck they identified was the flow of information and decision making from Olney's office. Decisions had historically funneled up to the 13 Room unit manager level for approval before any direct action was taken. This included decisions relating to budget, schedule, technology, quality, cost, and safety—virtually everything relating to the operation of the organization was brought to the unit manager. The group decided to formally eliminate this step and begin empowering the first-level supervisors with the decision-making authority and responsibility to address these issues. This was further augmented by having these supervisors directly involved in setting the annual goals for 13 Room, including goals for quality, delivery, cost, and safety.

Upon completion of the study sessions, the staff set out to describe a vision and the operating principles for 13 Room. The vision that was developed looked three to five years out and was focused on five areas of responsibility: site, management systems, operations, personnel, and planning. To further the role expansion of the first-level supervisors, each of Olney's five reports became responsible for managing one of these areas in addition to their regular responsibilities. The supervisor responsible for personnel, for example, developed the group's affirmative action goals, determined training needs, assured conformance to state and federal laws with regard to labor practices, and oversaw the compensation program. The supervisors regarded the chance to absorb these responsibilities as being "exciting opportunities" rather than "just more work." As one supervisor succinctly put it, "I was having fun for the first time in years."

During this period more and more emphasis was put on the importance of supervisors working toward developing the capability of their work groups. Initially this was primarily done in the form of increased information sharing. Olney began modeling this important aspect of the supervisors' role by sharing pertinent business information at monthly assemblies. During these meetings, open to everyone in the organization, Olney would share the latest financial, quality, cost, and schedule data for the unit, as well as review strategies and customer feedback and address any other issues that might be of interest to the audience.

The Organization Is Structured into SDWTs

The supervisors were starting to act like an SDWT of team leaders. They determined that a reorganization of the reporting structure would help facilitate information sharing and problem solving. Under the reorganization, teams were formed based on the flow of the product (formerly teams had been formed and managed based on shift). This new structure created some immediate advantages, including far greater visibility of bottlenecks and problem areas. It also had the advantage of creating a stronger sense of team identity among the operators. The newly formed groups were called *core teams*.

Team Meetings and Training Are Critical

The operations team leaders began to hold regular meetings with their core teams. These meetings became focused on problem identification and resolution. They also served as opportunities for team leaders to share with their teams what they had learned from the study group sessions. In this way the meetings began to develop the capability of the work teams themselves. This was the critical piece of the overall role expansion equation: the team leader role could expand only to the extent that the work group role absorbed many of the traditional supervisory responsibilities.

To further develop the skills and abilities of core teams, the team leader group became directly involved in developing a training package that included statistical process control, just-in-time (inventory and waste reduction) concepts, group interaction, goal setting, and consensus decision making. The training sessions, which were divided into 12 different modules, were taught by the team leaders themselves.

13 Room Is Declared a Business

To more fully describe how much the management of the operation had changed, the 13 Room staff declared their operation a business. From a legal standpoint nothing was really different—13 Room was still a manufacturing unit within Eastman Kodak—but from a psychological stand-point, everything had changed. Olney took on the title of "CEO" and each of his staff members became a "director." They began to develop measurements, including financial data, that looked at 13 Room as if it were an independent business. They extended the focus of their role on more strategic, longer-term issues and put even more emphasis on developing their work groups. As one "director" described it:

> **The question we had begun asking ourselves was, "If this were my business what would I do?" After we declared ourselves a business it really began to feel like it was our own.**

Results

The results of this effort are impressive. In a single year:

- Overall product conformance to specifications improved 27 per-cent.
- Statistical process control improved 228 percent.
- Output increased 12 percent.
- Costs were reduced 11 percent.
- Uptime increased 2 percent.
- Safety increased 67 percent.
- The department achieved the highest rating of any production unit in Kodak's annual quality of work life survey.

No less impressive is the profound nature of the changes to the management role. Operations team leaders are now directly involved in strategic planning, goal setting, customer and vendor relations, and the continual development of their teams. "Our role today is so different," stated one team leader, "that if a foreman from 10–15 years ago were to come here and see what we're doing he'd have a stroke."

Summary

We have much to learn from the 13 Room transition to self-directed work teams. Unlike many other organizational changes of this type, which have traumatized supervisors, the process at Kodak left leaders personally empowered. The common thinking that suggests that empowering workers means disempowering team leaders proved wrong in this case. As a result of unusually high trust between the management team leader and the operations team leaders, coupled with specific acts that empowered them all to perform important new responsibilities, these team leaders saw the transition as a personal win rather than a career loss. As these changes were supported organizationally through formal title changes (and by recognition systems reinforced through performance appraisals and project reviews with Olney and other team leaders), they became real.

In analyzing this example in detail, four critical factors that led to the successful transition from the supervisory role to the team leader role clearly stand out. These factors are encapsulated in the following principles:

1. Create an expanded role (not a diminished role) for team leaders.
2. Develop a true self-directed work team for team leaders, not just for workers.
3. Manage by vision and principles rather than by policies and procedures.
4. Make developing capability a priority.

Each factor will be covered in more detail in the next chapter.

Overcoming Common Transition Difficulties: Four Learnings from the 13 Room

"The worst thing you can do to a team is to leave it alone in the dark. I guarantee that if you come across someone who says teams didn't work in his company, it's because management didn't take an interest in them."

James Watson, *vice president of Texas Instruments*

THE 13 ROOM change process demonstrates how an organization can avoid many of the problems suffered by team leaders in transition. Consider the following:

Create an Expanded Role for Team Leaders

All too often the role of team leaders in self-directed work team organizations is described in terms of what they should not do (the wingwalker problem). Supervisors should not dictate; they should not make decisions for their group; they should not railroad decisions through; they should not take credit for the accomplishments of the group; they should not manage the attendance policy and vacation schedule, and so forth. On the other hand, even the list of shoulds is typically filled with terms that have become clichés, like *coach, leader,* and *facilitator.* These terms, though perhaps accurate, are often not helpful to managers and supervisors who find themselves struggling with exactly how they should be spending their time and focusing their energies on a day-to-day basis. As a result, many supervisors faced with the transition to self-directed work team practices have a fairly concrete notion of what they should be giving up, but only an abstract idea of what they should be moving toward.

Avoiding the Wingwalker Problem

The wingwalker problem was clearly avoided in the 13 Room transition. Members of the supervisory team saw themselves as the creators and architects of the new work environment rather than victims of it. They were first involved in expanding their own knowledge of technical processes and high-performance work systems through the study group. This helped them to develop the vision and operating principles for the organization. Once the vision and principles were defined, the supervisors became directly involved in translating them into a business plan with clear goals, objectives, and strategies. Each step in the process built on the previous one, expanding both the personal capabilities of the team members and the horizons of their role as team leaders. It became natural for the operations team leaders to begin relinquishing many of their former administrative responsibilities and much of their technical expertise to their team since the expansion in the capability of the team allowed the leaders to further expand their own roles. The management team leader (Olney) did exactly the same thing for the team of leaders.

Using Symbols to Reinforce the Changing Team Leader Responsibilities

While to some the act of declaring I3 Room a business and forming a board of directors might seem silly, its significance on both a symbolic and literal level cannot be ignored. Symbolically it represented a clear break with the supervisory practices of the past and suggested a greatly expanded role for the team leaders. On a literal level it was representative of the kind of work that the former supervisors had begun to do: it was strategically oriented, directed more toward customer and vendor interfaces, and more fully focused on the development of people.

Develop a Self-Directed Management Team

The transition to self-directed work systems is generally described as being a traumatic, gut-wrenching experience for supervisors at all levels in an organization. It is viewed as requiring individuals who are introspective enough to recognize their own personal biases and the impact that their management styles have on their teams. In short, supervisors need to acknowledge how they must personally change before they are likely to become effective in the new team environment.

Applying SDWT Principles to Team Leaders

The I3 Room case helps to illustrate a dramatically different approach—one in which the management team served as the primary support mechanism during the transition. Instead of being a group of independent first-level supervisors focused on the success of their functional organization and competing for the limited attention and resources provided by higher-level supervision, these team leaders were treated as a self-directed work team themselves. They had common goals and multifunctional tasks, and they were responsible for making decisions and solving problems as a team.

Certainly one-on-one meetings between Olney and members of his staff were important, but far more critical was the interaction and feedback that the operations team leaders received from each other on an ongoing basis. Initially Olney, the management team leader, modeled this behavior by asking staff members to provide him with candid feedback about his performance during one of their team meetings. As Olney recalls,

It was several months into our effort and several things were going wrong. So I went into the staff meeting and said, "I need some help. Give me some feedback." The initial response was silence. Not a word. Then I prodded the group a little and suddenly it all came flooding in. I left the meeting with a list of 30-some items.

At the next meeting Olney went through the items and described those he felt were his responsibility and those he felt were the team's responsibility. He described what he was going to do with those items he felt were most important for him to personally address; he also facilitated the group through decisions on how to address those that were more the responsibility of the team.

The Importance of Example and Feedback

The 13 Room case demonstrates the power of feedback in a constructive, nondefensive manner. This power was further augmented by a two-week course, attended by the entire management group, that was focused on how to give feedback effectively. The common experience greatly enhanced members' ability and desire to give constructive criticism and support for one another's efforts. One manager described his relationship with the team succinctly by saying, "When I committed to the future state of this business I was accountable to the unit, not to Ralph [Olney]. My reinforcement comes from them."

The team that was formed among the group of managers was further enhanced by the members' responsibility structure. Since each member had the dual responsibility of managing both a manufacturing operation and what traditionally would have been a sitewide staff responsibility (site, personnel, planning, operations, managing), a tremendous amount of interdependency existed among all the members. If, for example, a training issue emerged in one core team, the manager responsible for personnel would work directly with that group and its direct supervisor to address the problem.

Manage by Shared Vision and Principles

By having the team leaders develop the vision and guiding principles as a team, Olney assured a common acceptance and common understanding of the direction of the organization. This was augmented by Olney's ability to model the importance of managing by principle, one of the key attributes of team leaders, which we discuss at length later in the book. Rather than directing or regulating with policies or procedures (the preferred means of operating a traditional organization), Olney used the principles the team leaders had developed instead. During staff meetings, for example, Olney would ask questions that ensured that the principles were being considered before decisions were reached. This continued modeling led to the formalization of a proposal and business plan format that required that the relationship between the guiding principles and recommended actions be thought through and consistent. The management team saw an essential part of its role as being guardians of the vision and operating principles of I3 Room. This gave team members another shared responsibility and kept them focused less on their individual teams and more on the shared purpose of the newly organized business.

Develop Capability

One of the things that immediately strikes the outsider who observes members of I3 Room is the emphasis put on developing the capability of the team. The phrase *building capability* means developing the business, interpersonal, and technical abilities of the workforce far beyond the level considered adequate in a traditional organization. The phrase is uttered constantly. To the management team and core group members, the words are not lip service. They are truly obsessed with the idea. "*Everything* we do here," noted one team leader, "is directed toward developing more capability in each other."

Building Team Leader Capability

Developing capability takes on many forms in I3 Room. Initially, much of the capability development was directed at the management team. This was initiated in the study group sessions where, over the course of 6 months, 12 management books were read and thoroughly discussed. "It was like going back to school again," one team leader reflected on the intensity of the sessions. The books served as eye-openers to what is possible in a high-performance work team environment.

The expansion of knowledge was tightly coupled with an expansion of responsibility. The management team was encouraged to begin applying what the members had learned and was given the necessary authority and responsibility to see the changes through. The team itself became engaged in developing the vision and principles for the operation and ultimately setting the business plan. Olney was particularly effective at encouraging this expansion and challenging the capability of each team member. According to one team leader, "He shares responsibility, which is very different from delegating. I have as much input as anybody."

Building Team Member Capability

Capability building was no less emphasized among the core group members. This was begun first by increasing the flow of information to the operators through monthly information sharing meetings. At these meetings Olney would share the current financial, quality, and output performance, as well as strategies that were being pursued or feedback from customers, with everyone in 13 Room. This flow of information was soon augmented by improvements in the computer information systems that gave operators up-to-the-minute status reports on the performance of the entire unit.

Training

In addition, a 12-module training program was begun that covered topics ranging from the basic concepts of self-directed work teams to the intricacies of process flow mapping and statistical process control. It is noteworthy that these training sessions were not conducted by a separate training department, but by the management team themselves. The sessions were cleverly designed, often using a game show format to make the learning experience more fun. The module on statistical process control, for example, followed a format identical to *Jeopardy;* teams were given the answer and then scrambled to be the first ones to push the buzzer and give the correct question.

The Importance of Ongoing Learning

The expansion in capability continued (and continues) in virtually all areas of the operation. Operators took complete responsibility for developing the training manuals that depict the correct methods for performing each sequence in the unit. They also determined the means for conducting cross-training and set a realistic implementation schedule. More recently they have begun redesigning the work area to more effectively utilize existing space, and they were directly involved in creating a new performance evaluation document and describing the process for its use. Some team members have volunteered to become the subject matter experts for their core groups in the area of quality management. These individuals embark on an intensive one-year program in which they work with and learn from the process engineering department directly about the complexities of color film manufacturing. After the completion of their program they return to their core teams, where they share their knowledge with their teammates. In this way the entire capability of the team is enhanced through the members' experience.

As the capability has increased, so have the expectations that both management and peers put on one another. As one operator noted, "There was a time when you got rewarded for just knowing your name." Clearly that is no longer the case. The obsession with developing capability has greatly enhanced the current performance of 13 Room and promises to do so well into the future. As one engineer noted, "The problem now is keeping up with the demands for more knowledge. We aren't able to develop the capability in them as fast as people are able to assimilate it."

Summary

Four simple lessons are important themes to remember when introducing self-directed work team leader practices: create an expanded role, develop a self-directed management team, manage by vision and principles, and develop capability. Kodak was able to engage its supervisors where other companies have only frustrated them. More importantly, the expansion of the supervisors' roles, as well as their participation in the transition process itself, improved the implementation of the SDWTs throughout the organization. The 13 Room experience demonstrates the importance of applying the concepts of high-performance work teams to management groups. In this way many of the typical transition difficulties reviewed in earlier chapters are rather neatly resolved before they become problems. We have also learned from Kodak that the role of the team leader is critical for empowerment. The SDWT of team leaders would not have happened without Ralph Olney. And the self-directed core teams would not have happened without the operations team leaders—Richard Burke, Miles Kavanaugh, Herb Melcher, Norm Roegiers, and Gerry Shepard.

In the next several chapters we will explore in more detail leader characteristics and the role of leaders during the implementation. Many of these things have been highlighted briefly in this study. But the ability to effectively manage by principle, develop team capability, and model appropriate behaviors takes more than what we have discussed so far.

In the next chapter we will consider both the visible and the invisible parts of being an effective team leader.

PART III

The Power of Values and Assumptions

The Visible and Invisible Elements of Team Leadership

"The most difficult thing for me was giving up control. I was far more traditional than I thought I was."

Bob Condella, *director of the Administrative Center of Corning Inc.*

O<small>NE OF THE</small> reasons the role of the SDWT leader is difficult to explain is that it is something more than just actions and activities. It includes the way leaders think and the things they value. We talk too often about the team leader's role as something that we *do* instead of something that we *are*. We focus on management behaviors or on styles without also discussing the things leaders care about, like their personal values and vision, or a set of core beliefs that influences their actions. The resulting picture is incomplete. It is not wrong, but it is not entirely right either. It is like trying to explain why a glove moves without discussing the hand inside it.

Problems with Focusing Only on Actions

Focusing exclusively on the behavioral part of this role implies that we want team leaders to learn a standard set of participative behaviors, or to mimic the style of other successful leaders. This is a deceptive if not a dangerous practice because an action that is entirely appropriate in a given situation may be completely counterproductive in a slightly different one. And the problem with trying to exactly copy someone else's style, of course, is that pretending to be something you are not is an unhealthy, unsatisfying, and ultimately unsustainable effort. It is a sham.

Situational Leadership Does Not Help Much Either

Even the idea of situational leadership—the notion of selecting and applying a particular leadership style warranted by the situation—is not very helpful in clarifying the team leader role. Of course, different situations require different approaches. But telling someone to change his or her style suggests a sort of mechanical selection from a set of preprogrammed responses. That never felt very authentic to me. It comes off like playacting instead of really manifesting convictions. It is sort of like walking around in an uncomfortable, ill-fitting mask just because it has the required expression for the moment. Peter Vaill, an authority on high-performing organizations, expresses this idea succinctly. He writes:

> I would say a lot more clearly how bankrupt I think situational management is for understanding leadership in high performing systems. It is true that in high performing systems, leaders' styles "fit" the needs of the situation. It is not true that in high performing systems leaders have made any very concerted effort to change their style to fit the needs of the situation which is what situational theory says you're supposed to do. Leaders of high performing systems seem to understand instinctively that if you tinker with your style, you'll undercut your effectiveness.

> So where does that leave us?

The Role Is More than a Style of Managing

We need more discussions about the inside stuff of managers; about what some team leaders call "managing with your gut." Understanding this role requires more than an understanding of the things we can see team leaders do. It requires looking at what happens inside of the leaders as well. We have generally avoided these kinds of discussions about what goes on inside people's minds, however, for some pretty good reasons:

1. Things like management beliefs cannot be observed. Since they cannot be observed, they cannot be touched, photographed, verified, or quantified. That makes them hard to talk about and impossible to measure.
2. What team leaders care about can be pretty personal. Delving into these issues may seem intrusive.
3. Things like values and vision sound pretty soft. They do not grab the attention of many busy, results-oriented leaders like well-reasoned prescriptions about what to do and how to act.

Despite our discomfort with probing the internal stuff of team leaders, however, we need to do this to understand the role of the SDWT team leader and to show how it differs from the classic role of the supervisor. Supervisors have become frustrated with the contradictions and confusion caused by emphasizing only the visible parts of this role. That means we must look inside at the intellectual and emotional parts of management.

A Model for Discussing the Things You Cannot See

For purposes of this discussion it may be helpful to divide the various aspects of the management role into two parts: observable things (like an individual's behaviors, style, and statements) and unobservable things (like someone's values, assumptions, paradigms, and vision). (See Figure 8.1.) These unobservable things are examples of the core beliefs of the team leader. They include the invisible elements that create a personal code of rightness and wrongness in conduct.

In the model, the different elements of the team leader's role are divided into two boxes: the invisible box and the visible box. Elements in the boxes interact with each other. If a leader really *assumes* at a gut level that team members have good ideas (things in the invisible box), for example, then the leader's *behavior* (things in the visible box) will likely reflect these biases. Thus the team leader who assumes that the clerks will do a good job hiring their peers is much more likely to invest in the training necessary to prepare them to manage the hiring process than the supervisor who doesn't believe they can do it.

In later chapters we will review the importance of these invisible elements of the role required to be successful as a team leader. At this point, suffice it to say that most unsuccessful team leaders have problems not with behavior or skill deficiencies, but rather with the invisible stuff of leadership. Jim Wessel, a vice president at Becton Dickinson, noted that some of that company's more problematic transitions were in the area of changing thinking, not just changing actions. "We had to get over the mind-set that said, 'I'm not in control, so it must be out of control,' " he says.

Just as the invisible elements of the role affect the visible elements, the reverse is also true. If a team leader actively practices the *behavior* of soliciting ideas from team members, for example, then that leader's *assumptions* and *values* about this topic will likely be influenced by these experiences. To go back to the hiring example, assume that a new team leader from another area is transferred in to work with the team in the middle of the hiring process. Even if she hadn't assumed that the members of this team could have done hiring (and probably wouldn't have

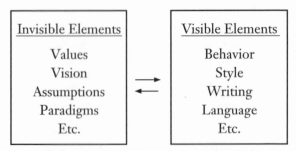

Figure 8.1 The invisible and visible elements of the team leader role.
Adapted from "Managing in the High-Commitment Workplace," Kimball Fisher, *Organizational Dynamics*, Winter 1989.

empowered them to do so if it had been her decision), her assumptions change when she sees them succeed ("Hey, they did a great job, I'll do this again!").

Summary

Describing the role of the team leader requires more than a discussion of typical activities and behaviors. It requires looking at things that go on inside the team leader. Thus, both things that are visible (like behaviors or management style) and things that are invisible (like assumptions and values) are important aspects of this role. Obviously, we cannot see what is in anyone else's "invisible box" except as it is demonstrated through visible behaviors. But we need to understand clearly how important the invisible elements are in driving effective team leaders. We also need to explore how a few commonly held values in traditional organizations inhibit the effectiveness of the team leader.

The next chapter focuses on some of these values that can either inhibit or accelerate team leader effectiveness.

Theory X Assumptions and Control Paradigm Thinking: You Can't Get There from Here

"In warfare, commanders like Captain Queeg, who rule by intimidation and monitor every maneuver from the top, have sometimes won battles and even wars. But from the German blitzkrieg to Asian guerrilla struggles, the most adaptable forces, and the most effective . . . have been those in which soldiers and subcommanders understood the objective and could be trusted to work toward it on their own."

James Fallow, *author*

O N THE MORNING of July 1, 1916, British troops launched what was to become a horrifying suicidal assault on the Germans at the Somme. During the attack, troops emerged from their trenches and began marching in orderly rows directly into German machine gun fire. Several problems could be faulted for the unthinkable slaughter of that day. But Author Paul Fussell argues in *The Great War and Modern Memory* that 60,000 of the 110,000 British soldiers were killed or wounded during that battle largely because of the British class system and the assumptions it fostered:

> **The regulars of the British staff entertained an implicit contempt for the rapidly trained new . . . "Kitchener's Army," largely recruited among workingmen from the Midlands. The planners assumed that these troops—burdened for the assault with 66 pounds of equipment—were too simple and animal to cross the space between the opposing trenches in any way except in full daylight and aligned in rows or "waves." It was felt that the troops would become confused by more subtle tactics like rushing from cover to cover, or assault-firing, or following close upon a continuous creeping barrage.**

Our Thinking Affects Our Behavior

Fortunately, business leadership assumptions rarely result in carnage of this magnitude, but our beliefs about people *will* affect our ability to work successfully in an SDWT environment. Our values, assumptions, and management paradigms will ultimately become our behavior. To test this idea, ask yourself the question, "Do I know what is important to my boss?" Unless we are new or dysfunctional employees, we almost always know what our bosses *really* care about through the subtle clues they give us—not the stuff they say they value, but what they really care about. They can use new behaviors, techniques, styles, or vocabularies for a short time, but ultimately they reward or punish us according to what they truly value. And sometimes we know what they value better than they do. The same is true of each of us. Until our beliefs about people change, for example, our actions toward them aren't likely to change. A Monsanto manager once told me that the difference between successful and unsuccessful SDWT leaders was more in what they thought than in what they did. It's perfectly natural. As a Pop Warner football coach once told me: "Watch their navels, not their heads; their bodies will follow their navels." Similarly, our actions will follow our gut-level beliefs and values.

If we honestly believe that everyone wants to do a good job—or, in the words of Johnsonville Foods CEO Ralph Stayer, that "they want to achieve greatness"—we will treat people differently than if we are skeptical of their motives or abilities. There is a lot of truth to the biblical adage, "For as he thinketh in his heart, so is he." That is why the invisible elements of the team leader role are so important. This change requires a whole different way of management thinking, because blocking the pathway to effective team leader behaviors is the gate of personal values, assumptions, and paradigms. Without first unlocking the assumptions of the traditional supervisory gate, the traveler cannot progress far on the journey toward becoming a team leader.

In this chapter we will review some of the invisible elements of leadership that are so important to the team leader. Specifically, we will examine the problems caused by Theory X assumptions and control paradigm thinking. To introduce these topics, consider the following example.

The Invisible Team Leadership Elements in Action

When Ricardo Semler became president of Semco, Brazil's largest marine and food processing machinery manufacturer, he had a problem. The company was close to financial disaster. After a few years of "hard work" and "good luck," however, Semco became one of Brazil's fastest-growing companies, with a profit margin of 10 percent on sales of $37 million in 1988. What happened to turn the company around? Says Semler: ". . . most important were the drastic changes we made in our *concept* of management." Specifically, Semler credits the three fundamental values on which some 30 management programs are based: democracy, profit sharing, and information.

Grand values like these that aren't acted on, of course, don't have any currency in the workplace at all. In fact, to the predictable detriment of the organization, they only create cynicism and mistrust. Some supervisors individually, and some organizations (apparently speaking for supervisors collectively), have articulated such values or principles or enlightened assumptions about the workforce for years. Semler calls this "participatory hot air." I call it the *stated values*. What is important, of course, are the *demonstrated* values and assumptions—the values we enact.

Demonstrated Values Are More Important than Stated Values

When Semler, for example, *stated* that he assumed that all workers were adults, he *demonstrated* the value by abolishing the norms, manuals, rules, and regulations that were inconsistent with that assumption. Flextime was established, dress codes were eliminated, and collective decision making was introduced. When it was time to make a decision about relocating the marine division into larger facilities, the division closed up shop for a day, loaded up buses of employees, and took them to evaluate the three factories for sale nearby. Interestingly, the employees favored a different building than the culture and management team leaders (Semco calls them "counselors"). They moved into the building the team members wanted, however, and the division's productivity per employee improved significantly, jumping from $14,200 per person per year in U.S. dollars to $37,500 in four years.

Says Semler, "Employee involvement must be real, even when it makes management uneasy." He speaks from personal experience. Employees convinced him to abort an acquisition process that he was sure was the right thing to do for the business. Reflecting back on this trial of his "democracy value" and "adult worker assumption," Semler believes that the future of the acquisition would have been clouded because the people who had to make it work didn't think it was the right thing to do. So it was probably the best decision to stop the process. But that didn't make it any easier to swallow at the time. He wanted it and they didn't. He was the owner of the company and could easily have forced his will on the organization. But reinforcing the values was more important to him than having his way.

Would the Semco turnaround have been successful without these actions? It's unlikely. Would Semler have been able to take the actions with a traditional set of values and assumptions about the role of managers? It's doubly unlikely. "Corporate civil disobedience" (Semler's words) requires a courage and conviction that is born from a different set of invisible gut-level beliefs. It's a completely different mind-set. Let's explore the differences by reviewing a particular piece of management wisdom that has withstood the test of time.

Theory X and Theory Y Revisited

Most supervisors are familiar with Douglas McGregor's famous Theory X (autocratic) management and Theory Y (democratic) management. But many still think these are management styles or techniques rather than management assumptions. These people miss the point. Theory X managers are not necessarily mean or harsh; they simply assume that people are naturally lazy and need to be supervised. Some of the nicest, most gentle supervisors I have known were Theory X supervisors. Conversely, some of the toughest and angriest supervisors I have known are Theory Y managers who assume that people want to achieve and consequently hold them accountable for it. The distinction between Theory X and Theory Y refers not to management styles or behavior, but to assumptions that we have about people (see Table 9.1).

Team leaders are Theory Y managers. But what does that really mean? Without Theory Y assumptions we are simply incapable of being effective team leaders because we cannot allow ourselves to do what needs to be done in a team environment. Whenever I have had Theory X assumptions about team members I have worked with, for example, I have resorted to blaming, accusing, and nonparticipative behaviors, which only limit the capacity of the workforce by creating

Table 9.1   Differences in Management Assumptions

Theory X	Theory Y
Most people are lazy.	People like to work.
Most people need to be controlled.	People have self-control.
Most people need to be motivated.	People motivate themselves.
Most people are not very smart.	People are smart.
Most people need encouragement to do good work.	People want to do a good job.

Adapted from the work of Douglas McGregor, especially *The Human Side of Enterprise*, McGraw-Hill, 1960.

fear, confusion—or even worse, apathy—in the workplace. When we believe that workers are lazy ("All he does is waste time if I'm not watching him") or stupid ("She'll never learn the computer, she's a high school dropout"), we don't take the time to develop or challenge them. Consequently our assumptions actually limit these employees' potential performance.

Theory X in Action

Most of us know that our assumptions affect our behavior toward others. We can validate this, of course, in our own personal experience. It is blatantly clear to me when others have Theory X assumptions toward me. For example, U.S. federal and state income tax forms and procedures are clearly based on the assumption that people will cheat on their taxes. Some company paperwork or processes apparently assume that employees are not trustworthy (time clocks, certain kinds of expense reports, expenditure authorization processes, etc.). Have you had these experiences? How do they make you feel? Do you feel empowered?

A particularly frustrating experience with Theory X assumptions occurred outside the business setting. I was on an airplane that had been badly delayed when a harried flight attendant started chiding us over the P.A. system for standing in the aisles. "You know, people," she said caustically, "we can't push back until everyone is seated." What were her assumptions about the passengers? Did she think we were hoping to delay the flight further by lollygagging aimlessly in the aisles? It was clear to me that we were laboring as quickly as possible to get our luggage into the overhead bins so that we wouldn't miss our connecting flights. What we needed was some help with our luggage, not a tongue-lashing. Too often what we give team members is polite recriminations when what they need is help with the luggage.

We Get What We Expect

When we believe that workers need to be supervised, we will find ways to control them. For example, I once talked with several livid union members who were told that they had to bring in a doctor's excuse for each time they took a sick day. Although there may have been abuses in the system, this particular company chose to tighten up the policy instead of dealing firmly with the abusers on a one-on-one basis. What do you think was the message delivered to the work force by that decision? The workers assumed that the message was, "We don't trust you and we will treat you like children." Unfortunately, if we treat grown-ups like children, they tend to act like them. One employee quipped that although he couldn't afford to go to the doctor for every flu or cold he got, he would satisfy the new requirement by getting a note from his mother.

Theory X Assumptions Can Be Anywhere in the Organization

Dave Hanna, while an organizational development executive at Procter & Gamble, noted an interesting, related phenomenon at executive levels in organizations. When managers were newly promoted, they would soon start complaining about how their bosses failed to realize the competence of the managers at their level. When they were promoted again, however, they soon forgot their earlier frustrations and began to question the competence of their former peers. Hanna began to realize that most managers had the assumption that the level of incompetence was always one level below them.

These assumptions prompt supervisors at all levels to create audit systems to check their subordinates. These systems then hinder the subordinates' ability to do the work and negatively affect their accomplishments. Instead of working, for example, the subordinates have to spend their time filling out reports or defending their decisions. This then reinforces in the superior's mind that the subordinates are incompetent. It's a vicious circle caused by Theory X assumptions.

How Theory X Assumptions Become Self-Fulfilling Prophecies

In his book *Managing in the New Team Environment*, Larry Hirschhorn makes a similar argument. He describes the psychology of control as a self-fulfilling prophecy. Supervisor Anne, for example, assuming that her subordinates need supervision, closely monitors worker Bruce's performance. Over time Bruce begins to assume that he must need to be supervised closely or else Anne wouldn't do it. So he acts accordingly. The supervisor sees how he acts and lays on more supervision to compensate for the lower level of self-initiated work. Bruce sees the increased supervision and his self-esteem suffers further, he loses more interest in the work, and so forth. It creates a negative performance spiral that injures self-esteem and causes unhealthy dependency. Anne's good intention to improve the performance of the operation either causes performance to suffer or requires her to continuously increase her supervision to a point of diminishing returns.

Try Some Different Assumptions On for Size

If you are like me and don't come naturally to a lot of these Theory Y assumptions, what do you do? When something goes terribly wrong (which is usually when our true assumptions about people surface), slow down and force yourself to assume that the event happened in spite of the team members doing the best they could with the skills, tools, and information they had at the time. You will approach the situation much differently than if you start from Theory X assumptions. I know this from personal experience. Try it sometime; it's worked for me.

Early in the start-up of our company we had problems with our training materials not arriving in time for the sessions. After several phone calls, in which I reprimanded (in a nice way) the "responsible" principal for not performing up to the standard of service we expected, I found out that the problems had been caused by a lack of timely notification about the sessions. In almost every case, the problem had been caused because I, not understanding the time required for mock-ups, printing, and shipping, had not given people enough notice to accomplish the work. I had been reminded again of something that I frequently forget: we normally need to fix the system, not the people. My assumption that someone else was at fault for the mistake was wrong.

Another invisible element of team leadership related to the assumptions we have about people is our paradigm of work. This deserves some elaboration.

Work Paradigms

Our life experience is translated into models or patterns of thinking, the dictionary definition of *paradigm*. Paradigms provide our own personal interpretation of reality and act like lenses through which we see and make sense of the world around us. During the time of Columbus, for example, the flat world paradigm was dominant. Consequently, maps were drawn accordingly and sailors would rebel when they had been at sea too long for fear that their captains were running perilously close to the edge of the earth. The earth-centered universe paradigm was so prevalent during the time of Galileo that the scientist's life was threatened when he suggested a sun-centered theory.

Our paradigms are so powerful that Thomas Kuhn, while writing a history of science, found that scientists (a normally rational and logical group of people) frequently ignored data that was inconsistent with the prevailing theories of the day. They actually screened out information that couldn't be explained by their scientific paradigms, ignoring the inconsistencies that, when finally understood, often later led to scientific breakthroughs. The adage, "I'll believe it when I see it," is wrong. When we understand the impact of our paradigms, we understand that "I will see it when I believe it."

Paradigm Paralysis

Joel Barker, a noted futurist, calls this phenomenon *paradigm paralysis*, a rigidity of thinking that doesn't let people see things outside their frames of reference. An example of this is the Swiss watchmakers who, because of their domination of the watch market for decades, were literally blindsided when digital watch technology took over the marketplace and forced the Swiss to lay off thousands and thousands of watch workers. Ironically, they not only didn't see it coming, they actually were the ones who had invented the digital technology that drove them to their knees in the 1980s. At a watch show, the Swiss R&D people displayed the digital watch they had invented, which, because it had no mainspring or hands, was not considered important enough to protect. Their analog watch paradigm blinded them to seeing the threat or possibility inherent in the digital watch. Seiko and Texas Instruments were at the show, and the rest, as they say, is history.

People Who Don't Have the SDWT Paradigm Don't Understand SDWTs

I saw this happen at P&G. After 20 years of successful experience with SDWTs, there were still some managers (some at very senior levels of the company) who couldn't see what made these organizations work so well. During tours when visitors came through the Lima, Ohio plant, for example, I saw several managers rationalize away the impressive business results of the facility. "Well, you guys are successful because of the new equipment you have," they would say, even though less successful plants had the same equipment. "This is primarily because people work harder in the Midwest than in other parts of the country," some argued, but there were successful SDWTs all over the country. Still others said it was because the plant was a greenfield, or start-from-scratch, plant, even though P&G had retrofit or brownfield success stories even back then.

Some visitors argued that anyone could do this if they could hire the kind of people we found at Lima. Somehow they did not realize that the technicians at Lima had become so skilled through years of special education, coaching, and experience they had received at work, all of which would be unavailable to employees in a more traditional workplace. These employees did not have all of these characteristics when they were hired. They had to learn them in the same way that team leaders learn how to make good decisions and solve problems: by doing. Genetic coding didn't create these extraordinary team members; their raw talents were refined in the crucible of personal experience and through the assistance of their team leader mentors who made sure that the development opportunities were provided.

Why didn't people understand? It wasn't because they were stupid. These were bright, successful managers. They were simply incapable of understanding things that were so inconsistent with their paradigm of management. They were literally blind—like the scientists in Kuhn's book were—to the data.

Control and Commitment Management Paradigms

Our work paradigms are firmly entrenched in our minds and then consequently manifested in our organizational structures and practices. Noted employee involvement expert Richard Walton, for example, identifies the primary difference between managers in traditional organizations and managers in empowered work systems not as their actions but as their paradigms about management. He suggests that most supervisors at all levels of organizations today operate with the "control" rather than the "commitment" paradigm, seeing their job as controlling the workforce through policies and punishment. It is a logical extension of Theory X assumptions. The successful team leaders I have worked with, however, see their primary responsibility as engendering the commitment of the workforce rather than eliciting compliance. They do this by teaching, coaching, and leading team members so that the workers' own self-control can replace the externally imposed controls of traditional supervision. The differences between the control management paradigm and the commitment management paradigm can be seen in Table 9.2.

The Pervasive Influence of the Control Paradigm

Most of us have been heavily influenced by the control management paradigm because it is the most prevalent operating paradigm of management in modern organizations of all kinds. Many of today's supervisors grew up in families where parents were bosses who set rules, made the decisions for the family, determined chores, allocated resources, and

Table 9.2 Differences Between Management Paradigms

Control Paradigm	Commitment Paradigm
Elicits compliance	Engenders commitment
Believes supervision is necessary	Believes education is necessary
Focuses on hierarchy	Focuses on customers
Biased toward functional organizations	Biased toward cross-functional organizations
Manages by policy	Manages by principle
Favors audit and enforcement processes	Favors learning processes
Believes in selective information sharing	Believes in open information sharing
Believes bosses should make decisions	Believes workers should make decisions
Emphasis on means	Emphasis on ends
Encourages hard work	Encourages balanced work/personal life
Rewards conservative improvement	Rewards continuous improvement
Encourages agreement	Encourages thoughtful disagreement

administered punishments. They went to school where teachers were bosses who made assignments, ran the classroom activities, determined grades, and decided when students could go to the bathroom. In the military they had bosses who, because of their rank, could issue orders that were to be followed precisely and without question. Churches and community organizations they were associated with were run by bylaws, commandments, and rules of conduct. Governments created vast bureaucracies to regulate and enforce national, state, and local laws. In the workplace there were clear chain-of-command hierarchies, with every higher level of management responsible for the work of those below that level. These workplaces were also permeated with laws, rules, regulations, contracts, and procedures.

Is it any wonder that so many of us see our role as controlling subordinates? I am not suggesting that the control paradigm is bad. In some situations it may be entirely appropriate. But it has clearly influenced contemporary management thinking because it has been so pervasive. It would be difficult to imagine a single supervisor who has not been immersed in the ocean of control paradigm examples that have washed over modern cultures.

The Language and Structure of Control

Even the language of many business organizations makes this paradigm explicit. Interestingly, the title *supervisor* sounds like "superior vision," "look over (the shoulder)," or "more important (than workers)." The title of senior financial people in the organization isn't *communicator*, but *controller*. Certain staff people are normally *auditors* rather than *teachers*, and senior managers are often promoted to being *directors* rather than *facilitators* of particular groups. Instead of a *chief learning officer*, we have *chief executive officers*. We use these titles in traditional organizations simply because they are logical extensions of our thinking.

There is additional evidence of the control paradigm at work. The traditional way to describe an organization, for example, is with an organization chart. This way of structuring organizations is so prevalent that software is now available that automatically draws a triangle-shaped chart of boxes and lines representing the cascading links in the management chain of command. Each level of the triangle has more authority and responsibility than the level below it. The boss is at the top of the pyramid, various levels of sub-bosses and their reports are sandwiched in the middle, and the base of the pyramid is composed of the people who do the work. What better example is there of control paradigm thinking? These organizational structures are put in place not to allow for easy communication and coordination of activities, as is often posited, but to provide an authorization path for decisions.

There is, of course, additional evidence of control paradigm thinking. We sometimes share information, for example, on a "need-to-know" basis. This selective information sharing usually follows hierarchical lines, because senior managers "need to know" while others apparently do not. Ironically, the people who must implement something often do not have access to the information necessary for effective implementation. Much of the progress that has been made in high-performance work systems has come about because modern technologies like the Internet and e-mail are status blind—something much more difficult for human beings to achieve.

Clear class distinctions are implied in the reporting relationships described as "subordinates" and "superiors." Pay systems are set up to reward people for rank. This causes an interesting pay delivery pattern. Imagine you are an anthropologist 200 years in the future who comes upon the pay plan of a major current American company. What conclusions would you draw from the ancient artifact of a company of the twenty-first century? Would you find it curious that the people who actually designed, built, or delivered the products and services of the corporation were among the lowest-paid in the operation? Would that be supportive of the written corporate statements you find that say that quality and customer focus are the primary goals of the operation? Would you wonder why such a corporation reserved its lowest rewards for the people who actually touched the product and worked with customers? Would you wonder what was really important in that operation?

Results Versus Control

This reminds me of another issue that deeply concerns me. I have heard people say that certain supervisors at all different levels of the operation cannot support empowerment because they are just too results oriented. This is plainly and simply untrue. This kind of management resistance comes because these supervisors are *not* results oriented. To be more precise, they value control more than results. Perhaps you know supervisors like this. They will not empower people because that is too "touchy feely," but they will spend thousands of dollars on consulting, training programs, or equipment that people know will not produce sustainable results. They will gladly waste precious time, energy, and money tangled in senseless bureaucratic red tape and protocols, but they would not think of "wasting time" in meetings to share information or decision-making responsibilities with others. Is that being results oriented? No, it's being control oriented.

Contrary to popular belief, in order for SDWTs to work, we need more leaders who are results oriented, not fewer. We need more leaders who will put company profitability over personal profitability. We need more leaders who will put satisfying customers over maintaining management policies. We need less control paradigm thinking.

And it isn't just supervisors who have this control management paradigm in their heads. One of the major transition obstacles organizations face is to help team members accept responsibility for solving problems and making decisions, tasks that were traditionally seen as the job of management. There is something comforting in knowing that someone else is responsible for solving your problems. Some team members are uncomfortable picking up "management responsibilities."

SDWTs Require the Commitment Paradigm

Does this kind of thinking and its manifestations in the workplace block effective SDWTs? Yes. Says Frank Merlotti, retired chief executive of Steelcase, "We tried to remove anything that got in the way of people communicating, discussing ideas. We wanted to get rid of the top-down thing." Lots of organizations are following suit. Many of the artifacts of a workplace culture based on the control paradigm rather than on the commitment one are disappearing. In fact, quickly becoming obsolete in the SDWT workplace are:

- The traditional concepts of rank and privilege (parking places, office differences, executive perks, etc.)
- Status-laden organization responsibilities, described in "up" terms (higher, more important, etc.) and "down" terms (lower, less important, etc.)

- The typical business language that implies superiority and inferiority depending on job titles
- Many of the other "us" versus "them" distinctions of the classical operation

There is an old saying that the eyes are the window of the soul. Similarly, language is the window of paradigm and assumption. Successful team leaders, for example, don't say, "I did this." They say, "We did this," or "The team did this." They don't say, "He works for me," or "She reports to me." They say, "We work together." They don't talk about "my employees" as though the managers were benevolent slave owners; they talk about "the teams" they work with. These kinds of statements reflect their internal conviction that they are working with the team as partners, not as superiors. Management titles are changed to reflect facilitative rather than directive responsibilities. More common than *manager, foreman,* or *supervisor,* for example, are *leader, counselor,* or *advisor.*

Team leaders use different metaphors as well. Traditional supervisors think about their jobs as a mechanical process. You can tell by the analogies and metaphors they use to describe their roles. For example, I have heard numerous supervisors talk about "driving," "steering," or "jump-starting" the organizations they manage. This implies a mechanical view of managers as the people in the driver's seat of the organizational vehicle. Those who think this way believe that they are solely responsible for making things happen. Cars, unlike people, are not self-starting and self-steering. Team leaders tend to use metaphors that are more organic. They talk, for example, about the importance of helping to "grow" or "nurture" the organization. Their language doesn't imply a mechanistic or superior relationship with others. It suggests a developmental or teaching focus.

Summary

The invisible elements of the high-performance team leader role (like values, assumptions, and paradigms) can help or hinder the leader. Certain common beliefs about workers, for example, can actually limit the team leader's ability to be effective. Theory X assumptions in particular severely inhibit team leader success in the empowered workplace. If we believe people need to be supervised, for example, we will find ways (excuses) to supervise them. This creates a basic incompatibility in the work system between the SDWT concept (the stated value) and the management process (the demonstrated value).

For many of us, other invisible things need to change personally and organizationally if SDWTs are to succeed. Most organizations are loaded with the artifacts (language, structures, policies, etc.) of the prevailing control paradigm. Though most supervisors have been immersed in the control paradigm (the brother of Theory X assumptions) for years, successful team leaders change themselves and their operations to manifest a different paradigm. That mind-set—the commitment paradigm—may be the crucial discriminating factor between successful and unsuccessful leaders of SDWTs. Although certainly some individuals and organizations require no significant changes to demonstrate to others in the workplace that their values are consistent with SDWTs, that is not true for everyone. What are those values?

In the next chapter we'll discuss some of the more specific nontraditional values and beliefs that seem to characterize successful team leaders.

PART
IV

The Role of the Team Leader

The Supervisor Versus the Team Leader: Sheep Herders and Shepherds

"But of a good leader, who talks little,
When his work is done, his aim fulfilled,
They will all say, 'We did this ourselves.' "

Lao-Tzu, *about 550 B.C.*

A FAVORITE STORY of mine illustrates some of the primary differences between the role of the traditional supervisor (at all levels of the organization) and the role of the team leader.

When I was in high school, my family moved to a large farmhouse in central Utah. The house had been finished in 1900 by a sheep baron who had proudly displayed blown-up photographs of his prize-winning long-haired sheep throughout the home. The photos were large, measuring nearly 36 inches tall by 48 inches wide, and were made to look even larger through the use of thick wood plank frames painted jet black. Some were watermarked or otherwise damaged, and all of them looked like the sheep were posed with the same unsmiling formality of most turn-of-the-century photographs (see Figure 10.1). Partly because of the pictures' value as a conversation starter, but also because they were an integral part of the history of the home, my mother and father kept some of the photos in their original locations on the staircase walls of the second story.

Probably because of the pictures, I started paying attention to tidbits I heard here and there about raising sheep. I found out, for example, about the importance of sheepdogs. During the long grazing drives into the rugged Utah mountains, sheep owners would use sheepdogs to circle around the flocks to keep them all together and heading in the right direction. Some called the better dogs "sheep herders," a title normally reserved for human beings, to designate their extraordinary skill in controlling the livestock by barking and nipping at the legs of the sheep.

Figure 10.1   The flock.

When the sheep wouldn't move, these sheep herders would get them going. When the sheep were heading in the wrong direction, the sheep herders would get them turned around. When an errant lamb strayed from the other sheep, the sheep herders were there to drive it back into the safety of the flock.

That summer I went to Israel for six weeks with a touring group of boy scouts. One day, when I was looking out the window of the old tour bus, I saw a small flock of sheep in the dusty hills by the roadside. The flock was accompanied by a lone shepherd carrying a staff and dressed in long desert robes. The shepherd, seemingly oblivious to the sheep in his charge, turned his back to the flock and walked briskly away. He didn't even glance backward. I thought his action was irresponsible: without sheep herding dogs to keep the flock from scattering, it appeared that he was abandoning the sheep. But I was surprised to see that the sheep were not wandering aimlessly. They were following him. For some reason these sheep did not need their heels nipped to move. They simply walked along with the shepherd until they were out of my line of sight. This was inconsistent with my paradigm of sheep herding, but it was a tremendous learning experience about shepherding.

Sheep Herding Versus Shepherding Management

This story can be related to the two different management roles— shepherd versus sheep herder (see Table 10.1). Now people, of course, aren't like animals. Supervisors don't act like trained dogs obediently coercing dim-witted sheep. Nor do team members mindlessly comply with the manipulative force imposed on them. Nevertheless, there are some parallels.

Table 10.1 Sheep Herders Versus Shepherds

	Sheep Herder	Shepherd
Technique	Directing	Developing
Work Focus	The flock itself	The flock's surroundings
Location	Behind the flock	In front of the flock
Purpose	Move sheep	Create shepherds
Methodology	Barking and heel nipping	Clearing the path
Result	Creates dependence	Creates self-reliance

Sheep Herders Drive Subordinate Flocks

The traditional approach to management, for example, is a lot like sheep herding. It often puts the supervisor in the role of regulating, enforcing, or directing subordinates. Supervisors in this role, regardless of their level in the organization, concentrate on driving the subordinate flock in some predetermined direction. They monitor work performance carefully and take appropriate corrective action when the flock veers off course. They become skilled in barking and heel-nipping techniques like performance reviews, layoffs, and more subtle organizational censures. While they become quite proficient at moving sheep, they tend to create flocks that are compliant, complacent, and dependent on the sheep herder.

Shepherds Lead and Develop

Shepherds, however, have more of a developmental responsibility than a directive one. They assume a position in front of the flock as leader and example, rather than behind the flock as driver and director. They also spend considerably more time and energy analyzing the environment surrounding the sheep to anticipate dangers and opportunities than sheep herders do. The analogy breaks down somewhat, of course, because the sheep in Israel were very dependant on the shepherd. Even though his tactics were noncoercive and they followed his lead willingly, the sheep were incapable of surviving without him. In SDWTs, however, shepherds actually create other shepherds fully capable of leading both themselves and other team members successfully. Although the team members may not know many of the skills required to be self-directing when they join the organization, the SDWT shepherd makes sure they learn these skills over time.

Problems with Sheep Herding

The problem with the sheep herding type of supervision is that, while it certainly can get the job done, it just does not fit with self-directed work teams. While skilled sheep herding may have been not only acceptable but actually admired by traditional supervisors and employees alike, emerging work teams now see this way of managing as at best redundant or at worst inconsistent with their own newly expanded responsibilities to regulate their own work flow and processes.

Sheep herder supervisors unintentionally create organizational cultures characterized by low risk-taking and low initiative. Since direction, rewards, and punishments come from the sheep herder, subordinates (whether they are operators or vice presidents) rapidly learn that the way to prosper is to wait to see what the boss wants to do and then do that. They wait for directions, move only tentatively when the path is unclear, and stampede obediently wherever they think the boss wants them to go (whether the direction is right or not). The desirable culture for SDWTs, of course, is very different. People take direction from the work itself, and rewards are seen as coming from customers, not bosses.

Shepherds Live in Traditional Organizations Too

Just because supervisors work in traditional organizations, however, they don't necessarily have to act like sheep herders. Excellent supervisors in traditional organizations have often mastered shepherding skills even though it may have been difficult for them to use such skills. Janice Klein, who has published extensive research about supervising SDWT organizations, writes that ". . . [I] believe that many managers in control systems also hold to the same paradigm [as successful managers in empowered workplaces] even though their work environment may limit their ability to act on those beliefs." Klein's research with Pamela Posey shows that the supervisors who are perceived to be the "stars" in traditional systems act like shepherds, not sheep herders, and are generally skilled in "working the system" (sometimes working around the system) to use self-regulating techniques with employees even though they may not be encouraged or rewarded by their superiors for doing so.

While successful supervisors in traditional organizations have often acted as shepherds even though it was inconsistent with the hierarchical and bureaucratic structures of their traditional organizations, SDWTs require the shepherding role from team leaders to make the work design completely functional. If only a select few act this way, while others continue the sheep herding role commonly observed in organizations today, the SDWT effort won't work.

Summary

Although excellent supervisors have often managed in nontraditional ways in traditional work systems, most supervisors have been trained and reinforced for acting more like sheep herders than shepherds. SDWTs need their leaders to be shepherds—people who lead, take risks, and develop other shepherds—not sheep herders who drive sheep with work rules and procedures.

In the next several chapters we will flesh out the specifics of the team leader role in more detail.

The Role of the Team Leader

"The new manager must serve as a motivator, coordinator, and diplomat as opposed to a controller, autocrat, and disciplinarian. These managers will lead by convincing people, not telling them, because their team members will be intelligent and not easily swayed by rhetoric or willing to do something just to maintain the status quo. Finally the new manager must be willing to put aside his or her ego for the good of the organization."

Larry D. Runge, *Abstract from "The Manager and the Information Worker of the 1990's"*

I T TOOK ME a while to figure out how to really "shepherd" at the soap plant in Lima. And I had some difficulty when I attempted to explain what I was learning to the frequent P&G visitors who toured the plant to observe our SDWTs. During the visits, for example, it was usually the technicians (hourly employees) who gave presentations about major projects they were managing, goals they had set and accomplished, teammates they had hired, equipment they had purchased, or cost savings measures they had implemented. The visitors noted that in the traditional plants, those were things that would be said and done by staff professionals, managers, or supervisors, but not by "workers."

"If the technicians do all that," they would ask, "then what do you do?"

I hated that question. At the time I didn't have a good way to explain the critical role of the team leader. This chapter is a belated attempt to respond to the query, "What do team leaders do?" It focuses on the general role and responsibilities of a team leader by comparing a traditional supervisory job description with one for a team leader. We will also look at the team leader as a boundary manager, and then conclude with seven important competency clusters for SDWT leadership.

Team Leader "Job Description"

What is the role of a team leader? Pamela Posey and Janice Klein have done much of the pioneering work on this question, especially as regards operations team leaders. They have found that many of the behaviors of team leaders and successful supervisors are the same. Three consistent attributes, for example, are associated with the most successful leaders in both traditional and empowered organizations.

1. The ability to create strong mutual respect between the workers and the leader.
2. Assuring that the job gets done.
3. Providing leadership in getting problems solved.

However, in addition to these attributes, SDWTs require some other things from their leadership as well. One distinguishing characteristic is the focus of their activities. A team leader's "job description" usually differs from that of a traditional supervisor because it focuses less on tasks and more on relationships. It also emphasizes fewer one-to-one interactions with employees and more team development, as shown in the example of a first-level job description in Table 11.1.

These job descriptions change because the role of the team leader extends beyond the role of the supervisor. While the supervisor is responsible for the performance of the day-to-day work, the role of the team leader expands to include responsibilities that go beyond the immediate accomplishment of the task. The team leader functions more as a work process architect than as a work operations monitor. Thus the primary target of the team leader's work expands from tasks (the work) to relationships (things that affect how the work gets done), and from individuals (a smaller part of the work unit) to teams (a larger part of the work unit).

The Boundary Manager

One of the best ways to describe the overall team leader role is as a *boundary manager.* The large circle in Figure 11.1 represents the team

Table 11.1 Examples of First-Level Job Descriptions

Supervisor	Team Leader
1. Plan, organize, direct, and control	1. Ensure that resources are available for team to produce on-time, quality product and/or services
2. Meet cost, quality, and delivery objectives	2. Develop team maturity—coach and counsel
3. Manage daily problems	3. Represent team in organization-wide activities
4. Coordinate activities and resources	4. Train and lead team in problem solving
5. Plan and implement improvements	5. Motivate team to achieve goals
6. Administer safety, housekeeping, and communications programs	6. Assume responsibility for indirect tasks

Adapted from Klein and Posey's "Traditional versus New Work System Supervision: Is There a Difference?" in *Revitalizing Manufacturing: Text and Cases,* Janice A Klein, Irwin, 1990.

boundary. The boundary is simply the make-believe line that differentiates the team from the environment surrounding it. The team leader manages that boundary. What does that mean? Let's review a little organization theory to establish a common point of reference, and then I will answer the question.

SDWTs Are Open Systems

Figure 11.2 adds some things to the picture of the team we looked at earlier. Team members must take inputs (like raw materials or information) of some sort and transform them into desirable outputs (like products or services). To do this they add value to the inputs (assemble, organize, edit, etc.). This is called the *transformation* or *throughput* part of the operation. Figure 11.3 shows that outside the organization boundary is the environment (customers, competitors, other teams, etc.). Social scientists call this way of looking at organizations *open system theory*.

An information systems (IS) team, for example, may be responsible for turning data into useful information. The members collect and compile the data, and program it into computers. These bits of raw data are organized into useful reports, which are distributed to the team's customers. According to the open system model, the raw data is the input. The throughput process is the series of tasks that transforms the raw

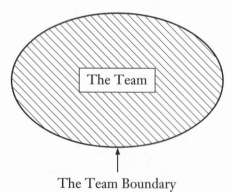

The Team's Environment
(All the things outside of the team itself)

The Team Boundary

Figure 11.1   The team boundary.

The Team's Environment

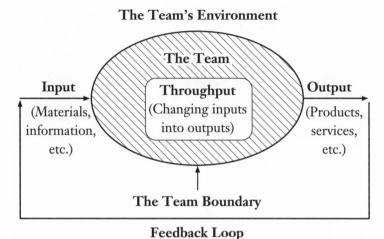

Feedback Loop
(Feedback from environment about outputs)

Figure 11.2   The team as an open system.

data into a delivered report. The report is the output. The customer must feel that the report meets a need that is equal to or greater than what must be paid to get it from the IS team. If the information system team does this better than the alternatives for providing this service, then they are successful. If they don't, they won't survive in the long run.

The Team's Environment

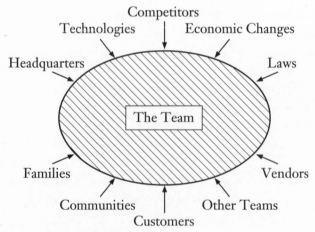

Figure 11.3   The team's environment.

SDWTs Manage Inside the Boundary

Now let's get back to the original question: what does it mean to be a boundary manager? Traditional supervision usually focuses attention on the transforming process or throughput portion of the team's responsibilities. In the IS example, that would include supervising activities such as the compiling of data and the accurate entering of that data into the computers. Supervising the day-to-day throughput operations of the team, however, is largely done by team members themselves in self-directed work team settings.

Team Leaders Manage the Boundary

This allows the team leader to focus on the environment surrounding the team, much as the shepherd looks beyond the flock itself and into the fields, which hold potential danger and/or opportunity. Rather than spending his or her primary energy on the throughput process, the team leader focuses more attention on boundary issues, such as interface problems with other teams, customer and vendor interactions, dealing with other corporate groups, assessing competitors and market opportunities, working legal or community issues of importance, forecasting new technologies, building communication bridges with other groups, forging important alliances, bringing training and development opportunities to the team, and so forth (see Figure 11.4). Those are the things at the boundary of the organization represented by the circle. As a boundary manager, the team leader manages these elements in the team's environment in a way that positively affects the team's ability to be successful.

One way to further describe the boundary manager's role is to look at sample boundary management responsibilities (see Table 11.2). The primary role of the boundary manager, of course, is to help the team adapt successfully to the environment. To do this, he or she acts as an organization designer, an infrastructure builder, and a cross-organization collaborator. Each of these aspects of the boundary manager's role is a departure from the traditional role of supervisors at every level of the organization.

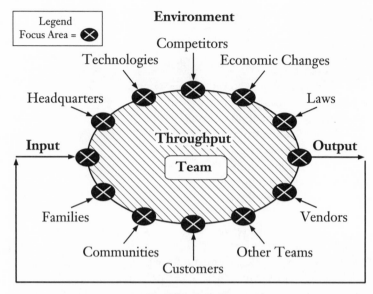

Figure 11.4 The boundary manager's focus areas.

Boundary Management Is a Nontraditional Role

SDWTs won't function properly if supervisors at any level continue to work inappropriately inside of the team boundary. Ralph Stayer, CEO of Johnsonville Foods, tells a story of how he couldn't get the quality of the company's product to be as high as he wanted until he stopped managing throughput and left that to the teams. Johnsonville is a producer of high-quality sausage. As the CEO, Stayer continued tasting the sausages on a regular basis to demonstrate his personal commitment and concern for quality. The teams didn't assume full responsibility for product quality, however, until Stayer stopped tasting the sausage and turned that task over to them. Rejects dropped from 5 percent to five-tenths of 1 percent when the teams fully assumed the responsibility of throughput management.

Supervisors "Taste the Sausage"

There are lots of ways that supervisors "taste the sausage" and hinder SDWT development. Most do it through requests for information

Table 11.2   Examples of Boundary Manager Tasks

Sample Boundary Tasks

Hosting customer visits
Introducing team members to key external contacts
Buffering the team from corporate pressure
Sponsoring joint vendor-team projects
Bringing in information from headquarters
Evaluating market trends
Anticipating technology shifts
Building communication linkages
Bringing in customer feedback
Forging alliances
Solving problems between teams
Bringing in technical training
Inviting vendors to provide training on the equipment they sold the team
Getting resources for the team from other parts of the company
Brokering team members out into community service activities
Bringing in concerned citizens to discuss community problems
Evaluating competitive offerings for similar products and services
Building systems for direct data links to and from customers/vendors

(reports) and by expressing concerns about throughput problems they see. When the team itself requires this kind of information to monitor its throughput, it is *essential* to take the time to compile some facts and data. But when the information gathering is mandated by supervisors and is for the sole benefit of the supervisors, it actually causes more problems than it solves. In many circumstances, people have discovered that the process of filling out status reports for management, for example, cost *significantly* more in lost time and salaries than the value of any improvements that came out of the process. Team leaders avoid this trap.

In today's fast-paced world, these kinds of imposed supervising processes on the throughput take too long to be useful anyhow. Team leaders don't bottleneck the teams by making them wait to take action until the team leader is in the loop. That defeats the purpose of self-directed work teams. But this isn't easy for many of us. Laments a controller at Tektronix, "What you've got [in an SDWT] is a manager who doesn't know what is going on." We aren't used to that. Most of us really enjoy being in the thick of things. Team leaders can be partly consoled by the fact that, by the time they hear about something, it's probably too late to do anything about it anyway.

Supervisors Work *In* the System, Team Leaders Work *On* the System

Boundary managers don't taste sausage. That's not their role. While supervisors at every management level usually work *in* the system, team leaders work *on* the system instead. That means working on things that affect the ability of the organization to be successful. One way to do this is as an organization designer. Team leaders believe that team members are already doing the best they can within the constraints of the system they are working within. So they focus on improving—or redesigning—the system. This virtually always requires working across the boundary.

Bill Snyder, a former operations team leader at American Transtech, acted as an effective organization designer and saw dramatic improvement in an SDWT. The labor cost per unit went from $180 to $100, quality remained consistently high, throughput improved by 100 percent, and employee morale soared—all in the first 6 months of Snyder's tenure. What did he do?

> **I provided feedback on all the goals once a week. I expected them to explain variances. I arranged for the marketing person to collect customer feedback and read it out at the weekly meeting. I arranged for team members to get technical training and apprenticeship opportunities. I initiated the development of a reward system that enabled team members to earn weekly cash bonuses based on team and organization performance. In short, I didn't do, I designed. The design elements helped us all to succeed.**

Organization Design

Snyder "didn't do" the traditional supervisory tasks of telling people how to accomplish the significant improvements they achieved together; that is working *in* the system as a supervisor. Instead, he worked *on* the system. He brought in marketing information and technical training from the environment so that people could be informed and skillful. He also changed the team bonus. By doing these things he designed system improvements. Though organization designers don't often do the design work themselves (they usually involve others in the spirit of empowerment), they do ensure that it gets done. And they ensure that it gets done in a way that incorporates open systems thinking. This is more difficult than it sounds. The general tendency for organizations is to make improvements based only on inside needs and wants. The boundary manager knows that other elements outside the teams must be considered for effective organization improvement. For example, anyone who has ignored customer needs during this process has done so at some peril to his or her operation.

Of course, the extent to which team leaders can act as boundary managers depends on the maturity level of the team. Some teams still need a lot of help to learn how to manage the throughput of the operation. This needs to be done before the team leader can take on the new responsibilities of boundary management. Many of the full responsibilities of boundary managers, in fact, don't come until later. They evolve as the team gradually develops the skills and experience to monitor the throughput process itself.

Infrastructure Building

Boundary managers help with this maturation process (which is detailed in later chapters). One way they do this is by ensuring that effective infrastructures are in place to support SDWTs. This is a key part of the organization designer's responsibilities as well. The infrastructures help the teams manage throughput, and they can form an institutionalized way for team members to stay focused on the needs of the environment. As Snyder recalls:

> . . . a timely information system . . . [provided] quality and profitability results on a daily or weekly basis. As long as the system measured the right things, and as long as the results were good, I could focus my attention elsewhere (unless the team asked for help). Certain peers were rankled by my confidence and freedom, and would warn me that the teams were "fooling around" and "taking advantage" of me in my absence. Those same teams were lowering their costs by 40% and achieving higher quality results

than they had in years. I wasn't worried, and I told my peers that they shouldn't be either.

Substitutes for Hierarchy

These kinds of infrastructures are important for effective team operation. Ed Lawler, a prolific management writer and employee involvement expert, calls them "substitutes for hierarchy." Absent these systems the teams would be thrown into chaos, not competitiveness. Like it or not, hierarchy and bureaucracy have performed an important coordination function in most organizations that must still be accomplished somehow in the SDWT workplace. A number of companies have reported problems when hierarchical controls (management authorizations, policies, procedures, etc.) were withdrawn from teams prematurely without anything to replace the clarity and direction that those controls provided. Boundary managers act as organization designers to ensure that teams have these substitutions for hierarchy in place.

Cross-Organization Collaboration

Boundary managers do other things as well. Rosabeth Moss Kanter, an author and business school professor, describes this new role as managing channels of influence, networking horizontally, and managing external relations—or in her words, "brokering interfaces instead of presiding over empires." What does this look like? Whereas supervisors focus on optimizing their own departments or sections, team leaders (as boundary managers) are much more interested in optimizing the whole operation, even if that means suboptimizing their part of it. They act as cross-organization collaborators rather than empire builders because their knowledge of the environment shows them that collaboration is essential to survival. For more examples of how a boundary management approach differs from a traditional supervisory approach, see Table 11.3.

Seven Competencies of Boundary Managers

The overall role of the SDWT leader is to be a boundary manager. This includes not only being an organization designer, infrastructure builder,

Table 11.3 Differences in Approach Between a Supervisor
and a Boundary Manager

Sample Situation	Traditional Supervisor's Approach	Boundary Manager's Approach
Orienting new team members	Focuses on clarifying the new job description, specific job tasks, rules, procedures, and policies pertaining to the department.	Focuses on customer requirements, vendor issues, quality standards, ethics, and interface issues with other teams.
Problem with another group	Works on solving the department's part of the problem. Reminds the other group to solve its part of the problem.	Brings the groups together and facilitates a joint problem-solving process.
Lack of skill in operation	Ensures that good technical training is completed.	Brokers in business training, interpersonal training, and technical training from his or her network of corporate and community resources.
Problem within the group	Engages in active problem solving that may or may not involve other department employees. Focuses on getting the problem solved as quickly as possible.	Provides relevant resources or information from external sources so the group can solve its problem itself. Focuses on accomplishing the purpose of the team rather than just fixing things that are broken.

and cross-organization collaborator, but a lot of other responsibilities as well. Boundary managers, for example, often play the role of translator, as they try to help team members comprehend the fuzzy and chaotic reality of the outside world. They also block certain disruptions from entering the team, shielding it from inappropriate distractions or unnecessary confusion. As diverse as these different team leader responsibilities appear, all of them seem to require a common set of personal competencies.

A number of generic attributes are important for effective team leaders, such as a clear understanding of what it takes to be successful, excellent communication abilities, and a strong interpersonal and technical skill base consistent with the organization's culture. Specific behaviors exhibited by successful SDWT leaders I know, however, include some other things as well. These leaders:

1. Articulate a vision for the organization.
2. Get good results.
3. Actively facilitate and develop team members.
4. Aggressively eliminate barriers to team effectiveness.
5. Understand and communicate business and customer needs.
6. Effectively coach individuals and teams.
7. Set a personal example.

These behaviors can be developed into seven clusters of competencies and values, which further clarify the required skills for a successful team leader (see Figure 11.5):*

1. Leader
2. Results Catalyst
3. Facilitator
4. Barrier Buster
5. Business Analyzer
6. Coach
7. Living Example

* These descriptions and the "Team Leader Role" model are part of the Fisher Group "Leadership Skills" training program © 1999 by The Fisher Group, Inc. All rights reserved. Used by permission.

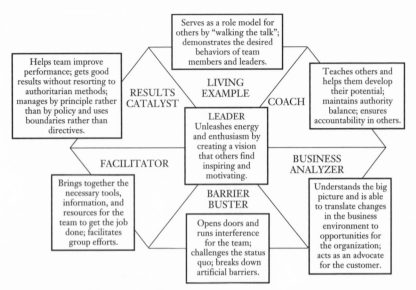

Figure 11.5 The team leader role.
Leadership Skills training program, The Fisher Group, Inc. © 1999. All rights reserved. Used by permission.

What do these clusters mean? Let's start at the center of the model and work around it counterclockwise.

1. The *Leader* unleashes energy and enthusiasm by creating a vision that others find inspiring and motivating.
2. The *Results Catalyst* helps the team improve performance, gets good results without resorting to authoritarian methods, manages by principle rather than by policy, and uses boundaries rather than directives.
3. The *Facilitator* brings together the necessary tools, information, and resources for the team to get the job done, and facilitates group efforts.
4. The *Barrier Buster* opens doors and runs interference for the team, challenges the status quo, and breaks down artificial barriers to the team's performance.
5. The *Business Analyzer* understands the big picture, is able to translate changes in the business environment to opportunities for the organization, and acts as an advocate for the customer.

6. The *Coach* teaches others and helps them develop to their potential, maintains an appropriate authority balance, and ensures accountability in others.
7. The *Living Example* serves as a role model for others by "walking the talk" and demonstrating the desired behaviors of team members and leaders.

Summary

There are a number of role similarities between successful supervisors and successful team leaders. But leading SDWTs requires some special perspectives and competencies. Team leaders are boundary managers who act as organization designers, infrastructure builders, and cross-organization collaborators. They don't "taste the sausage."

While supervisors work *in* the system, team leaders work *on* the system. As boundary managers, team leaders perform responsibilities at the interface between the team and the team's environment. This allows them to help the teams stay focused on the big picture instead of becoming mired in the day-to-day throughput tasks for which the SDWTs now have primary responsibility. It also allows team leaders to get needed resources and information from outside of the team.

We have found that successful boundary managers have a number of general attributes and skills. They have highly developed competencies in the areas of leadership, getting results, facilitation, barrier busting, business analysis, coaching, and setting an example. Without skills in these areas, team leaders are not likely to be successful boundary managers.

Because of their importance to the team leader, each of these seven clusters of competencies will be described in more detail in the next few chapters.

CHAPTER

12

Essential Competencies for Team Leaders: Leader, Results Catalyst, and Facilitator

"The greatest people are self-managing; they don't need to be managed. Once they know what to do they'll figure out how to do it . . . what they need is a common vision . . . leadership is having a vision (and) being able to articulate that, so that people around you can understand it . . ."

Steve Jobs, *two-time CEO of Apple Computer*

A RUNNING CRITIQUE of large organizations is that they are typically overmanaged and underled. While in a traditional operation this is unfortunate, in a high-performance work system it can be disastrous. SDWTs need leadership to be successful—but inappropriate management can destroy them. In this chapter we will review the first three clusters of competencies of team leaders: (1) leadership, (2) getting results, and (3) facilitating. Each of these clusters has some competencies and/or attributes associated with it that are important to the leader.

Acting Like a Leader

Nothing has been studied so thoroughly or written about so consistently as leadership. What is a leader? Two leadership characteristics are particularly important to SDWT boundary managers: (1) they are masters of change, and (2) they are visionaries.

Leaders as Change Agents

Leaders are masters of change. They are so committed to continuous improvement that they constantly challenge the status quo. They empower those around them to do what is right rather than allowing them to succumb to the momentum of the "way we usually do things around here." The team leader has the skills required to make these changes in a way that minimizes counterproductive disruptions, motivates people to achieve, and creates the support of enough followers to accomplish an honest modification of the culture. Tichy and Ulrich call this unique bag of skills needed to move a lumbering organization in a new direction *transformational leadership*, a term that captures the scope and significance of this characteristic. Simply stated, leaders create big, sustainable change. One of the primary ways they effect change is through vision, the second important element of leadership.

Vision: Gotta Have One

Leaders are visionaries. In fact, managing by vision is one of the key characteristics of a team leader. Vision is a leadership tool. Like a hammer, it can drive a nail or smash a thumb. But when it is used effectively it makes a big difference.

One Apple Computer plant manager describes Steve Jobs, cofounder of Apple, as such a visionary: "Steve had his problems," he said, "but I can still remember how he could inspire and motivate us with his vision. He would get us together and tell us that Apple products were going to *change the world*. He made that happen." Think of what Apple accomplished in those early days of the company. I was working as an intern with IBM in 1979 when good IBMers were laughing at this upstart little company with its toy computers. I remember being in meetings when senior managers declared that microcomputers would never replace mainframes in the office. They were wrong. Jobs's vision motivated people to break the office technology paradigm and change the world. Although Apple wouldn't win the minicomputer hardware war, Jobs's vision of a user-friendly computer would later be imitated by the Windows programs that would dominate the industry he started. After he left Apple, however, his offbeat company would falter.

Perhaps more instructive than Apple's start-up was the near-death experience the company had just before the new millennium. Most analysts had written it off. Sales were disastrous, third-party software development was nil, and even the confidence of die-hard Mac addicts was waning. But Steve came back. Few leaders get to start a company, leave it, and then come back and rescue it from the brink of extinction. But Jobs's remarkable turnaround of the company in 1999 is testament to the clarifying, motivating, and restorative power of leadership vision.

Another remarkable example of the power of vision is the story of Microsoft's entry into the Internet. Few people remember that Microsoft was a no-show in the early days of the Web. Companies like AOL and Netscape were very influential, while Microsoft was criticized publicly in business journals for not participating in the development of the information superhighway. Within a matter of weeks, Microsoft was involved. Within a matter of months the company's presence was so dominant that competitors started to cry unfair competition. How did it happen? Insiders say it was because Bill Gates's personal vision for the company was clearly and compellingly shared with company employees. Somehow, through the power of his vision Gates turned the huge Microsoft battleship 90 degrees. It practically flew out of the water.

How Have Leaders Influenced You?

Think of leaders who have inspired and motivated you to do your best. How did they do it? Chances are that they believed in you, they were honest and trustworthy, and they had a vision you believed in. Although they are often controversial, great leaders bring about great change with these visions. Dr. Martin Luther King Jr. inspired millions with his "I have a dream" speech that asked us to judge each other not by the color our skin but by the content of our character. Gandhi moved millions with his vision of nonviolent change. Lech Walesa changed a nation through a vision of worker solidarity. Mikhail Gorbachev dismantled the former Soviet Union with his vision of *glasnost* and *perestroika*. John F. Kennedy focused the unchanneled creativity of a nation on putting a man on the moon.

This kind of vision is important for any human organization, and it is certainly a useful tool for operational, management, and culture team leaders. Whether the team is a Fortune 100 company or a small group of office workers, a good team leader has a vision of what that team could accomplish that will allow him or her to provide clarity of direction and values. The vision must be concise enough to be focusing but broad enough to allow the creative autonomy necessary to accomplish it.

Pioneer Hi-bred International is a Dupont agricultural research subsidiary that started developing new corn breeds in 1913. While employees appreciate the company requirement to be a profit-making entity, what really inspires most of them is the simple but compelling leadership vision to "feed the world." Phil Rittenhouse, while a plant manager at Corning, had an unusual and compelling vision for his plant. On vacation in India with his family one year, he found hand-scrawled on a monument a paragraph that described what the graffiti writer thought was required to help India achieve its own economic and spiritual potential. Rittenhouse modified it somewhat and presented it as his vision of the factory. "(The operation) will be made of what we are. As we are big so will (the organization) be. We want to enjoy success. We want jobs and fair rewards. We want people who are going to stand up for what they think is right and not submit humbly to wrong. We challenge ourselves to do big things. We cannot command success, but success often comes to those who dare to act." The vision captured the attention of the plant. It was also so different from the traditional mission and objective statements that the employees were used to that it clearly signaled a departure from the norm.

Nested Vision

Since every team leader uses vision as a tool to motivate and focus team members, there is a risk of a serious problem. If multiple visions empower multiple teams to head in lots of different (read *inconsistent*) directions, an organization can be ripped apart.

A concept that is useful to coordinate multiple visions is called *nested visions*. If the vision of culture team leaders is broad enough, then the vision of management team leaders can fit inside it. If the vision of management team leaders is not too restrictive, then the vision of operations team leaders will fit inside it as well. Thus the visions nest inside of one another. Like Russian matreshka dolls, the smaller visions fit inside larger and larger visions. Each is completely whole and developed, but each is consistent with the size and shape of the others it fits within. This process also makes it more likely that the visions will become shared visions in the operation because there is consistency of message.

Shared Vision

Just having a vision isn't good enough. Obviously, if the vision isn't (1) communicated and (2) agreed to, then it won't make any difference at all. Leaders know this. Shared vision is the only vision that drives the nail home. How do you create shared vision?

Sometimes just articulating a well-crafted picture of the future is enough to create shared commitment to achieving it. This seems to work especially well for leaders who have a certain amount of charisma and are trusted by team members. Many team leaders, however, prefer an alternative process that enrolls the team members in the modification/creation of the vision. How? Some share their vision in an informal setting and then invite others to modify it to the extent required for them to support it. Others use a joint visioning process, in which they work with the team to create the vision together from scratch.

A Joint Visioning Process Example

Let me give you an example to illustrate both a joint visioning process and the nested vision concept. In one large, progressive organization, company representatives were commissioned by culture team leaders to jointly create a companywide vision for empowerment. The representatives included people from manufacturing and distribution units, nonmanufacturing units, the union, and management. After some discussion, they wrote a companywide vision (see Figure 12.1). Although this example of a vision deals with one particular attribute of an organization (empowerment) rather than with a vision of the whole purpose of the organization (the normal use of vision), I think it is instructive.

The involvement process automatically made the vision a shared one. And the vision these people came up with was of secondary importance to the fact that they had created it together. The magic wasn't the

---

Vision

Create a sense of urgency to change the environment across the entire company to unleash and focus the full potential of all employees in our drive to serve the customer and to be the best in the world in every one of our plants and businesses.

Employees will be provided with all the information to understand their business (customers, suppliers and products) and to focus on our competitors as the common adversary.

All employees will be the best trained, most flexible, productive and secure in their areas of employment.

All employees will be trained and empowered to make operational decisions across a very broad range of tasks for which they and their work groups will be responsible.

Every unit will develop and implement a plan to continuously design or redesign their operations to ensure that we beat our competition.

All employees will participate and share in the success and financial prosperity of the business.

Leadership Skills training program, The Fisher Group, Inc. © 1999. All rights reserved. Used by permission.

Figure 12.1 Sample of a company-wide vision of empowerment.

document itself, but what happened in the room leading up to the development of the document. As individuals personally and collectively committed to the vision, the employees created implicit agreements to help each other change the culture. As you can see in Figure 12.2, an information systems division of the same company came up with its own unique vision of empowerment, which although more specific than the corporate one is still consistent with the broad direction. You can also see that the division vision leaves plenty of room for individual teams to create clear and motivating visions of their own. Interestingly, in both of these vision documents the participants have chosen to include some statements of their values as well. As they have taken action toward operationalizing the statements on these sheets of paper, they have started to make significant progress toward creating empowered work teams.

Vision

Information Services will be an organization in which employees are vested with both the responsibility and authority to deliver total customer service.

An integrated, well-communicated division direction guides each individual's actions such that a sense of commitment, dedication and power exists within each employee.

An openness exists throughout the organization which facilitates communication, minimizes bureaucracy, and speeds decision making.

Responsibility for the success of the empowerment effort rests with all I/S employees. Responsibility for creating an empowered environment rests with the I/S management team.

Increased responsibility, authority, and accountability reside at the action initiation or customer interface points within the organization.

Coaching, mentoring, and collaboration skills are emphasized and are the dominant organizational style.

Processes are simplified to allow broader involvement in direction- and priority-setting.

Continuous improvement is expected and is measured by a periodic Empowerment Survey.

Figure 12.2 Sample of a division-wide vision of empowerment.

The Results Catalyst

The second competency cluster is getting results. When all is said and done, great leaders are judged neither by the promises they make nor by the commitment they inspire from others. Great leaders get results. The way they get results, of course, is what differentiates a good traditional supervisor from a high-performance leader. Team leaders get good results without resorting to autocratic, authoritarian methods.

Managing by Principle Rather than by Policy

One of the most important skills for getting results in a high-performance work system is managing by principle rather than by policy. No other activity better symbolizes the difference between traditional organizations and self-directed work teams than limiting organizational edicts and focusing on results instead. The leader emphasizes the end rather than the means to accomplishing it, and trusts team members to use their intelligence and experience to get good results. Team leaders at every level want to develop an entrepreneurial spirit, often called *ownership*, in others by encouraging them to find their own best way to get the job done.

Traditional, nonparticipative systems are typically managed through policies and procedures. While rules ensure consistency and control of the business, an undesirable side effect is that they also restrict creativity, flexibility, trust, and commitment, which are keystone attributes of competitive organizations.

While some rules are necessary, of course, a reliance on rules as a primary vehicle of management often leads to memorized answers and rigid solutions. In a worst-case scenario it can create a culture of unthinking compliance that can be damaging to the operation.

Consider a true and terrible story. Not long ago in the midwestern United States, a young man was injured by stray bullets from a drive-by shooting. With the help of a friend he managed to walk to a nearby hospital, where he fainted from lack of blood on the steps leading into the building. His friend ran inside to get help.

Hospital employees informed the friend that hospital policy prohibited them from leaving their stations to help bring the victim inside. While hospital employees looked on, an ambulance was called to transport the young man the final few yards into the emergency room. But by the time the young man was inside the hospital it was too late. Ironically, the policies and procedures that should have facilitated the hospital's core mission of saving lives had actually cost one.

A furious community demanded explanations and was told that there was good reason for the policy. It protected hospital employees from a dangerous neighborhood and ensured that people were always at the work stations where patients needed them. But hospital administrators acknowledged that in this case the policy was wrong. Had the nurses and technicians felt free to use common sense and run the 30 yards or so to help the boy on the steps, he would probably be alive today. In another interesting irony, politicians demanded that new policies be developed to ensure that this situation never happened again, when in my opinion it was an overreliance on policies that caused the problem in the first place.

Break Some Rules

Few things are as demonstrative of the team leader attribute of managing by principle rather than by policy as when the leader makes a visible alteration of a well-known written or unwritten rule. For example, when R. J. Boyle of Honeywell wrote a you-don't-have-to-wear-a-tie-when-it's-hot memo to his division, he sent a message that *principles*, like maintaining a professional image with customers (the reason for the dress code), were more important than rules like "Everyone needs to wear a tie to work every day." If this is done enough, people remember that the principle is more important than the policy. Eventually they will feel free to challenge policies that unintentionally inhibit organizational effectiveness rather than mindlessly complying with something that doesn't make sense.

Managing by principle is more difficult than managing by policy. At the Lima plant we managed by three particularly important principles:

- Do what is right.
- Get results.
- Do it together.

Are these kinds of principles more vague than policies would be? Are they subject to individual interpretation? Do they apply differently in one set of circumstances than they might in another? The answer to all of these questions is yes. That is why principles are difficult to use. It is also why they work. On many occasions team members would say, "Hey, wait a minute, what we are doing now is what is cheap or easy but not what is right." Or, "Hold it, we are making a decision that affects another team, we should make this decision together with them." In virtually every situation these kinds of discussions led to results that were far superior to what would have occurred if employees were simply complying with a management rule.

Using Operating Guidelines

An effective way to reinforce guiding principles is to establish *operating guidelines*—agreements for group interaction that are supported by all team members. By setting operating guidelines, the team can create positive norms for team effectiveness. Key reasons for establishing operating guidelines include the following:

- If the team does not deliberately set operating guidelines, then the team's norms (habits) become the guidelines by default.
- Operating guidelines foster trust and openness.
- They establish common expectations for team member behavior.
- They provide a common vision of how the team will operate.
- They foster continuous improvement.

Facilitating Skills

The third competency cluster is facilitating. Team leaders realize that people, like seed corn, will be productive only as long as they have the resources that are necessary. Although not all seeds are germinated— just like all team members aren't productive all the time—most will bear fruit in favorable conditions. Team leaders, therefore, facilitate higher crop yield by creating the favorable conditions. Fertilizing, administering pesticides and herbicides, irrigating, being responsive to destructive molds and diseases, harvesting, and so forth are the ways that farmers ensure that the seeds have the resources necessary to produce as much corn as they are internally capable of producing. Conversely, withholding resources can cause corn to wither and weaken. The unsuspecting team leader who, even unknowingly, withholds information, authority, autonomy, budget, training, or whatever resources are necessary to get the job done, lowers productivity even as he or she may be struggling so hard to "make" people be productive. Trying to make people productive is like a farmer "making" corn grow: it isn't a good use of time.

We have already mentioned that team leaders believe that most people will do what is right. Therefore they focus most of their time and attention on how to provide people with the appropriate resources, experiences, and information needed to do the job successfully rather than on how to influence opinions. They enable people to be successful. They assume that most problems are the result of a lack of resources rather than of a desire to subvert the operation. Team leaders also understand that motivation is internally generated. They realize that while they need to *allow* people to be productive, they cannot *make* them productive. Hence the title *facilitator* rather than *director.*

How Do You Facilitate?

How does the team leader facilitate? The facilitator's ongoing objective, of course, is to actively solicit and channel the participation of others. This facilitation may take the direct form of asking for participation: "Jim, I know you have a lot of experience on this; what do you think we ought to do?" As team members become more comfortable with the participative process, it may take the form of requesting more thorough proposals that require a significant breadth and depth of organizational understanding.

Team leaders also actively focus on the development of others. That was the war cry we heard at Kodak's 13 room so often: "Develop capability." Instead of taking over conversations and making the decisions, the team leader walks to the chart pad, grabs a pen, and starts asking people where the team should go from here. Instead of doing things for the team that the members could learn to do for themselves, the team leader teaches them how to do it. He or she becomes skilled at understanding the dynamics of a work group and knowing when and where to intervene. He or she develops expertise in teaching people processes that will help them solve problems and make decisions themselves instead of just giving them a solution or decision to implement. He or she takes advantage of every teaching moment that presents itself.

When I had team members come to me to ask me to solve a problem, I would say, "Sure!" and bring them along with me. After a while, they knew it made more sense just to go solve the problem themselves without dragging me into the middle of it.

Training

Training becomes a crucial element of the facilitator's responsibility, especially in the early stages of SDWT implementation. Most team leaders seriously underestimate the time commitment required for this. Says Bob Condella, director of the Administrative Center of Corning:

> **The biggest mistake we made was that we did not train enough. People need a lot of help in the beginning. People need more help and more tools (than we thought). We spent about 10 percent of our time in training. But when I went out and benchmarked, companies were spending about 20 percent.**

Training is an ongoing responsibility as well. Both Tektronix and General Electric found that, if you include all types of training (classroom, mentoring, cross-training, business meetings, team meetings, etc.) the ongoing requirement for training time is in the neighborhood of 10 to 20 percent of every person's workweek. That is almost a whole day a week dedicated to learning. It is a far cry from the traditional organization's training record of 0.5 to 2 percent. Farsighted companies like Motorola are already establishing goals for team member training, which helps the organization understand that training is part of the work to be done rather than something that takes people away from their work. And they are backing it up with resources as well. Motorola spends 2.5 percent of its annual payroll upgrading the skills of each of its 96,000 employees. William Wiggenhorn, Motorola's corporate vice president for training and education and the president of Motorola University, acknowledges that the facilities that don't reinforce the training have a negative return on investment. But plants that reinforce the training receive a $33 return for every dollar spent, including the cost of wages. Motorola expects these training budget increases to continue as empowerment requires further buttressing of basic skills and an expanding curriculum of business skills for employees on teams.

Career Development

Facilitating career development also takes on a new and important twist in the SDWT. In these flatter organizations, there are fewer and fewer opportunities for promotions. Therefore, lateral development takes on more importance than vertical development. That means that the team leader is responsible for ensuring that team members get experience across the operations, rather than just remaining inside a traditional functional silo or being limited to one area of narrow technical expertise. This knowledge may come partly from classroom training, but it requires much more. Typically, team leaders ensure that processes are in place that require the regular rotation of responsibilities to give team members actual experience in a wide variety of technical and leadership assignments across the team and then into other teams as well.

Summary

Team leaders facilitate both individual and team effectiveness by focusing on things such as career development and training, and by helping people solve problems and make decisions themselves. They manage by principle rather than by policy because they realize that this approach provides clarity without reducing the ownership that comes from personal involvement. They encourage the development of operating guidelines as a vehicle for self-direction. Team leaders, of course, also demonstrate specific leadership skills. In particular, they are visionaries and change agents. They know how to coalesce people around a shared vision that is nested with the organizational leadership. These groups of competencies—leadership, getting results, and facilitating—are important parts of the team leader role.

In the next chapter we will review the final four competency clusters of the team leader role: barrier busting, business analysis, coaching, and modeling.

The Barrier Buster, Business Analyzer, Coach, and Living Example

"All coaching is, is taking a player where he can't take himself."

Bill McCartney, *defensive coordinator, San Francisco '49ers, Super Bowl season*

I N THIS CHAPTER we will consider the last four team leader competencies clusters in more detail. They are:

1. Barrier busting
2. Business analysis
3. Coaching
4. Modeling

With this discussion we will finish the review of the seven competency areas that make up the role of the SDWT leader.

Eliminating Barriers to High Performance

The first competency cluster we will discuss in this chapter is barrier busting. One of the quickest ways to make team members feel empowered is to identify and eliminate organizational barriers to higher performance. Perhaps no activity is more energizing to a team than isolating a particularly restrictive policy or practice and working with the team leader to modify or eliminate it. It doesn't matter whether these are real or only perceived barriers. Barrier busting builds trust in the team leader and credibility for the change effort.

One note of caution, however, is that this cuts two ways. Unsuccessful efforts to make these kinds of changes will slow and stop the progress of empowerment. It is far better to build some momentum by biting off a few smaller projects that have a reasonable chance of success than by going after the big high-risk one right out of the barrel.

Quality of Work Life Concerns

Early concerns identified by teams are often related to quality of work life. When the sanitation department of New York City began its empowerment efforts several years ago, for example, workers were much more interested in putting in clear thermal curtains to keep the cold winter air out of their work areas than they were in improving technologies or cutting costs. But that came later. After the workers came to trust the team leaders who helped them improve the quality of their work life, they then went after things like new cutting torch technology and painting techniques. These ideas eventually saved the city millions of dollars associated with maintaining the largest nonmilitary fleet of vehicles in the United States. Barrier-busting team leaders made it happen by freeing up worker time and project resources to work on improvements (they created an R&D department), which were unavailable with the more restrictive work practices of the past.

Eliminate Unnecessary Policies

Barrier busting is tricky business. It needs to be handled in a way that doesn't disenfranchise key resources to the team. Blaming corporate staff groups for stupid policies, for example, often makes staff members unwilling to help the team later on when their expertise may be essential. Similarly, the clumsy dismantling of long-standing corporate artifacts can upset important senior leadership. [We used to call these types of efforts CLMs (Career-Limiting Moves).] Nevertheless, when done with sensitivity and when supported with good business information, barrier busting can create enormous psychological and business gains. Even the little wins make a difference.

For example, with the help of some team leaders, a small team of union executives at a P&G plant was able to change a policy relating to travel to nonunion plants and an unwritten rule about sharing profitability information inside the plant. Busting these barriers rebuilt trust in the facility between management and the union, which had eroded away over decades. In a Tektronix division, a management team leader helped eliminate a requirement that people report their time using a particular method that required very detailed record keeping. Sadly, the team leader discovered that the reports generated from this time-consuming activity were compiled, distributed, and virtually ignored. The previously unchallenged policy was significantly simplified. This resulted in a savings of thousands of employee hours a month. Moreover, it created a flurry of activity. When team members saw that management was willing to get rid of inhibiting practices, they surfaced a number of barriers that they had always thought were unmovable. Although some were, in fact, barriers that resulted from legal requirements that could not be changed, a number of others were simplified. Production output increased, quality improved, and development speed increased.

Analyzing Business

The next cluster of competencies has to do with business analysis. More than anything else, business analysis is the process of gathering and then disseminating business information. While it is true that the effective team leader must be skilled in the process of evaluating and analyzing, the most common inadequacy associated with this competency cluster isn't whether the analysis itself is good or bad. It is whether that analysis is shared with the team effectively or not.

Let me explain. My fourth-grade teacher first taught me the importance of sharing information. Mrs. Anderton was a very large woman who wore a thimble on the middle finger of her right hand to plunk on the foreheads of errant students (I was on the business end of that thimble more than once). She suggested one day that "democracy would not work." After a dramatic pause that captured my attention as a young patriot (willing to risk even the thimble for a developing belief in democracy), she continued. "Unless people are informed," she said.

Democracy without information is nothing more than uninformed mobocracy. Democracy only works when people are informed. "I am a firm believer in the people," said Abraham Lincoln. "If given the truth, they can be depended upon to meet any national crisis. The great point is to bring them the real facts." Bringing them the facts is the key. You might better have a few people making good decisions autocratically than a lot of people making stupid ones democratically. There is nothing good about that.

Empowerment Without Business Information Is a Sham

Teams cannot work toward self-direction without understanding their businesses *well*. Business literacy efforts, real-time data about customers and markets, and information from other parts of the organization are the lifeblood of high-performance work systems. I already mentioned that Corning has been using the word *partnership* to describe its SDWT work. I like the word because it helps people be honest about the effort by asking a simple question: "Am I treating others (and am I being treated) like a business partner?"

Would you join a business partnership if your soon-to-be partner told you that although you would have equal access to decision making, he was not going to be able to share all the business information with you? Would you placidly accept his reasoning that it is just too time-consuming or expensive to do this? What if he said that he wanted to wait until he had all the facts before he shared them with you, or worse, that he feared you wouldn't be able to understand the information anyway? I wouldn't be a partner in an operation like that. Nor would I want to be a partner in an organization that buried me in reams of useless information.

It is becoming increasingly clear that the primary competitive advantage of the information age is knowledge. Companies of all sizes have been scurrying around to implement large knowledge management systems that help share business analysis data with people. These systems also attempt to transfer knowledge internally. Large consulting firms such as Anderson Consulting have recognized the importance of these systems and have deemed them proprietary.

We Need Better Knowledge Management Systems

Team leaders cannot share good business information, of course, unless they have access to it. Unfortunately, many businesses are sadly lacking in information that can be used to manage the business at each team's level. At the same time they are also inundated with e-mail, voicemail, intranet and Internet data, and various reports that are clogging the arteries of the operation. Not enough of some information, too much of other types of information. The challenge for the team leader is this: how can we get the right information to the right people at the right time?

Technology alone is not the answer. Having the ability to share information well is not the same as actually doing so. Some companies have spent millions of dollars putting knowledge management systems in place with little payback. Others have used low-tech alternatives like public whiteboards, effective cross-functional meetings, and job restructuring to better advantage. Absent good discipline, gathering and disseminating information can rapidly devolve into a waste of a lot of time. Even worse, poor information transfer can turn into something akin to internal hemorrhaging.

What Kind of Information Do SDWTs Need?

What kinds of things do team leaders need to understand and then bring to the team members? Leaders need to have a good understanding of the business variables at the boundary of the team, including specific facts and data relating to at least these eight topic areas:

1. *Customers/Markets:* Who are they? What do they need from us?
2. *Technologies/Technical:* What are the options? How do they affect us?
3. *Competition:* Who are they? How are we different from them?
4. *Environment:* How do we eliminate contaminants?
5. *Political/Governmental:* What laws affect us? Are there community concerns that could affect us?

6. *Demographics:* What are the changing requirements of the work-force?

7. *Suppliers:* Who are they? How do they affect our work and customers?

8. *Economics:* How is the economy? How does that affect us?

It is a sad commentary on businesses today that many team leaders cannot answer basic questions relating to these areas. Many times I have visited with team leaders at different levels of organizations who could not name end-use customers of the products or services they provided. Others haven't known their competitors and their strengths and weaknesses. Many have been unaware of government regulations that affect them or of the new technologies that were available to help them accomplish their work more effectively. While answers to these questions are generally available in certain compartmentalized functional areas of these organizations, they were not widely known. The knowledge transfer system isn't working.

There are, of course, some refreshing examples of leaders that do disseminate knowledge well. After Bill Gates expressed concern that managers didn't know enough about their competitors, Jeff Raikes, then manager of the word processing business, got to know Pete Peterson, his counterpart at WordPerfect. He put a picture of Petersen's children on his desk and continues to send them birthday cards each year. The pictures, of course, were only a symbol of the thoroughness of Raikes's investigation into the competition. Family photos do not substitute for good competitive information.

Institutionalized Methods for Joint Business Analysis

The bottom line is this: business information needs to be disseminated throughout the organization, and there need to be institutionalized methods for regular discussion of these and other topics relating to the internal workings of the business. That is what creates a forum for joint business analysis. It is for this reason that many SDWTs in manufacturing settings have shift overlap meetings every day and why other types of teams may meet several times a week. These meetings provide an opportunity for sharing real-time information. They also become the primary forum for ongoing skill training and for group problem-solving and decision-making activity. Where the supervisor relied on controls to coordinate and focus work activity, the team leader now relies on information instead.

Customer Advocacy

An essential part of business analysis is customer advocacy. Customer advocacy is one of the main ways to help the team stay focused on the purpose of the organization. Says Paul Allaire, CEO of Xerox, "You can't get people to focus only on the bottom line. You have to give them an objective like 'satisfy the customer' that everyone can relate to."

Customer advocacy helps the team keep the proper perspective and allows it to solve problems and make decisions with the bigger picture in mind. When the customer advocate does his or her job, we don't see as many dysfunctional internal squabbles that can cripple the productivity of a team. People know they can't afford much of that. We focus on quality, cost, and speed not because of upper management, but because of customers.

Stew Leonard, a grocery store manager, doesn't just say that customer feedback is important; he actively solicits and applies it. The suggestion boxes in his store are stuffed with hundreds of customer suggestions a month, which are typed and distributed to employees on a daily basis. A few results of these suggestions include fresh fish being taken out of the packaging and put on ice, and customers filling containers with strawberries and eggs themselves instead of purchasing them preboxed. The result? Sales have more than doubled for these items.

Team leaders take actions like these to reinforce the importance of keeping the focus on customers. They bring internal and external customers into team meetings to talk to the team members, and they coordinate site visits so that team members can see how selected customers actually use their products or services. There is no substitute for first-hand interaction. The "we have customers" concept in the abstract is not meaningful to anybody. Why do sales and service employees talk about customers so much? Because they deal with them on a day-to-day basis. They know when they are happy or unhappy, and they are typically rewarded for some measure of customer satisfaction. Everybody needs to feel like a salesperson does about customers. What does it take to make them feel that way? The same advantages salespeople enjoy: information, interaction, and rewards.

Team Leaders Develop Customer Empathy

Team members need to see customers as real people like themselves who want value for their money. They need to know their names and experience their problems. One steel mill, for example, reported that a visit to a nearby bicycle manufacturing company that used its steel helped employees have more empathy and enthusiasm for the importance of quality and delivery issues. Tektronix reported improved (more practical and user-friendly) designs and customer relations when engineering team members visited end users. One team leader brings in a different customer each month for a plantwide assembly so that team members across the facility can hear from customers on a regular basis. Many team leaders have had success with sit-down meetings with their teams and visitors from other teams who act as internal customers for their services. These meetings serve to clarify expectations, define deliverables, and resolve problems that may ultimately affect the cost or quality of a product to the end-use customer.

Misusing Customer Advocacy

Aetna found an interesting problem with this customer advocacy process, however, that is worth mentioning: too much emphasis on the demands of the *internal* customer (like another downstream department inside Aetna) was causing problems for the external customer. The teams, anxious to please the internal customers, were sometimes complying with requests for additional services that ended up increasing the cost to the final customer. Not good. Aetna resolved the problem by eliminating the focus on internal customers and emphasizing end users. Although this may not be necessary in all organizations, the clear message is to make sure that all internal vendor/customer relationships are aligned so that they serve the final end user.

Some company teams talk about their management as their customers. This is the classic mistake of using the commitment paradigm vocabulary to reinforce the control paradigm organization. Bosses aren't customers and never will be. They work for customers just like everybody else.

The bottom line is that organizations exist to serve customers who pay for products and services. Companies that remember this are much more likely to be successful than those that get tangled up in day-to-day work priorities. They can't continue to make decisions that improve their own work situation at the expense of the customer. American automakers suffered for decades because of the popular perception that they traded off quality for production in the 1960s and 1970s. This is ironic because arguably General Motors was "born" when this group of small automakers decided that they could survive against the powerful production machine built by Henry Ford only by listening to customers and by offering them an alternative to black Model T cars. As another example, Burger King has carved out a piece of McDonalds' market by letting customers have it their way.

Team leaders help team members establish work priorities by keeping the customer up front. This helps people make trade-offs in favor of quality and service and, perhaps most importantly, provides a purpose for their work beyond just getting the job done. Team members with this understanding have a completely different orientation to their work than an autoworker who described his view of working prior to empowerment as "an eight-hour interruption of my leisure time."

Coaching Teams

The third competency cluster we will review in this chapter is coaching. Coaches recognize that they need to develop individual players on the team and help the team learn how to work together effectively. Like the other competencies of team leaders, coaching is important in any organization. The reason it is especially important in an empowered work system, however, is that everyone plays a much larger role in running the business. Decisions are made at the point where action is taken on them. Responsibilities are given to those who are most directly affected by the consequences. Business direction is influenced by those who need to implement it. The rule of thumb is that people are given as much responsibility, authority, and autonomy as they can handle. The amount they can handle, of course, depends on how effectively they have been developed and will therefore change over time.

Many one-on-one performance coaching skills are readily transferable from traditional organizations to SDWTs. But coaches in these team-based operations also need to be proficient in working with the whole team as a unit. Coaches need to help team members build their skills. Although people need a number of particular technical and social skills, a few fundamental areas require some special coaching attention. Team leaders develop teams that:

1. Produce good results.
2. Exhibit teamwork (work together effectively).
3. Demonstrate self-sufficiency (producing and maintaining a high level of results with little external influence).
4. Communicate effectively (keep everyone well informed).

These focus areas form a foundation upon which the more specific skills tailored to the operation can be built.

One of the most difficult and most important skills to build into a team is the skill of learning how to learn. This thinking skill is critical to continuous improvement and self-direction. How do we coach it? One way is by asking questions instead of giving solutions.

Socratic Coaching

Allowing team members to build inner skull muscle tone is more important than any other development activity. Coaches refrain from judgement statements like, "That won't work." Instead, they ask questions like, "What is the problem you want to solve?" or "How will you know when you have solved it?" or "What information did you base this conclusion on?" Socratic coaching is a skill not to be undervalued in the SDWT environment. If done well, it teaches, strengthens, and empowers.

Relying on this technique too much, of course, can cause serious problems. Coaches who continually ask team members, "What do you think?" frequently lose their effectiveness when people eventually stop coming to them for advice. Better questions focus on where information can be found or on teaching particular thinking processes that help people make good decisions. There was one division manager at P&G, for example, who had a reputation for always asking, "What other solutions did you consider and why did you reject them?" After the second or third interaction with this management team leader, operations team leaders began to understand that he was teaching us to think through things carefully and not always settle for the first satisfactory (but maybe suboptimal) solution.

High Expectations

Coaches also recognize that there is a time and a place to be tough. When I think back on people who have been great coaches in my life, they have always had very high expectations of me. And they let me know when I wasn't performing to my level of capability. They did this in the right way, of course, by sharing good data and clear examples with me. Delivering feedback is an important coaching skill. And there are more effective and less effective ways of doing it.

Performance Appraisals Are a Lousy Way to Coach

Traditional performance appraisals are undoubtedly one of the least effective coaching techniques. They are depressing, nonsupportive, artificial, and untimely. I can just imagine what would happen if we applied this technique to professional basketball teams. Would the NBA work better if coaches gave each player a thoroughly documented performance review at the end of each season? I don't think so. What team members need is ongoing effective feedback during the game. Several team leaders I work with regularly share customer and peer feedback with teams to let them know whether they are on track or off track. Professional sports teams use videos of their games to help players self-review performance, and orchestras listen to their tapes for the same reason. Similarly, charts, graphs, and project reviews can help teams monitor their progress against performance goals and objectives, while internal and external customer visits can offer some real-time feedback that is more likely to motivate than discourage.

Being a Living Example

The final competency cluster for the team leader is being a living example. Team leaders model the behaviors they demand from others. They also embody and symbolize the vision of the organization. It is hard to overstate the importance of this part of the team leader's role, as evidenced by the example of the Kodak team leaders and others. Team leaders simply must walk the talk, or in the words of some Boeing managers, they must at least "stumble the mumble." Team leaders understand that the eloquence of their example is far more powerful than their words.

Alexander the Great is said to have won the commitment of his soldiers by risking his own life alongside them. He was the first man to charge the Theban Sacred Band at Chaeronea, and plunged so often into the thickest of the battle that his soldiers, fearful of losing him, begged him to go to the rear. Alexander was also the first to scale the walls of the Mallians. The ladders broke after he and two others had leaped into the city and found themselves alone among the enemy. He collapsed from loss of blood just as his armies broke into the city and saved his life. On one occasion, to calm a potential mass sedition, he presented himself to his army and asked which of them could show more scars than he, "whose body bore the marks of every weapon used in war." He led by example. An old saw about the difference between leaders and managers in the Civil War said that you could tell which was which from their position relative to the charging troops. Leaders were in front. Managers shouted direction and encouragement from behind.

People simply do not care what team leaders say, they care about what they do. The best team leaders I know don't talk about how they value employee input, they solicit it. They don't give speeches about the importance of customers, they visit them. They don't pontificate about quality, they shut down work when the operations are just slightly out of spec. And they empower (by example) the team members to do the same things.

Team Leaders Aren't Above the Law

Team leaders don't hold themselves above the law. They realize that a double standard causes distrust and looks hypocritical. If sound business reasons dictate the need for certain policies, leaders adhere to them. If money expenditures require authorization, they go through the same process as the team does for approval. If vacations need to be coordinated, they coordinate their vacations too. Any policy that applies to the team member applies to the team leader as well. If it is silly for team leaders to conform to any of the policies, then it is silly for team members to conform to them. In fact, team leaders often find themselves eliminating these kinds of practices and policies in their role of barrier buster. Team leaders, in short, practice what they preach.

For example, John Adamoli, a vice president of a large company in the defense industry, wanted to do two things. He wanted to demonstrate that his role was to support the organization, not boss it around, and he also wanted to emphasize the importance of cross-training for the newly empowered project teams. Instead of just having a meeting to tell this to people, he took off his suit, went down to the production floor, and had employees teach him how to weld.

Summary

The role of the team leader in an empowered organization setting is to act as a leader, results catalyst, facilitator, barrier buster, business analyzer, coach, and living example. In this chapter we reviewed the last four competency clusters, ending with that of the living example. We have probably all heard the saying, "I can't hear what you say because what you do is so loud." This folk wisdom comes from years of practical experience in a variety of human institutions. Successful team leaders carefully consider whether their actions set the right example or not. Effective coaching is also a key competency for the team leader. Running practices and giving good feedback is a helpful way to build the capability of team members individually and collectively. Although the traditional method of formal performance reviews is not likely to help, one method of effective development is Socratic coaching. If used effectively, questions help team members learn and improve. The business analyzer acts as a customer advocate. Customer advocacy focuses team members on the purpose of their existence and helps them make good decisions. This requires, of course, that internal customers not be emphasized to the detriment of the end user and that people not see management as customers. The business analyzer also focuses a great deal of energy on getting the right people the right information at the right time. He or she deals with the complexities of effective knowledge management. Finally, the team leader is an effective barrier buster, eliminating both real and perceived barriers to higher performance.

This team leader role is necessary for the ongoing effective operation of a self-sustaining team. It is important to understand that the role is an aggressive and proactive one, not the commonly misunderstood one of a milktoast passivist whose only responsibility is to "stay out the way." More on that topic in the next chapter.

The Myth of the Marshmallow Manager

"Perhaps if there has been one failing within our organization over the years, it is that we haven't tried to dispel the notion that our success comes out of a computer. It doesn't. It comes out of the sweat glands of our coaches and players."

Tom Landry, *former head coach, Dallas Cowboys*

NOT LONG AFTER I arrived at the P&G plant in Lima, Ohio, the team members were having a problem with one of their peers. Thinking it the right thing to do, I encouraged them to resolve the issue themselves without involving me. I was reluctant to jump in and fix something that I thought was the responsibility of the "semiautonomous team."

We called this way of managing "the concept," and it was a characteristic of our business that we considered a competitive advantage. In fact, when I had been hired by a joint group of technicians and managers from the plant, the plant manager warned me that *the worst* thing I could do as a manager at Lima was to harm "the concept."

The team members were normally responsible for handling most disciplinary problems with their peers. They dealt with absenteeism, job performance, and other issues primarily through peer pressure and by using systems they had developed to ensure fairness. But this particular issue was a personal and very complicated one that they could not solve. In fact, the members finally convinced me that I should have solved that particular problem without their involvement at all. They needed me to handle the situation autocratically. At the time I was troubled because it seemed somehow inconsistent with "the concept." But as I became more experienced in the operation, I discovered that at certain times an appropriate management intervention was not only acceptable, but required for SDWT effectiveness.

Team leadership is an art, not a science. As a result, no precise prescriptions are very useful to the team leader, who ultimately learns the role only through personal experience. But some general observations can accelerate the learning curve. One particular dilemma faced by team leaders, for example, is knowing when to intervene in the team's affairs and when not to. Generally speaking, team leaders intervene to generate support and clarity around vision and values, as mentioned in earlier chapters. They also, as in the example of the personal problem with my team, intervene when teams are operating outside of their agreed-on responsibilities or skills. But for one reason or another, team leaders certainly will intervene. It is a primary value-adding responsibility of the leader. In this chapter I will show that team leadership is not passive, even though it sometimes appears that way. I will also introduce another of the important skills of the team leader: setting boundary conditions. Using boundary conditions is another gauge that helps the team leader know when to intervene in a high-performance work system.

Team Leaders Are Neither Permissive Nor Passive

I have talked to other team leaders who had the same misconception about their responsibilities as I did when I first started with SDWTs.

Team leadership is not an abdication of responsibility. It is a shared responsibility. And team leadership is neither passive nor permissive management. So why do some people mistakenly think that their primary responsibility as a team leader, in the words of one well-intentioned leader, "Is to just stay the heck out of the way!"?

If we watch effective team leaders work, it is easy to come away with the misconception that this role is passive. Commitment-eliciting managers delegate a lot. They sometimes refuse to get involved in certain "management-type" decisions that they believe belong to the team. They avoid taking responsibility for the throughput activities of the team. It may appear like gutless acquiescence or responsibility dodging to the casual observer. In fact, to some observers these team leaders look like marshmallows—soft, squashy, and indecisive.

Marshmallow Managers

What do I mean by *marshmallow managers?* They are the supervisors who act sweet and sticky; they seldom take a stand under pressure, and they change their opinion easily to whatever is popular and noncontroversial. They can be operational, management, or culture team leaders who justify personal inactivity by saying, "That is the team's responsibility (not mine); they do whatever they want to do." It is often assumed erroneously that the switch from supervisor to team leader is a switch from "kick butt and take names" (in control) management to "going marshmallows" (out of control). Even if it looks that way to some, nothing could be further from the truth. Even shepherds carry a stick. Let's consider an example that demonstrates why the role might appear to be something it is not.

Why Team Leadership Sometimes Looks Passive

As one circuit board plant was starting up, the plant manager, Gene Hendrickson, chartered a large task force to make decisions about the design and operation of the cafeteria. The task force struggled for months, taking some of the members' precious production time to argue about the vendors, services, and facility layout of this cafeteria. External observers of this process (and, in fact, a few of the task force members) were baffled. Was this the way to engender commitment? Does participation mean that the team leader just lets go of decisions and lets people waffle around undirected for a while? Why spend hundreds of people-hours investigating something so trivial that it could have been decided by a single supervisor in an afternoon?

What people did not understand was that this team leader had a vision for his organization that included a workforce with the ability to make business plans and decisions. What appeared to some as unremitting chaos was in fact a carefully orchestrated training process in business information gathering, evaluating alternatives, communicating with others, and sticking by tough, unpopular decisions. Since it was a process of guided self-discovery, however, instead of a three-day workshop or some other highly structured activity, people could not see what they went through as training until later. All they saw from the team leader at the time was restraint, abeyance, and delegation.

The Role Can Look Confusing to Outsiders

Observers of this process could have been confused about the role of the team leader. It is easy to see the seemingly passive actions of leaders in examples like this one and to assume that they are marshmallows. On the contrary, successful team leaders are usually people of passion who have values and trust, which allow them to be patient in the time-consuming development of team members.

In the case of the plant cafeteria decision, people did in fact become capable of making significant business decisions over time. Three years later a similar group from the plant created the business plan, a sophisticated piece of market evaluation and business strategies, to direct the entire operations for the following 12 months. It was voted the second-best business plan of the Tektronix businesses by the senior managers of the company (who were unaware that it was developed by a group of mostly nonexempt employees).

Team Leaders Aren't Marshmallows

A contrasting story, told in the same plant, deals with the time Gene Hendrickson was trying to decentralize the plant engineering function. He had tried several times to encourage the engineers to relocate from their centralized office area to their respective production teams on the manufacturing floor. But his encouragement was to no avail. The engineers just didn't want to move. They liked their offices away from the noisy work floor and appreciated the collegial opportunity to review technical problems with other nearby engineers.

Hendrickson, however, had a different vision for the plant. So he came in with a moving crew one weekend and physically muscled the engineers' desks out into the plant. His behavior was in the classic style of the autocratic manager. Without even consulting the engineering team members, he took action. Was this action consistent with the role of an SDWT leader? Was this effective boundary management, or was Hendrickson messing inappropriately with the operational duties of the team?

Ironically, most of the same engineers later declared that it was exactly the right thing to do at the time (even though they were very upset with Hendrickson when he did it). Said one, "We never would have gone out there (to the production floor) if he wouldn't have forced us to. Now that we have seen the benefit of being right there when the problems happen we can see that it was a smart thing to do. I like it." Was this the action of a marshmallow? Hardly. Effective team leaders are just as strong and passionate and bullheaded as traditional supervisors. But they demonstrate their strength in fundamentally different ways.

Setting Boundary Conditions

Instead of controlling specific team member activities, for example, team leaders clarify the boundary conditions within which team activities are performed. These boundaries include things like project costs, schedules, or customer requirements. In much the same way as managing by principles, this provides people the autonomy required to generate personal commitment instead of the robotic compliance that is generated by externally imposed controls. It also obsoletes the requirements for many externally imposed controls like supervision, policies, and procedures. Team leaders are ferocious about these boundary conditions. They aren't marshmallows. Their ferocity comes from a knowledge that the survival of the team depends on their ability to meet these requirements. How do you use boundary conditions?

Let me give you an example. One company decided to redesign the manufacturing floor, and wanted to empower employees to do this task.

Traditionally, if employee input was sought at all, it would be highly restricted in conformance with numerous policies and procedures about equipment placement, power usage, mandated construction processes, management authorizations for spending capital, and so forth. In this case, however, team leaders wanted to complete the project in a manner that would be more consistent with the SDWT concept, which had recently been introduced in the operation. So, they developed boundary conditions for the project instead. These boundaries included the following:

- A requirement that the new design enhance the production of quality products.
- A project budget.
- A time by which the project had to be completed.
- The need to incorporate technical resources from engineering into the design process if necessary.
- A requirement that the team study leading-edge inventory and production management concepts and incorporate what it learned into the design.

There were a few other minor boundaries, but that was about it. Team members felt they had lots of flexibility about how to accomplish the redesign task. They felt trusted to do what was right for the business. They needed additional skills and support to be successful, of course, but the boundaries marked the field they were to play on.

Good Boundary Conditions Clarify

As team leaders clarify true business boundaries and hold the team accountable for them, team members are able to cut through the ambiguity of the workplace to accomplish things. Like the lines on a football field, boundaries define what is in bounds and out of bounds; they enable team members to assess their progress, and show them where the goal is located. Without these boundaries team members are likely to get frustrated and demotivated, but with them they can work together to create a series of winning plays.

These boundaries are much broader than directives. Directives, the tools of traditional supervision, dictate what is to be done and how to do it. Boundary conditions simply clarify the key constraints that must be considered. They provide clarity without unnecessarily limiting the alternatives the team can choose to accomplish the work to be done. Sometimes they actually encourage people to do things differently. Like the fence surrounding parts of the Grand Canyon, they provide a feeling of security that allows people to explore options right up to the edge of the boundary. Absent these, we often keep away from the edge of our experience and knowledge, sticking to the tried-and-true things we have done before. And although the tried and true may be more safe, it may not be what is needed.

The Natural Consequences of Being Unresponsive to Boundary Conditions

The fact of the matter is that boundaries exist whether we make them visible to team members or not. And there are natural consequences if boundaries are not observed. If you are late to the market, you lose some market share. If you go over budget, you have to increase the price of the product to the customers and thereby possibly reduce sales. If you miss quality boundary conditions, customers may not purchase the product at all. There is little need for artificial punishment in an SDWT environment when boundaries are set well. The punishment is simply the natural consequence of not responding to the boundary. Team leaders help team members avoid the problems that result from walking blindly into these known barriers. Enough unknown problems will surface during any significant project to keep teams' attention without the needless frustration of crashing into walls that are foreseeable and avoidable.

Summary

Empowered teams don't need marshmallow managers; they need principled leadership that is clear, motivating, and firm. Marshmallows, in fact, are likely to get toasted in these environments, which require often heated, vision-directed assertiveness. Team leadership isn't permissive or passive management. It is true, however, that the role often requires constraint, patience, and delegation, things that are frequently misunderstood by outsiders who aren't familiar with the history and situation of the work group. This leadership is not a science; it is an art. Because of this, it is difficult to explain when to intervene aggressively and when to back off. Only experience teaches that. But team leaders do use some processes that help to focus the team and at the same time clarify when certain management interventions are appropriate.

These leaders use boundary conditions, for example, as a way to help teams control themselves. And when the time is right (usually when boundary conditions, vision, values, or agreed-upon operating norms are violated), they take strong unilateral action, which looks to some like a return to autocracy. While supervisory action that takes back control from the team should be avoided at all costs, appropriate management interventions that reinforce values are necessary. These actions strengthen rather than diminish the SDWT process.

In the next chapter we will discuss how the team leader changes boundaries over time to adjust to the maturity level of the team.

The Five Stages of Implementing Empowerment

"When we were getting ready to start up the Richmond facility, I visited what we thought were the state-of-the-art plants operating like this. They all told me that one of the biggest mistakes they made was to give up too much too soon. People's ability to participate increases over-time if they are developed properly, but giving too much responsibility before they are prepared can cause some real problems."

Ross Silberstein, *former vice president and director of manufacturing, Sherwin-Williams Automotive Aftermarket Division*

ONE OF THE difficulties of describing the role of the team leader comes from the fact that it is a moving target. So far we have talked about the different competencies of the team leader role as though the role were static. But the role actually evolves as the team matures. It is difficult to act like a boundary manager instead of a supervisor when the team is less mature. At that point, more assistance on elements inside the team boundary is required, allowing little time for the team leader to focus on the team's environment. Primary emphasis during the early stages of team maturity is on being a trainer; then emphasis moves toward coaching as the team gains more experience with the skills it has been taught. Leadership competencies become more crucial as the team matures and requires less intensive coaching.

Although a number of factors may prompt the use of different team leader competencies, none are more significant than the maturity level of the team. As I mentioned in earlier chapters, the value set of the team leader is not situational. It provides the continuity and authenticity required for true SDWT leadership. But skills and role requirements will change with the maturity level of the team(s). For this reason, I would like to suggest a team maturity model that allows us to discuss how the team leader role changes over the typical life of the SDWT operation. We will consider the role prior to high-performance work team implementation and show how each successive stage of maturity has its own unique challenges. We will also begin to consider the tasks to be performed during the five stages. Later chapters will detail the tasks required for operations, management, and culture team leaders during the maturation process.

The Cycle of SDWT Maturity

This model of the typical evolution of self-directed work teams was devised for purposes of this discussion. Life, of course, is not as neatly segmented as any model. There are no boxes and arrows in the workplace, and perfectly clear lines don't separate one maturation step from the other. It is a lot messier than that. But this model does facilitate a useful discussion about how the team leader role evolves.

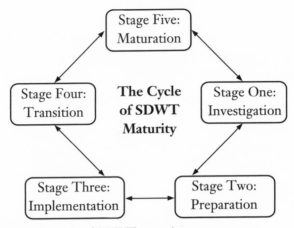

Figure 15.1   The cycle of SDWT maturity.
Adapted from Kimball Fisher, "Management Roles in the Implementation of Participative Management Systems," *Human Resource Management*, Fall 1986. © Copyright
by John Wiley & Sons. Used by permission of the author.

Self-directed work teams go through five identifiable stages during
the evolutionary process (see Figure 15.1):

1. Investigation
2. Preparation
3. Implementation
4. Transition
5. Maturation*

As major empowerment changes are made, the team may continue
to cycle through these stages multiple times. Some teams complete a
full cycle of the maturation process in just a few months. Some take
years. Some never complete the cycle at all because they get blocked at
one of the earlier stages. Critical events may also move teams backward

---

* In earlier publications I have used slightly different names to describe the five stages.
The original names for the stages were conception, incubation, implementation, transition,
and maturity. I have modified them here to promote clarity. I also changed from earlier references to different team leaders. Culture leaders used to be called executive managers,
management team leaders integrative managers, and operations team leaders interface managers. The terms used in the book are, I think, easier to remember and a little less hierarchical.

in the maturity cycle. Changing team membership, for example, always moves a mature team back to the transition stage where new responsibilities and operating contracts must be renegotiated.

The Five Stages of SDWT Implementation

During each of the five stages, team leaders need to play a different role in order to maximize the effectiveness of the organization. The five stages of self-directed work team system evolution are:

Stage One: investigation. In this stage the idea of either developing a new start-up high-performance work system or of changing an existing organization to more empowered work teams is explored. It typically involves a relatively small cadre of people and will produce a few "charismatics" who will champion the concept through the early stages of work system development.

Stage Two: preparation. In this stage the organization goes through the planning/designing and preparation required to successfully transform the organization. This is the stage for generating and demonstrating organizational support for the champion's vision.

Stage Three: implementation. The new work structures that are manifestations of the shift in the management paradigm are born. Changed or developed are the job design, work rules, formal statements of work ethics/values, policies and procedures, performance appraisal systems, team structures, pay and promotion policies, skill development practices, information passing mechanisms, and so on.

Stage Four: transition. This marks the "completion" of implementation and the beginning of adjusting to and becoming competent in the new work system. The work teams themselves are growing, so that they can take on the responsibilities required for maximum organizational effectiveness. Authority and autonomy transfer from team leaders to team members as skills warrant it.

Stage Five: maturation. A key attribute of this "final" stage is, ironically, that even though the work systems are "completed" in the sense that they are fully functional, they continue from this stage forward to evolve and change. That is what Albert Cherns calls incompleteness, or in other words, continuous improvement of the work unit. Analogously, though adults are chronologically mature, they continue to learn and change in response to the things around them. Work units, like the human beings who work in them, are never finished.

Challenges During the Five Stages

Each stage, of course, has its special challenges. While many of these challenges overlap the stages and typify most change efforts, a few are especially characteristic of one of the five stages. The primary challenges for each stage are listed in Table 15.1.

Stage One: Investigation Challenges
(Challenge = Understanding It)

When Procter & Gamble started up the Lima, Ohio soap plant in the late 1960s, only a handful of other organizations with similar "whole-scale" self-directed work teams existed. Predictably, upper management was disappointed that the behavior and results of the new organization did not meet its step level improvement expectations for this new type of plant for a full two years after start-up. During this time people were going through the difficult and time-consuming process of learning new skills. Even though information about these kinds of "up-front

Table 15.1 The Primary Challenges for Each Stage of the SDWT Maturity Cycle

Stage	Primary Challenge
One: investigation	Understanding it
Two: preparation	Accepting it
Three: implementation	Making it work
Four: transition	Keeping at it
Five: maturation	Keeping it continuously improving

Adapted from Kimball Fisher, "Management Roles in the Implementation of Participative Management Systems," *Human Resource Management*, Fall 1986. © Copyright by John Wiley & Sons. Used by permission of the author.

investments" of whole-scale attempts at self-directed work teams is now available, other organizations still encounter similar "disappointments." Like other major business transformations (mergers, technology shifts, market changes, etc.), starting high-performance work systems requires an investment. Understanding not only what *self-directed work teams* means, but also the costs and risks associated with this kind of transformation, minimizes downstream surprises.

Stage Two: Preparation Challenges (Challenge = Accepting It)

During this stage acceptance for the transformation needs to build to critical mass. Trust is a necessary prerequisite to this acceptance.

In one organization in the midwestern United States, a survey indicated that a lack of "trust" between employees and management was the single biggest concern shared by members of the organization. Subsequent efforts to modify work systems to more self-directed ones were implemented more rapidly and with less resistance in areas where there was a higher perceived level of trust than in areas where there was a lower trust level. Lower-trust areas quickly reached impasse as supervisors waited for non-managers to display the ability and interest to be involved in business decisions. Meanwhile, those in nonmanagement positions waited for supervisors to start including them. Nothing happened during the standoff. A lack of management change to participative behaviors, in fact, was frequently mentioned as the primary inhibitor to the implementation of work system modifications.

Working through the trust crises that often occur at Stage Two and then gaining the acceptance of the self-directed work team paradigm are the most typical and difficult challenges of preparation. Acceptance comes as people see (not hear about) the management paradigm shifting from supervision to team leadership. This shift needs to occur *prior* to the implementation of self-directed work teams.

Another major challenge of the preparation stage, of course, is to appropriately prepare for implementation. While team leaders should *diligently* avoid a planning trap that generates paper but little action, they will need to complete appropriate "pre-work" (reallocating resources, reevaluating business charters, thinking through alternative structures/modifications, etc.) to make implementation successful.

Stage Three: Implementation Challenges
(Challenge = Making It Work)

Even with trust, excellent plans, information systems, and resources in place, actually implementing the new work system is tough. Quarterly stockholder reports cause many American and European companies to be overly concerned with short-term results. Thus, serious threats to the survival of self-directed work teams can occur when the implementation causes temporary disruption of the work flow. As the proverbial waters get rough, some team leaders may abandon ship and revert to autocratic management, or even worse, give up, go marshmallows, and turn everything over to ill-prepared subordinates.

This is a stage of turmoil where all employees try to figure out the specifics and test the limits of the emerging system. The concern of a senior officer at Honeywell that implementing participative management systems was much like wrestling with jellyfish is not uncommon for employees as they explore new behaviors and try to make sense out of this work evolution.

While team members are often resistant to the concept of self-directed work teams at first (primarily during the preparation stage), the main resistance to the concept at the implementation stage will usually come from supervisors, for reasons that we have already described in earlier chapters. Transformation efforts in parts of Corning, Tektronix, Mead, Weyerhaeuser, Clark Equipment, and P&G have been slowed when supervisors at all levels were concerned by the perceived implications these changes had on their jobs. One internal consultant in a high-tech firm undergoing a transformation to high-performance work systems lamented:

> **It took us a while to realize that you cannot assume that managers will fall in line and support this just because their bosses do. They need to buy into the new roles and let go of the old ones because *they* want to or it won't work. And there has to be something in it for them in order for them to be willing to let go.**

Inordinate confusion about what kinds of things people will do in a high-performance work system (or pretending that there will not be a sense of loss for the earlier roles) makes mourning the death of the previous management paradigm more difficult and painful than necessary, potentially prolonging implementation.

Stage Four: Transition Challenges
(Challenge = Keeping At It)

A dilemma of the implementation cycle is that SDWTs perform successfully only when all the participants have the skills and information they need. This means that, even though team leaders start practicing empowering behavior in Stage Two, they are really not self-directed work team leaders until the management or nonmanagement team members are fully prepared to participate successfully during Stage Four.

Making this skill and perspective transition usually takes tremendous time and energy. In the words of one manager of an organization in the transition stage:

> It is a gut-wrenching experience to watch people learn how to make business decisions when they haven't made them before. A team will decide to not stay at work one afternoon in order to get more time off or something. You sometimes have to step in and stop it. And it gets tricky to intervene and head off poor group decisions while fostering the belief that you still want them to take risks and to participate.

A plant manager describes this common frustration of the transition stage like this:

> The best way to learn how to make [higher-level] business decisions is by making them. People learn by making bad decisions, but it is hard to sit by and watch them making bad decisions when you could step in and fix things so easily yourself. But sometimes you need to let them fail. I do a quick risk analysis every time I watch people start to learn these things. Unless the likely negative outcome of their decisions really outweighs the positive learning experience they will have by falling on their faces a few times, I don't interfere. That is often a very difficult thing to do.

Stage Five: Maturation Challenges
(Challenge = Keeping It Continuously Improving)

One of the biggest challenges of this stage is the successful perpetuation of an appropriate self-directed work team system. It is easy to "rest" after people make it through the transition stage, when they finally settle down into roles and responsibilities that they now have come to understand, accept, and handle competently. Unfortunately, in today's competitive and turbulent environment, to rest may mean to become stagnant and uncompetitive.

Another thorny challenge of this stage, of course, is to help people continue to grow and develop. People who have "grown up" in a self-directed work team environment hunger for additional opportunities. They want to be challenged as much as in the earlier years when they were learning a variety of nontraditional skills and participating in the "higher-level" role they may not have been able to or allowed to do in their earlier work experiences. As they progress through the new skills and roles, reward systems often become obsolete. Since promotions are generally becoming less of an option as organizations become flatter, creative ways to meet this challenge are often necessary.

Leadership Tasks During the Maturation Process

Leadership responsibilities vary somewhat depending on the position of the team leader during the implementation and maturation process. Management leaders, for example, are typically the ones who champion the changes with implications beyond single teams.

An apocryphal story is told in the northwestern United States about a management team leader who wanted to make changes in the way people thought about their new responsibilities in the self-directed work team system. After gaining acceptance for a significantly reduced number of different job descriptions, he took the thick book of current job descriptions out into the parking lot, poured gasoline on it, and burned it to cinders to symbolize the death of some of the restrictive involvement barriers. While this kind of activity may be overly histrionic for many organizations, it evidences the passion for change often required of champions during the implementation stage.

Culture leaders provide broad boundary conditions for implementation and encourage the appropriate challenging of the status quo during Stage Three. They continue to emphasize values, key business focus areas, and essential organizational objectives. They find ways to recognize appropriate implementation activities. Having management and operations leaders address audiences of their peers about their successes to date, for example, reinforces the difficult behavior changes and makes letting go of comfortable habits and institutions more tolerable.

Summary

Although we have talked about the competencies of team leaders as though they all applied equally all of the time, this role is not static. It evolves and changes depending on a number of variables. In this chapter I have highlighted the most important reason for team leader role evolution: the maturity level of the team. Different team leaders have different responsibilities during the maturation process, as we will see in the next few chapters.

We have reviewed the five-stage SDWT implementation model, which helps to characterize this evolutionary process. During each of the five stages, team leaders face a unique set of challenges demanding different skills and behaviors. During the investigation stage, the primary challenge is understanding SDWTs and what is required for effective implementation of them. During the second stage, preparation, the challenge is accepting the new paradigm and practices. During implementation, the primary challenge is making the systems and processes work. During the fourth stage, transition, the challenge is sticking with it. And in the final stage of maturation, the challenge is continuous improvement.

This five-stage model is not intended to suggest that the SDWT maturation process is an orderly or linear procedure. It is not. The reality of life in these operations is messy and nonlinear. Teams don't always become more mature over time. Sometimes they actually become less mature as they spend more time together. But utilizing this maturity construct does provide a vehicle that allows us to discuss the important topic of the changing role.

In the next chapters we will continue this discussion in more detail.

Leadership Roles During the Early Stages of Team Maturity

"The decisions take longer, and sometimes it takes longer to get things done. It's frustrating, because sometimes it takes people longer to see something than I'd like. But you can't say, 'Well, okay, your 36 seconds are up. We're going on.' You've got to take time to explain things. Sometimes you end up doing that several times."

Roger Smith, *former CEO of General Motors*

I USED TO have a picture on my desk that was torn from a magazine. It showed the outstretched hands of an airborne acrobat several inches away from a flying trapeze. The caption read, "Timing is everything." Those words can also describe the team leader's role during the cycle of work system maturity. What is appropriate in one stage may be disastrous in another. Timing is everything.

During each of the five stages, team leaders need to play a different role in order to maximize the effectiveness of their organization. In this chapter we will explore the roles of team leaders in the investigation, preparation, and implementation stages. We will also look at how operations, management, and culture team leaders generally play distinct roles during the early stages of the implementation process. Many of the team leader activities mentioned in this and the following chapter have already been discussed. Now they will be put into a kind of sequence that helps the team leader understand what behaviors are most appropriate during the various stages of implementation.

Operations team leaders, for example, progress through a series of roles that change subtly but distinctly in each of the stages. In the earlier stages these leaders primarily coach and develop the work group members' technical skills (function-specific skills such as work technologies, business fundamentals, etc.) and self-management/regulation skills (group decision making, giving and accepting feedback, confrontation resolution, working in a multicultural group, and so on). In later stages, however, leaders spend a bigger proportion of their time managing external forces affecting the ability of the teams to be successful (getting resources for projects, lobbying for participation in key corporate activities, monitoring competitors' activities in the marketplace, etc.). Similarly, management team leaders and culture team leaders have different roles at different stages. Playing the wrong role at the wrong time can have a very negative impact on the organization's effectiveness.

Investigation Roles

The leadership role at this stage is primarily performed by management and culture team leaders. Most of the successful transition efforts I know about are actually started by management team leaders rather than culture team leaders. In fact, the most senior managers (presidents, vice presidents, etc.) are often only consulted rather than being seen as driving the change. But where culture leaders do become actively involved in at least managing the symbols of the change process, the transition is simplified and expedited considerably.

Here are some suggestions for culture leader activities during Stage One. Culture leaders can examine the organization's culture to determine

Table 16.1   Culture Leadership Roles During Early Stages

Stage	Examples of Culture Leader's Role
Stage One: investigation	• Assessing compatibility of culture with SDWTs • Creating culture bridges • Tying self-directed team evolution to real needs • Developing a common vocabulary • Making self-directed team issues salient
Stage Two: preparation	• Building trust • Providing opportunities for people to discuss SDWTs • Modeling appropriate behaviors • Showing support for workplace evolution
Stage Three: implementation	• Encouraging appropriate deviation from the norm • Providing broad implementation parameters • Emphasizing overarching values/business focus/objectives • Recognizing success

Adapted from Kimball Fisher, "Management Roles in the Implementation of Partici-pative Management Systems," *Human Resource Management*, Fall 1986, © Copyright John Wiley & Sons. Used by permission of the author.

whether it is compatible with the SDWT paradigm (see Table 16.1). Cultural modifications will probably be necessary for any significant progress self-directed work teams make toward maturity. But if high-performance work systems are fundamentally opposed to the basic assumptions forming the culture of the organization, change may require such dramatic measures that it will become a very unattractive alternative. Frankly, it is better not to start than to abort the process in midstream. Once started, SDWT methods create expectations for continuing involvement that, if later violated, can create an environment of nearly violent distrust. In such situations it will be difficult, if not impossible, to go down the self-directed work team road again with the same people.

Create Bridges to Span the Chasm Between Old and New Cultures

If the gap between the existing culture and the self-directed work team paradigm can be bridged, culture team leaders can minimize the predictable frustrations associated with culture shifts by providing the culture bridges that somehow link the two. As an example, the late Howard Vollum, one of the founders of Tektronix, was being interviewed for the company paper when the interviewer observed, "It sounds like you might be in favor of the type of participative management being tried at [name of facility]." "Sure," Howard answered, "That's not new to [name of facility]. It was here at the start. Then we kind of got away from it. I think it's very important that we get back to it." These kinds of statements by respected leaders can make the journey more like coming home than like jumping off a cliff into an unknown abyss.

Demonstrate Support for the Change

Culture leaders also need to demonstrate appropriate support for the paradigm shift. People will watch for signals from culture leaders and act accordingly. One good way to show support is to raise the issue of SDWTs in important meetings and coaching sessions, and then encourage management and operations champions to rise to the challenge of carrying the empowered organization toward maturity. How do you do this?

In one operation, culture leaders hosted a 2-day meeting for the 200 top managers of the company. During this "People Involvement" session, managers heard the convictions and broad expectations of senior management. Then representatives from each business group shared progress and ideas on high-performance work teams. These kinds of activities evidence the culture leader's desire to make change happen without necessarily dictating a specific course of action.

Create a Common Vocabulary to Facilitate Communication and Learning

It is also helpful for culture team leaders to provide a common vocabulary for key aspects of the work system evolutionary cycle. This enables people to communicate about what otherwise may become a set of values, assumptions, and systems that become difficult to explain to others. Common vocabularies allow cross-fertilization of ideas and help to demystify self-directed work team concepts. Establishing some sort of management network can help to communicate and formalize this language.

Couple Team Design to Business Changes

During Stage One, management team leaders analyze the organization for the appropriateness of some sort of high-performance work system. They identify the costs and risks of moving forward, pass information to and gain commitment from the key people, and justify and empower resources to design the work system (see Table 16.2). It is particularly helpful for management leaders to determine the most appropriate timing for Stage Two and Stage Three at this point.

Several successfully transformed organizations have credited their success in part to coupling the implementation of self-directed work teams with other significant changes. New organization start-ups, new product introductions, new technologies, equipment, or methodologies, or reorganizations, and the like are ideal times to make self-directed work teams happen. After all, self-directed work teams are a way of doing

Table 16.2   Management Leadership Roles During Early Stages

Stage	Examples of Management Leader's Role
Stage One: investigation	• Completing SDWT feasibility analysis • Supporting the real need for evolution • Championing the SDWT concept • Lining up commitments/resources for the next stages • Determining appropriate timing for introduction
Stage Two: preparation	• Building trust • Demystifying SDWTs/facilitating clarification activities • Articulating vision • Modeling appropriate behaviors • Ensuring training and development • Facilitating "implications for us" analysis • Ensuring that good communication processes are in place • Providing necessary resources
Stage Three: implementation	• Championing SDWTs • Recognizing successes • Clarifying roles/expectations

Adapted from Kimball Fisher, "Management Roles in the Implementation of Partici-pative Management Systems," *Human Resource Management*, Fall 1986, © Copyright John Wiley & Sons. Used by permission of the author.

things rather than things to do. They are a means to the end of organizational effectiveness, not an end in themselves. Buying a new facility, introducing a new product, or reorienting the organization to focus on customers in a high-performing way is a much more appropriate focus than implementing self-directed work team systems for their own sake.

Preparation Roles

This is the first stage of widespread management involvement. Preparation is a period for discussion and clarification of self-directed work teams. Culture leaders train management leaders, management leaders train operations team leaders, and operations leaders train nonmanagers in the fundamentals of self-directed work teams. People discuss the implications of moving toward self-directed work team maturity for themselves individually and for their teams. Employment continuity discussions are often required to build trust and allay fears of hidden agendas.

Create a Common Vision to Facilitate Change

This stage produces organizational acceptance for the change. Management and operations team leaders therefore need to make self-directed work teams "real" by articulating their vision for the self-directed work team future in their organization (see Table 16.3). Jerry, the manufacturing manager in a 200-person manufacturing organization of a division within a large electronics company, decided that he wanted to learn more about socio-technical systems. After attending a few seminars on the subject and discussing it with some experienced external and internal resources, he wanted to implement a high-performance system in conjunction with division plans to change to a different manufacturing process.

Jerry determined that the time was right for the transformation. This type of self-directed work system would build naturally on a fairly recent organizational change that had split up functional groups into product-oriented work teams. It was also consistent with the new technology, which required teams to be more flexible and more involved with certain production decisions. Jerry felt that the basic division and company values were congruent with participatory work alternatives.

Table 16.3   Operations Leadership Roles During Early Stages

Stage	Examples of Operations Leader's Role
Stage One: investigation	• Studying SDWTs
Stage Two: preparation	• Giving input to work system design/values and transformation plans • Learning team leader behaviors • Modeling team leader behaviors • Sharing information with teams • Implementing technology changes • Making SDWTs real for teams • Feeding back facilitating/inhibiting factors for implementation preparation
Stage Three: implementation	• Implementing transformation plan • Ensuring team training and development (technical and SDWT skills) • Getting resources for training and development • Championing operations changes • Institutionalizing information-passing mechanisms

Adapted from Kimball Fisher, "Management Roles in the Implementation of Participative Management Systems," *Human Resource Management*, Fall 1986, © Copyright John Wiley & Sons. Used by permission of the author.

Concurrently with his discussions with management, he began sharing his ideas of what the organization would be like in the future. The product of these discussions came to be known as "Jerry's vision." This vision was clear enough that people could picture what the business would be like and how they would act differently in it. It was referred to frequently during the preparation and implementation stages as a focus and a justification for the work.

Share Business Information and Line Up Resources

During Stage Two, management leaders ensure that all appropriate information is provided to effect implementation. They see to it that the right people are involved in the process and sufficient resources are allocated to produce the desired results. It is often appropriate to bring in external consultants or internal subject matter experts to minimize the "reinvention of the wheel" and to help the organization avoid some of the common roadblocks that get in the way of these kinds of efforts.

Make Technology and Operating Principle Changes

Technology changes that facilitate the work system implementation (automation of boring, repetitive jobs, introduction of new products/ services, or relocation of equipment of decentralized areas, etc.) are spearheaded during this stage by operations leaders in a way that is consistent and illustrative of the self-directed work team paradigm. Principles or values that guide the organization and define appropriate behaviors are developed and agreed to throughout the organization.

Implementation Roles

Operations leaders play a number of important roles during the implementation stage. Establishing and then maintaining forums for knowledge management and training becomes pivotal. At the very least, these managers will need time for the discussion of business information. Many organizations find that they can only meet the dramatically increased information needs of their work teams by institutionalizing daily team meetings. While these meetings will be frustrating and ineffective at first, they can become the forum for group decision making as teams are coached in their appropriate use by their operations leader. Without the information distributed during these meetings, teams are incapable of doing the operations analysis and redesign that is the hallmark of this stage. Team leaders actively facilitate these processes, often with the help of other internal and external consultants. They deal with the elements of the implementation as they arise. Rather than trying to anticipate all of the interrelated aspects of the SDWT process, leaders are sensitive to the needs of their teams and help them work on the things that need to be worked on when they need to be worked on. Generally speaking, team leaders work on reward systems last to ensure that the pay design and delivery mechanisms support the organization design.

Begin Appropriate Training and Development

This phase requires intensive training in the technical areas of the new or recently changed jobs. Operations leaders also coordinate training in SDWT technologies and skill building in group decision making, problem solving, and so on. The operations leader focuses on the development of new teams so that they will be able to be self-regulating and manage their part of the business effectively during the latter stages. One thing to be aware of is that these development activities are best undertaken just prior to the time when team members actually use what they have learned. Giving the teams skills training much before they need it is a waste of time. Most people already know more than they are allowed to do anyway.

Summary

Team leader roles change during the cycle of SDWT maturity. During the investigation stage, for example, culture leaders can do a number of things to clarify what SDWTs are and to empower people to move toward them. They build bridges between the old and the new culture. They demonstrate their active support of high-performance work systems and create a common vocabulary to facilitate learning. They couple the SDWT initiative to real business needs and changes, but they don't actively participate in developing the specifics: other people are empowered to do that. It is during the preparation stage that management and culture team leaders create a common vision that guides and motivates team members. All team leaders work to help clarify the SDWT concept and eliminate misconceptions and fear during this stage. They line up resources and make appropriate preparations for implementation. And they facilitate technology and operating principle changes to grease the skids for SDWTs. The implementation stage requires team leaders to create ongoing forums for information passing and training. The actual implementation of appropriate team structures and systems is facilitated by team leaders at this stage.

If the appropriate preparation work has been done, this stage can be fairly straightforward. But it is never simple. Most agree that this stage feels like going two steps forward and one step back. Since the process is always tailored to the operation, it contains large blocks of unique and unpredictable activities. It is messy, invigorating, and tiring. But in this stage the team leaders begin to see some of the early results of the high-performance work teams.

In the next chapter we will review the changing role of team leaders in the transition and maturation stages of team maturity.

Leadership Roles During the Later Stages of Team Maturity

"Forget structures invented by the guys at the top. You've got to let the task form the organization."

Raymond Gilmartin, *CEO of Becton Dickinson*

Once teams are implemented successfully in Stage Three, the role of the team leaders changes again. In this chapter, we will discuss the evolving role of team leaders in the later parts of the maturation cycle. In the early stages of the cycle, the culture leaders play a predominant role. While culture team leaders offer ongoing support and input through the cycle of self-directed work team maturity (see Table 17.1), the primary roles in Stages Four and Five are played by the management and operations team leaders.

Table 17.1 Culture Leadership Roles During Later Stages

Stage	Examples of Culture Leader's Role
Stage Four: transition	• Supporting appropriate work
	• Transferring authority and autonomy to business teams as skills expand
Stage Five: maturation	• Providing development opportunities

Adapted from Kimball Fisher, "Management Roles in the Implementation of Partici-pative Management Systems," *Human Resource Management*, Fall 1986, © Copyright John Wiley & Sons. Used by permission of the author.

Transition Roles

Transition is an uncomfortable stage during which organizations often know what they are supposed to do but have not yet become skilled enough to do it. Expectations for involvement precede the skills required to be successfully involved. People who are still learning make mistakes.

Managing Skepticism

Early in Stage Four, management leaders find themselves continually encouraging skill development and risk taking. They spend significant time nursing the skinned knees of those who have tried and failed, but who must get up and try some more. These "failures" fuel the fires of those people who never really thought that self-directed work teams would work. Management leaders continue to patiently answer the challenges of these remaining skeptics who observe the shortfalls of the transitioning system (see Table 17.2).

Protecting the New Team

Later during the transition, management leaders often find themselves in an umbrella-like protection role of defending the organization from the "acid rain" influence of well-meaning observers who see people struggling to develop new skills and perspectives. These outsiders encourage the organization to revert to the more predictable and less painful roles of the recent past. The management leader holds off the pressure until members of the organization have the skills in place to be

Table 17.2 Management Leadership Roles During Later Stages

Stage	Examples of Management Leader's Role
Stage Four: transition	• Encouraging skill building and risk taking • Transferring authority and autonomy to teams as skills expand • Helping people learn from mistakes • Providing protection from outside forces
Stage Five: maturation	• Facilitating continuous improvement • Leading system-wide changes • Providing skill development opportunities • Dealing with destructive behavior

Adapted from Kimball Fisher, "Management Roles in the Implementation of Participative Management Systems," *Human Resource Management*, Fall 1986, © Copyright John Wiley & Sons. Used by permission of the author.

successful. This is particularly difficult when the host organization, of which the transitioning group is a part, still has one foot firmly set in the established culture.

When the Lima P&G plant was starting up, for example, it initially received a lot of pressure to revert back to a traditionally managed operation. Why? The results during the first two years of operation were poorer than expected. The division manager, however, was convinced that results would improve dramatically as plant personnel became more experienced. He finally convinced corporate management to be patient and allow the facility to progress along the learning curve without pressure to abort the process and return to the management practices of traditional P&G locations. As predicted, results improved dramatically in the third year, when the training investment began to pay returns. Had the experiment been stopped during the first 2 years, the plant would never have had the 30 to 50 percent improvements over the traditional plants it has sustained since its third year of operation. The division manager saved the SDWTs, which would have surely been dissolved prematurely without his direct intervention.

Operations leaders serve as trainers early in Stage Four, and then make the transition into a resource role as the teams become more self-sufficient (see Table 17.3). They transfer authority and autonomy to others when those people have the skills and information to use it successfully. During this stage operations leaders begin to change their pri-

Table 17.3 Operations Leadership Roles During Later Stages

Stage	Examples of Operations Leader's Role
Stage Four: transition	• Assessing team member skill development • Transferring authority and autonomy to teams as skills expand • Changing from internal to external focus • Continuing skill training/feedback
Stage Five: maturation	• Assessing the need for resources for teams • Getting resources/being a resource • Providing skill development opportunities as needed • Assessing external environment • Funneling data to teams • Dealing with destructive behavior • Managing external interfaces • Facilitating continuous improvement of team • Facilitating appropriate work system evolution

Adapted from Kimball Fisher, "Management Roles in the Implementation of Partici-pative Management Systems," *Human Resource Management*, Fall 1986, © Copyright John Wiley & Sons. Used by permission of the author.

mary focus from developing their subordinates' skills to managing forces outside of their team(s). Changing behaviors from an inward to an outward focus is difficult. It is not unusual for leaders and their teams to experience some frustration as the teams are weaned from the leader and as the management role starts to focus on boundaries.

Maturation Roles

At maturation the organization has reached the minimum acceptable level of SDWT performance. People in the organization have become competent and more comfortable in the system. Artificial barriers are continuously challenged and changed as they become issues. People develop closer ties to their internal and external customers. Management leaders assess the organization periodically for behavioral congruence with the values on which the system is built. They deal appropriately with aberrance from those values.

Although the team leader obviously needs to spend time facilitating the effectiveness of the group (particularly as new people rotate into the group), the operations leader's role shifts from that of trainer to that of environment scanner. In this stage, the team leader becomes a fully functional boundary manager. He or she looks at the external environment to note business trends and opportunities that need to be relayed back to the group. For example, the leader may discover important projects being developed in other areas of the company that affect the operation. He or she will want to get one of the team members involved early in the project to ensure that the team's input is considered. At other times the operations leader may find him- or herself protecting the team's "turf" when staff members or other managers want to usurp decisions that should be made by the team.

Facilitating Continuous Improvement

In this stage, the team leader determines how to best help the established, maturing team. This is an art form. As the team is maturing, the leader changes his or her approach to the team so that it corresponds to the team's changing needs. How do leaders know when teams are maturing? Typically the types of business and interpersonal tasks the teams are able to complete successfully act as the best indicator. One clue is how they respond to the requirements for increased responsibility and ownership. Ernie Turner, an operations team leader at a high-tech company, describes the typical evolution during the maturation stage as follows:

> At first, the team comes to you and says, "Here's a problem, what are you going to do about it?" Later they come to you and say, "Here is a problem and here are some of the things we think can be done about it." Still later they say, "Here is a problem and here is what we think we should do." Eventually they say, "There was a problem and here is what we did."

There is great satisfaction in seeing the team develop to this level of capability. Even when this point is reached, however, continued assistance is often necessary to keep the team growing. Tasks once thought impossible become more routine. The primary roles played by both the management and operations leaders at this stage, therefore, are encouraging continuous improvement and warding off organizational stagnation. As people develop higher-level skills they need to be presented with increasingly difficult challenges.

Summary

One of the challenges of being a team leader is the responsibility of playing the appropriate role as the team matures. Team leaders normally progress from coaching and training roles in the early stages to facilitative and leadership roles as the team matures. Full boundary management responsibilities are assumed only in the later stages, after the team has been well prepared to handle the responsibilities of work-directed rather than supervisor-directed assignments. In the later stages of the five-stage cycle of SDWT maturation, operations and management team leaders help the teams through the transition to full maturity. They manage skepticism and pressure from the people who see the normal mistakes that accompany transition and that try to force the SDWT backward to more comfortable traditional roles. As teams reach maturity, team leaders help them to continuously improve. These responsibilities are difficult but necessary for team leaders in all parts of the organization.

In the next chapter, we'll go into more detail about specific tasks that team leaders perform. We will consider a story that illustrates three typical days in a team leader's workweek as the team reaches maturity.

PART V

The Team Leader Workout

CHAPTER

Three Days in the Life of a Team Leader

"You cannot do to your people what was done to you. You have to be a facilitator or coach and, by the way, we're still going to hold you accountable for the bottom line."

Paul Allaire, *CEO of Xerox*

L ET'S LOOK AT a few days in the life of a team leader. He is a hypothetical operations team leader of a team nearing maturity.

Monday, 7:00 A.M.: Team Meeting

Cindy, one of the team members, grabs a pen and walks up to the chart pad to get the meeting organized. The team has shift overlap meetings at which the team members, called *associates*, review the previous shift's activities and share business information. Cindy writes down three agenda items: *computer problem, vacation coverage,* and *customer feedback.* The team decides to wait on the computer discussion because it will require advice from a technical expert from another team. After a short and emotional discussion about vacation coverage, three team members give their report on last week's visit to a customer site in a neighboring town. As they are starting to leave the meeting, the team leader asks who is going to contact the technical expert for the computer problem discussion. John, a team member, volunteers to get the person here sometime this week.

Monday, 7:25 A.M.: Unplanned Feedback

The team leader catches Cindy walking out of team meeting and congratulates her for stepping up to the chart pad and facilitating (she had been uncomfortable getting up in front of people until very recently). Recalling the computer discussion, the team leader asks if Cindy wants to know a simple technique to make sure that things don't fall through the cracks in meetings. She says yes. "It helps me to think of the three w's," the leader replies. "Facilitators can ask the question, *'who* will do *what* by *when?'* " Cindy agrees that could work and thanks him for the idea.

Monday, 7:30 A.M.: Area Walkthrough

As he is walking through the work area, the team leader sees what he thinks may be a problem. Two members of the team are arguing about something. "Can I help?" the leader asks. "No," says Tom, "we'll work it out." The team leader walks through the area, chats with the associates, delivers reports to some people, and gets invited to play in a softball game for charity.

Monday, 8:05 A.M.: Business Coordination Meeting

All the team leaders meet together with associate representatives for what used to be the facility manager's staff meeting. Cross-facility issues are discussed that require coordination across multiple teams, including staffing, quality problems, training issues, an emerging pay concern, and some general information from headquarters. The facilitation of the meeting is rotated every week, and the team leader's turn is coming up next Monday.

Monday, 10:15 A.M.: Desk Work

The team leader squeezes in some time to get back to his desk to pick up voicemail and e-mail messages, return phone calls, and do some project work. He calls back a staff manager from headquarters who tells him that headquarters needs some up-to-date information about the budget. When the team leader tells the staff person that he will transfer him to the team's budget coordinator, the staff manager is confused. "Aren't you the manager?" he asks. For the millionth time in the last two years, the team leader politely explains the team concept and then tells the staff manager that Rita, an associate, has more up-to-date information than he does, because she authorizes and tracks the team's spending on a day-to-day basis. He makes a few more calls, jots down some notes on his pad about the compensation project he has been working on, and arranges for a sales rep to give a brief presentation at next Monday's business coordination meeting.

Monday, 11:00 A.M.: Drop-In on Human Resources

On his way to the cafeteria the team leader drops by the HR cubicles to see if Bill is there. Bill, a former supervisor, has been helping the teams with their training needs. The team leader wants to take Bill up on his suggestion to do some training on hiring laws and skills. The team is going to start interviewing soon for an opening. "When could you do the training?" the team leader asks. Bill suggests that it be just before the team has its first interview and says that he could be available either this Thursday morning or next Monday afternoon.

Monday, 11:08 A.M.: Problems

The team leader's pager goes off and he uses his cell phone to call the team's work area. Tom answers and tells the leader he better come over and help settle an argument. In the workplace to greet him are Tom and

Joe, who have both been assigned to the supplier quality improvement project. Tom speaks first and says, "Joe thinks we need to take a trip down to see this vendor, but I don't think it will be worth it. Besides that, I'm still behind in my work, and I don't think it's fair to ask the team to cover for me again since I was just on the customer visit last week." Joe impatiently interjects, "Well, I think we need to do what's best for the business." The team leader asks Joe why he thinks a visit would be best for the business. "Because," Joe replies, "this stuff has been causing us problems for three weeks. If we can see their processes and get face to face with these guys I think we can resolve the material problem." "Well," says the team leader, "what is this problem costing us?" Joe picks up some reports and does a series of calculations that take a couple of minutes, checking periodically with Tom to see if he is doing the math correctly. "It's more than I thought," he says. "Looks like we're losing about two thousand a week." "What do you think, Tom?" asks the team leader. "Jeez," says Tom, "That's really serious. I guess we better do something." Joe commits to working it out with the team over lunch and getting something set up with the supplier ASAP.

Monday, 11:35 A.M.: Lunch with Team Leaders

The team leader apologizes for being late and then walks over to the refrigerator to get his lunch. He enjoys these periodic lunches with other team leaders. Today they have a speaker, a professor from the university who is talking about some new technologies that may be appropriate for their business someday. Most of the time they just get together and blow off a little steam or talk about how things are going with their teams.

Monday, 12:30 P.M.: Desk Work

The team leader returns to his desk to make arrangements for a coaching session and for project reviews later in the week. The phone rings and he answers it. It is Joe telling him that the team can cover either Joe or Tom (but not both) to go to the vendor right now. The team decided Joe should be the one to go. The vendor has also been contacted about a meeting tomorrow morning. The team leader says he feels a couple of members probably ought to go on the visit and volunteers to pick up a company car and drive Joe down. "Good," says Joe, "pick me up at 6:30." "How about I meet you at The Pancake House for breakfast at 6:00?" counters the team leader. "We can do a little planning about how we're going to approach this meeting." "OK by me," says Joe. "You buying?"

Monday, 1:00 P.M.: Safety Meeting

A near miss precipitates a meeting sponsored by the safety committee. Everyone is required to attend one of the three scheduled sessions to review the incident.

Monday, 2:00 P.M.: Area Walkthrough

The team leader walks back through the area to see how things are going. Two or three people see him and ask him questions or request help. Things seem to be running pretty smoothly. He leaves several copies of the professor's handouts about the new technology on the breakroom table with a note that says he will be happy to review this with team members if they are interested. The associates start coming in for their break.

Monday, 2:30 P.M.: Breakroom Talk

Several team members are talking about a problem they had this morning. They isolated the problem, corrected it, and got up and running with only a short interruption in production. "I remember when we used to just call maintenance and then come in here and park it until things were fixed," says Cindy. "Yep," adds Joe. "Things have sure changed around here." The team leader agrees. He thinks back to a similar production problem only a few years ago. Back then, it was the supervisor's job to solve problems and make decisions. By the time he lined up the maintenance people, got the problem fixed, and rounded up the operators to get them back to work, they had lost half a day. Today they were down for 20 minutes, and he didn't even know about it until it was all over.

Monday, 2:40 P.M.: Area Walkthrough

The team leader walks back to the work area with several team members and sees Rita updating the whiteboard with the team goals on it. "How's it going?" he asks. "OK," she replies, "but we're never going to meet this cost reduction goal without some new software." "Can you cost justify it?" the leader asks. "I'm not sure," says Rita, "but I'll run the numbers and let you know."

Monday, 3:30 P.M.: Team Meeting

After the associates complete the pass-down of information to second shift, the team leader reviews the options for the hiring training. The group agrees to the Thursday time slot, and spends the rest of the meeting figuring out how to cover for the associates who will be on the interview team. As they are leaving, Cindy realizes that no one has volunteered to close the loop with Bill about the training. "Wait a sec," she says, "who will talk to Bill and when can they get it done?" The team leader flashes her a thumbs-up signal as Tom says he'll drop by HR on his way out tonight.

Monday, 4:00 P.M.: Desk Work

The team leader walks back to his desk (a cubicle right in the middle of the production area) and reviews e-mail. Nothing urgent. He gets on the Internet and downloads some information for the compensation project and for a speech he has to give tomorrow, interrupted only twice by calls. "Amazing," he thinks to himself at one point. "Forty-five minutes straight without an interruption." It wasn't that long ago that he felt like he was fighting fires all day long.

Monday, 5:30 P.M.: Return Home

After dinner the team leader goes into the garage and picks up a woodworking project he started a few weeks ago. He is soon lost in the sound of the table saw. Turning his work around in his hands a couple of hours later, he says to himself, "Boy, it's nice to watch something progress so quickly." He wishes his work were more like that sometimes. "That's life," he chuckles as he walks into the house.

Tuesday, 6:00 A.M.: Breakfast and Travel to Supplier

After a quick breakfast, Joe and the team leader get in the company car. During the two-and-a-half-hour drive they plan their approach to the supplier problem. They go over the data Joe prepared yesterday afternoon and brainstorm ideas for structuring the meeting to eliminate blaming and to focus on resolving the problems. The team leader asks Joe what he wants to accomplish during the meeting and how he will know if the meeting is successful. Together they generate some indicators of success. Joe also talks about his family, and the two compare notes about raising teenagers. They decide that resolving supplier problems is a whole lot easier.

Tuesday, 9:00 A.M.: Supplier Meeting

The supplier meeting begins with a tour of the facility. After the tour Joe and the leader sit down with the supplier and Joe presents the data about the quality problems. After a two-hour conversation they are nowhere. Joe is getting frustrated. "Well, something has changed in the last few weeks," he reiterates. "If nothing else, I know that the bags you ship the material in have changed from a clear color to a purple color." The team leader didn't know that. "That's right," says the supplier. "We did have a new stretch-wrap machine installed in the packaging department that just came on line six weeks ago, but I don't see what that would have to do with product quality." The team leader and Joe ask if they can see the packaging department. When they arrive, Joe asks the operator if he has noticed anything recently that might account for their problems. "Maybe," replies the operator. "This new film is a different gauge and it has more static electricity. We also use more heat to seal the package now." The team leader and Joe ask if they can take home some product before it is wrapped and after it is wrapped to see if there is a difference when it is used in their process. "Sure," say the suppliers, "let us know how it works out." They know it is a long shot but it is all they have to go on for now.

Tuesday, 1:00 P.M.: Drive Back to Work

On the way home the leader and Joe critique the meeting and share their disappointment that they didn't get the issue resolved. "I did learn some things, though," says Joe. "They have one of the same RR7 machines that we do, but they set theirs up different than ours. I'm going to talk to the team about trying it their way when we get back." The team leader spends the rest of the trip talking with Joe about his work. Joe confides in the team leader that he doesn't get along very well with Tom. When the team leader asks if it interferes with work, Joe answers, "Yeah, sometimes." They talk for nearly an hour about how to give feedback to somebody you work with every day to minimize the possibility of getting a negative reaction. "Or," says the team leader, "you can ignore it and hope it gets better by itself." "Slim chance of that," says Joe. "Slim chance," echoes the team leader.

Tuesday, 3:30 P.M.: Team Meeting

Joe and the team leader get back just in time for the afternoon team meeting of the first and second shift people. They share their experience with the vendor and show everyone the wrapped and unwrapped product. Joe proposes an experiment when they set up second-shift production tonight, and the team members agree. He also discusses the different setup the vendor uses on its RR7 machine. The team finishes the pass-down and John tells everyone that the technical person will be in tomorrow morning's meeting to work on the computer problem.

Tuesday, 4:00 P.M.: Return Home

After the team meeting, the team leader drives home to finish his speech for the City Club dinner and spend a little time with his wife and kids.

Tuesday, 6:30 P.M.: City Club Dinner

On behalf of the company, the team leader accepts an award for "corporate citizen of the month." He says a few words, thanks the City Club, and has a great dinner with his wife. He is glad that the work of the facility to improve its image in the community has been recognized, and he is flattered that the members of the Business Coordination Team asked him to go and represent them at this dinner. The bronze plaque will make a nice addition to the "Wall of Fame," a growing collection of awards recognizing the many accomplishments of the facility.

Wednesday, 7:00 A.M.: Team Meeting

John facilitates the meeting so that the pass-down from graveyard to day shift can be done as quickly as possible, allowing most of the team meeting to be devoted to the computer problem. Mary, the technical person, works with the team on brainstorming several possible causes for the intermittent hardware malfunction and they narrow it down to two probable causes. The team agrees to collect specific data on the computer's performance until Friday, when Mary will come back to the work area and help troubleshoot. Joe also excitedly reports that second shift called him last night to let him know that the experiment showed that there was a definite difference between the vendor material that had been wrapped and the material that had not been wrapped. He says he will call the vendor later today.

Wednesday, 7:20 A.M.: Area Walkthrough

During the walkthrough Rita stops the team leader and hands him several sheets of paper. "What's this?" he asks. "The cost justification for the software," she answers. "It pays out in 3 months with a rate of return of over 40 percent." "Sounds pretty good," says the team leader. He remembers when the operators wouldn't even know the meaning of those words, let alone be able to do the calculations. "Let's move forward on this. How do you want me to help?" "Grease the skids, will ya?" requests Rita. "Ever since those guys on the midwest customer team went on that software buying frenzy a year ago, it's been hard to get requisition signatures for this kind of stuff. Headquarters wants to authorize all personal computers and software."

Wednesday, 9:00 A.M.: Desk Work

The team leader makes phone calls to get information for the marketing analysis project he is working on. He also calls his daughter to tell her that he'll swing by to say hello on his way to the dentist.

Wednesday, 10:00 A.M.: Dentist Appointment

The team leader feels a little guilty about not being at work—but not that guilty. He enjoys the brief chat with his daughter and the ride to the dentist. He does not enjoy his time at the dentist's office, however. Some things never change.

Wednesday, 11:45 A.M.: Lunch with the Boss

The team leader meets his boss, Jane, in the cafeteria. "How's it going?" she asks. "Okay," he replies, "but I could use some help on a couple of things. You got a minute?" "Sure," Jane says. The leader sits down at Jane's table and reviews the week's activities so far, then sees Rita come into the room. "Rita, come join us if you can," he requests. Rita and the team leader review the idea for new software with Jane. "You know," says Jane, "unbudgeted software purchases are a political hot potato right now." The team leader and Rita nod. "What will it take to get your support for this purchase?" asks the team leader. "Rock-solid cost justification," answers Jane. The team leader pulls out the sheets Rita gave him earlier and together they walk through the analysis. "Looks good to me," says Jane. "Go for it, Rita." The leader writes a note to himself to work with Jane to get this new policy from headquarters eliminated. He remembers when challenging corporate policies was a CLM (career-limiting move). Now it is expected.

Wednesday, 12:30 P.M.: Coaching Discussion

John has requested a coaching session with the team leader. In preparation for the discussion, John has asked the other team members to give him some feedback on his performance. This information has been compiled and summarized by the team leader. The discussion includes a review of the peer feedback and some observations that the team leader has already shared with John. The team leader makes a special point to reinforce John for doing a good job of arranging for the team discussion with Mary, the technical expert.

Wednesday, 1:30 P.M.: Market/Competitive Product Analysis

A cross-facility project group has been working for some time to complete a market analysis that can be used to update all the teams. The group meets and asks the team leader to purchase competitive products and put up a display for people to look at and experiment with. Nobody did this type of thing before, but the teams find market and competitive data very helpful to them now. A write-up on the analysis will be posted on the company's intranet. The project team reviews everyone's assignments and does a dry run of a presentation for the monthly facility-wide meeting next Friday. It is still a little rough, but all the pertinent information is there.

Wednesday, 2:30 P.M.: Breakroom Discussions

The team leader passes by the breakroom and is waved in by Joe and Cindy. "We tried Joe's idea and it cut setup time on the RR7 by 13 minutes," they explain nearly in unison. The team leader feels proud of his team. "I'm bringing the doughnuts tomorrow," he says. "How about we bring in Jane for the afternoon meeting and we tell her about the successful setup and the vendor test? Looks like your meeting, Joe. Let's brag a little." Joe is beaming so brightly that it looks like his face will catch on fire. "Okay," he says, "but I want Cindy and the second shift guys to do the talk with me too. It was a team effort, you know."

Wednesday, 2:40 P.M.: Work

On his way into the work area the leader sees team members buzzing like angry yellowjackets. "The !**#!* computer dumped last week's invoices," shouts John. "We need everybody we can free up to re-input them before the mail deadline at 4:00." The team leader fights back the urge to take over and control the crisis. It looks like John is doing fine. "I'm free," says the team leader. "Have a seat at terminal 2," says John as he exits the room. "I'll go get the technician and some more team members." The team leader sits down at terminal 2 and Tom sits down at terminal 1. Before long the three remaining terminals are filled by Rita, Paul, and Mary, the technician. Although the team leader doesn't have the speed or accuracy of the other team members, he holds his own and the data is all entered before the deadline—just barely before the deadline. "Not bad," says Cindy as she walks in and reviews the team leader's work, "but keep your day job." Her voice is tinged with grudging respect. The four of them missed the team meeting. Cindy brings them up to speed on what was covered.

Wednesday, 4:00 P.M.: Team-to-Team Conflict Resolution Meeting

The team leader arranged some time ago to have Bill from HR facilitate a conflict resolution meeting between the team and one of the second-shift teams down the hall. Bill runs the teams through an organized process that gives each a way to say what it needs from the other to meet their mutual goals of providing top-flight service and products to their customers. They finish the meeting with work to do, and though they are far from being best friends, the session helps to take the personalities out of their disagreements and focus both teams on getting the work done.

Wednesday, 5:45 P.M.: Return Home

Going back into the garage, the team leader picks up his woodworking project. He reviews the last few days in his head. "You know," he thinks, "even though we have a long way to go, we are really making some progress as a team." He looks at the accomplishments and commitment of team members and feels good. They are doing a lot of the things that only he or the staff people would have done before. And even though the transition was pretty hard on him, he feels as though he is getting the hang of this team leader thing. It took him several months to learn how to ask questions to get the team members to think through problems themselves, rather than just telling them what they should do. He liked getting rid of vacation and overtime scheduling chores. But it nearly killed him to turn over the budgeting and work scheduling tasks that he really liked and was good at. Still, he has to admit that he feels darn good about what it happening now. He likes the coaching and development of team members. It's a lot tougher to do his job than it used to be, but he wouldn't want to go back to the combative workplace of pre-SDWTs. "Yep," he whispers out loud, "things are pretty good."

Then he turns on the saw and goes to work on the block of wood in his hands.

Summary

Thus ends three days in the life of a team leader. But getting to the point where team leader skills come naturally isn't easy. Preparing to be a team leader is like preparing to run a marathon. Just as marathoners condition themselves for the long run, less experienced team leaders can build up stamina and speed through a transition training program. This process is described in the next chapter.

A Weekly Activity Guide for Team Leaders

"To win, we need to find ways to capture the creative and innovative spirit of the . . . worker. That's the real organizational challenge."

Paul Allaire, *CEO of Xerox*

MARATHON RUNNERS START their training programs with short runs that condition them for longer runs. After runners develop stamina, they then work on speed. In this chapter you will find a similar development schedule for team leaders. While some supervisors and managers are able to make the transition into self-directed work team settings immediately, most of us benefit from a staged development approach that, like training for a marathon, builds up competence and confidence over time.

Short Runs

Team leaders can do a number of things immediately that, like the short runs, will begin to develop stamina. Two important activities for team leaders during the early part of their development process are spending specific blocks of time with the work group and engaging in personal education activities. The team block time should be devoted to being with the team as the members work ("hanging around" time, as one team leader calls it), which allows the team leader to be available for spontaneous team interaction and support. Table 19.1 shows a short-run schedule with specific recommendations for a workout for the first four weeks.

Communication Skills

One of the especially important skills to strengthen during this time is increased communication effectiveness. If team leaders build this skill early, it will serve them well throughout their careers in high-performance work system settings.

In traditional organizations, employee attitude surveys frequently and predictably say that communications are poor. In many of those same

Table 19.1 The Shorter-Run Workout (Weeks 1 Through 4)

Monday	Tuesday	Wednesday	Thursday	Friday
• Schedule nonmeeting time to be in the work area (1 hour).	• Read some team leadership materials (1 hour).	• Schedule nonmeeting time to be in the work area (1 hour).	• Read some team leadership materials (1 hour).	• Schedule nonmeeting time to be in the work area (1 hour).
• Gather some relevant business information (30 minutes).	• Share relevant business information with team (15 minutes).	• Gather some relevant business information (30 minutes).	• Share relevant business information with team (15 minutes).	• Gather some relevant business information (30 minutes).

Special Activity

• At some time during the month, get training on SDWT basics and then visit an SDWT site (3–5 days).

organizations, however, members of management report that they communicate fairly well. How can this disparity exist? Because managers assess themselves on effort and intent, while employees assess business communication on results. "How much do I know about what is going on?" they ask themselves, with the nearly inevitable reply being, "Too much on some things and not enough on others." In SDWT organizations, effective team leaders close the gap between their intentions to communicate and the perceptions of team members about the effectiveness of business communication. This requires patience and tenacity. One culture team leader from Shell laments that this process can be tedious. "We gave the vision presentation more than 100 times." he said. "Remarkably, there were still people who said they didn't know what the vision was!"

Communication Topics

What do team leaders communicate about? Anything you would share with a full business partner. Topics like timely and ongoing quality, financial matters, and goal achievement status are a must on the communication "to do" list. The list also includes information about customers, the market, products, services, other team responsibilities and accomplishments, and so forth. Although much of this information can be communicated electronically, time spent face to face with the team builds the relationship that is so necessary for trust. Team leaders often have to go out, get the information, and then format it so that it is easy to understand. That is why this activity is called a workout. It is often a whole lot harder than it looks.

Team Meetings

Teams typically have some sort of team meeting every day. Without meetings, teams have no institutionalized forum for information sharing, problem solving, and decision making. Because these meetings are typically ineffective and frustrating at first, team leaders are often tempted to work to eliminate them in favor of more pressing business concerns. This can be very shortsighted. While there certainly is no hard-and-fast rule on the required frequency of these meetings, it is not uncommon to have short operational meetings daily (at every shift overlap for multiple-shift operations), with more extended meetings for project work as needed. Figures 19.1 and 19.2 are examples of operational team meeting agendas for a production facility team and an office team, respectively. In both cases the same agenda is used daily and the meeting length varies from 15 to 30 minutes a day. Operations that run 24 hours a day can have difficulty hosting these regular team meetings, but often find that setting up a chart pad stand in an area where several team members can have quick standing meetings throughout the day can help.

Meetings as a Substitute for Hierarchy

These meetings are used to coordinate many of the tasks that would be done by a traditional supervisor (work assignments, firefighting, paperwork, vacation, and overtime scheduling, etc.), and they are also used as a real-time opportunity to provide information, training, and coaching (see Table 19.2). One Shell manager suggests that "The biggest mistake companies make (in the transition to SDWTs) is to change the role of the supervisor before the team has effective processes that will substitute for (the administrative service provided by) the traditional supervisor."

This is true. The move to SDWTs is not an elimination of supervisory tasks, but is instead a structured transfer of those tasks to the team members. These supervisory tasks can be assumed only by teams that have institutionalized processes and methods for doing them. For example, a team with the responsibility to manage the cross-training of its members is more likely to be successful if it has a process (charts, assignment algorithm, etc.) with which to accomplish this responsibility than if it does not. Even though mature teams often appear as though they are

---

Core Group Agenda

Quality Report (results of daily monitoring/quality audit results weekly/customer feedback from quarterly reports or special visits)

Finance/Throughput/Waste Results (highlights key cost leverages)

Round Robin (brief review of projects/problems from yesterday/last shift)

Coverage/Job Assignments (team decides who will do what today)

Special Announcements (announcements regarding current topics)

Figure 19.1 Team meeting agenda example (production).

Ops Meeting Agenda

Schedule and Calendar Review (who will be where when)

Client Status (project progress/review of action items/customer feedback and requirements/who needs help/who is available to help)

Office Issues/Follow-up (team decides who does what today and high-lights upcoming issues requiring coordination)

Figure 19.2 Team meeting agenda example (office).

"making it up as they go," they virtually always start with a structured process that, after it becomes a habit, provides a mental map for action even though it may be invisible to the outside observer.

My team in Lima, for example, made job rotation and coverage assignments according to a formula that had been established and continually renegotiated for years. It included agreements for new employees to always start their assignments as "makers," who performed the core work process around which each of the other four jobs (unloader, analyst, boilerhouse, and maintenance) revolved. The new employees then rotated to other roles as they became available. Similarly, team members who had not been makers for a long time were usually

Table 19.2 Possible Meeting Topics

• External customer requirements	• Organization values
• Internal customer requirements	• Professional ethics
• Emerging technologies	• Goal status
• Budget review	• Information from other teams
• Vendor information	• Legislation review
• Project updates	• Information from headquarters
• Staffing issues	• Team effectiveness assessment
• Work assignments	• Role clarification
• Capacity review	• Planning
• Work flow and process update	• Community issues
• Competition updates	• Safety information
• Problem-solving activities	• Customer feedback
• Market trend information	• International concerns
• New product/service review	• Work charts and graphs review
• Profitability review	• Quality review
• Process simplification	

assigned by the team to cover for makers' vacations so that they could refresh their skills in the core work technology. Someone who is unaware of this prioritization methodology might assume that the team simply picks rotation assignments at random. But when they come to understand the unspoken rationale behind the decisions, they see the pattern of decisions created by a methodology that has become internalized and institutionalized by the team.

Longer Runs

The short-run workout develops basic skills and work habits that are strengthened in the longer-run workout. In this series of development activities, team leaders spend more time working with the team in non-traditional ways (as illustrated in the examples in Table 19.3), continuing many of the short-run efforts and adding some new exercises to increase stamina. In this workout for the second month, team leaders build an action-oriented team training and development focus on the base of solid information passing established in the first month's workout. Team leaders also practice coaching, empowerment, example setting, and customer advocacy skills.

An important part of this workout is beginning to facilitate team member training. Table 19.4 presents some examples of the kind of training topics to consider for team development.

Caution: although teams often require a great deal of training and many development activities to prepare them to be effective as high-performance work systems, clustering all of the training together and delivering it to the team in great training extravaganzas is like giving it a drink from a fire hose. All this information is too much to assimilate effectively. It is better to spread the activities out over time and to schedule them so that they occur just prior to an opportunity for the team to apply the new skills it has developed. Team leaders pace the training in social, technical, and business skills appropriately. After all, SDWT members spend about 20 percent of their time in some sort of training activities, in contrast to the traditional employee training time commitment of 2 to 3 percent. That is an order-of-magnitude difference in training time, which corresponds to the increased responsibilities of self-regulating groups and the increasing need for up-to-date skills and information.

Table 19.3   The Longer-Run Workout (Weeks 5 Through 8)

Monday	Tuesday	Wednesday	Thursday	Friday
• Identify team training needs and make some helpful training happen (1–4 hours sometime during the week).	• In a one-on-one coaching conversation, empower a team member to do something big (30 minutes).	• Find a way to be a good example of something you have told the team is important. Walk your talk (15 minutes–3 hours).	• In a team coaching conversation, empower the team to do something big (30 minutes).	• Schedule time to be in the work area (1 hour).
• Schedule time to be in the work area (1 hour).	• Help the team establish or review its success indicators and operational guidelines (1 hour to establish/15 minutes to review progress).	• Schedule time to be in the work area (1 hour).	• Talk with another team leader and get at least 1 good idea (30 minutes).	• Gather some relevant business information (30 minutes).
• Gather some relevant business information (30 minutes).	• Share relevant business information with team (15 minutes).	• Gather some relevant business information (30 minutes).	• Share relevant business information with team (15 minutes).	

Special Activity

- At some time during the month, get training on team leadership skills, such as setting boundary conditions, facilitating, barrier busting, and managing by principle. Practice the skills you learn (3–5 days).
- Develop and share your personal vision of greatness for your team (½ day).
- Take some team members with you on a customer visit or have a customer come in and speak to the team (1 hour–2 days).

Table 19.4 Examples of Team Training Topics

Social Skills	Technical Skills	Business Skills
Giving feedback	Operating equipment	Setting/tracking goals
Receiving feedback	Maintaining equipment	Understanding
Making decisions	Troubleshooting	economics
Solving problems	Using quality tools	Using financial ratios
Leading	Analyzing work flow	Planning
Facilitating groups	Redesigning work flow	Managing projects
Coaching	Selecting equipment	Identifying customer
Interviewing	Integrating	needs
Making presentations	technologies	Working with vendors
Resolving conflicts	Developing new	Working with the
Working as a team	products	public
	Cross-training	Providing customer
	Learning software	service
	programs	Understanding
		competitors
		Analyzing markets

The Speed Workout

After stamina is developed in the first two workouts, team leaders work on speed. In this third workout, more difficult skills—like soliciting personal performance feedback, barrier busting, networking, and defining boundary conditions—are emphasized (see Table 19.5). Elements from the earlier workouts continue to be reinforced. These activities tend to help the team progress toward maturity and effectiveness more rapidly as the team leader helps members focus their efforts and cut through impediments to improving their work processes.

Running the Marathon

After all the preparations, of course, the really important thing for the team leader/athlete is to run the marathon. Continuing to run helps the team leader to stay in shape. This particular series of races requires both speed and endurance, and with each new event come new learnings as well as the satisfaction of knowing you have accomplished something.

Table 19.5   The Speed Workout (Weeks 9 Through 12)

Monday	Tuesday	Wednesday	Thursday	Friday
• Schedule nonmeeting time to be in the work area (1 hour).	• Identify a barrier to the team's effectiveness and work to eliminate it (1 hour).	• Ask the team how you can help. Do what the members request (1 hour).	• Talk with other team leaders at your level and get at least one good improvement idea (30 minutes).	• Identify a barrier to the team's effectiveness and start to eliminate it (1 hour).
• Gather some relevant business information (30 minutes).	• In a one-on-one coaching conversation, empower a team member to do something big (30 minutes).	• Schedule time to be in the work area (1 hour).	• Ask the team how you can help. Do what the members request (1 hour).	• Schedule time to be in the work area (1 hour).
• Identify team training needs and make some helpful training happen (1–4 hours sometime during the week).	• Share relevant business information with team (15 minutes).	• Gather some relevant business information (30 minutes).	• In a team coaching conversation, empower the team to do something big (30 minutes). • Share relevant business information (15 minutes).	• Gather some relevant business information (30 minutes).

Special Activities

- At some time during the month, commission the team members to manage a major improvement project with clearly defined boundary conditions (2 hours–2 days).
- Take some team members with you on another customer visit or have another customer come in and speak to the team (1 hour–2 days).

Summary

Like a runner preparing for a marathon, the team leader can build stamina and speed by going through team leader workouts consisting of (1) short runs, (2) longer runs, and (3) speed runs. These workouts help team leaders build their own competence and confidence. Short-run exercises emphasize communication skill building and personal role education. The longer runs build on this foundation and focus on developing team members and on practicing the team leader skills of coaching, empowerment, example setting, and customer advocacy. The speed workout emphasizes all of the earlier competencies and provides practice time for receiving feedback, barrier busting, networking, and setting boundary conditions. Although these workouts certainly aren't very comprehensive, they can provide some experience in many of the essential tasks of team leadership.

This chapter has focused on some ideas for building team leader competencies. But even more important than *skill* building is *will* building. To complete this change, team leaders have to want to do something different. Skills alone won't help. I would argue, in fact, that many traditional supervisors already have the skills to be team leaders, but they just don't have the desire to use these skills. Later in the book we will focus on this important issue. We will address the question, "What does it take to help supervisors truly become team leaders?" First, however, we will review a common problem faced by most team leaders in the early stages of high-performance work system development.

In the next chapter we consider some alternatives for working with traditional employees who don't want to act like team members. We will attempt to answer the difficult question, "What do you do when people resist the change to SDWTs?"

PART
VI

Common Problems and Uncommon Solutions

When Team Members Resist the Change to a Self-Directed Work Team

"The economy is simply too important to be left in the hands of a few at the top of that (corporate) ladder. To solve our problems, we need reconciliation, cooperation, and the broad participation of all parties to the economic enterprise: workers, consumers, unions, the state and federal governments. Working together, we just might make a difference."

Christopher Meek, Warner Woodworth,
and W. Gibb Dyer Jr.

OVERALL, SUPERVISORS ARE typically more resistant to the implementation of self-directed work teams than team members themselves are. But the earliest and most vocal concerns about these work systems come from individuals on the teams.

It is not unusual for a work team, for example, to resist assuming responsibilities that are new to them. Workers may demand more pay for doing "management" work. They may see multiskilling as de-skilling. They may believe that SDWTs are a union-busting strategy or a method for eliminating seniority and protective job rules and classifi-cations. Office workers or staff professionals may protest the time they must spend away from their projects to work on team tasks or express discomfort about the new ambiguity that comes with group decision making and problem solving. "I liked it better when the director just told me what to do. That was quicker and simpler," they say, question-ing the sanity of other team members who seem to enjoy the additional responsibilities and worries of the new assignments required of a busi-ness partner. Teams of managers, newly empowered to assume strategic responsibilities previously reserved for senior management, may fear failure or be uncomfortable with the career risks associated with open feedback to upper management.

All of these concerns, of course, are perfectly normal during the early stages of transition. However, they must be resolved to the satis-faction of the critical mass of the team members for the implementation to be successful. Working through these issues keeps the implementa-tion process honest. It provides a living example of how the work cul-ture will function in the future. So how do you overcome this hurdle?

Change Model

A clear pattern is associated with successful individual change efforts. The elements of this pattern of successful transition can be visualized as a four-faceted diamond (see Figure 20.1). What are the four key com-ponents necessary for someone to change roles? People require:

1. *Clarity:* A clear picture of the emerging role and how it differs from the classic role of a worker.

Figure 20.1 Role change model.

2. *Felt need:* A personal desire to change to the new role.
3. *Support:* The organizational encouragement to create and sustain this personal role change.
4. *Self-awareness:* The ability to assess one's impact on others and make necessary "midcourse corrections."

Each of these facets is essential to the transition. For instance, even when a team member wants to change, is organizationally supported, and is aware of how he or she affects others, he or she will have little success without a clear understanding of what the new role entails. You can't get on the right train if you don't know where the trains are going. Each of the four facets deserves some specific attention.

Clarity

The first facet of effective role change is clarity about the emerging role. Even when the team members have been compelled to action with an exciting vision of the organization of the future, they need specific clarity about how that new organization will affect them personally on a day-to-day basis. "What will I do in the future that is different from what I do today?" is a question that must be answered to the satisfaction of the team members. Many of the effective role transitions at Apple, Corning, IBM, Weyerhaeuser, Chevron, and numerous other companies have used a training process to help with the clarification task.

Using Simulations to Clarify the New Role

One of the most effective training techniques is to use a simulation that demonstrates the difference between traditional roles and team member roles. These simulations are normally separated into two activities. In the first activity the participants create a product or deliver a service using traditional work roles. This part of the simulation takes from two to eight hours and graphically (and sometimes humorously) demonstrates the inefficiencies inherent in a traditional job-focused work system. Team members see how traditional work structures create the "that's not my job" syndrome, how compartmentalized departments restrict information flow, and how manager-dominated problem solving and decision making slows down a business. The best of these simulations further demonstrate how traditional operations affect quality, profitability, and morale.

The second part of the simulation then allows the team to redesign the workplace to better meet customer needs. Taking from two to eight hours, this phase demonstrates how teams can create a sense of "ownership" of the product or service that is not possible with traditional job roles. Instead of employees being assigned traditional job descriptions, which focus each individual on a narrow set of job responsibilities, the work tasks are managed and assigned by the team as a whole. People share responsibility for meeting the customer needs, and they make decisions and solve problems jointly as a team rather than bottlenecking everything through the supervisor. It is a commonsense approach to getting the work done, driven by the customer and the work itself rather than by the supervisor, rules, or regulations. It also shows dramatic improvements in business indicators of effectiveness.

Explain the New Team Member Competencies

In addition to this kind of general awareness training for team members, organization-specific training on roles and responsibilities is required. Visits to other SDWT sites can be a helpful way for team members to better understand these roles. But each organization has specific tasks that are unique to the SDWT members in their own operations. How can you deal with that? Consider the following general description of the role of a team member, which lists the essential competencies to be explained to members of an SDWT (see Figure 20.2). Using this model as a start, team members can construct the specific tasks and assignments for each pie segment themselves to provide additional clarity for their emerging role.

- *Customer advocate:* Strives to better meet the needs of the customer.
- *Trainer:* Trains others in job/skill areas; continually shares knowledge with others.
- *Resource:* Has a diverse and ever expanding set of skills; continually broadens knowledge base.
- *Skilled worker:* Demonstrates all the necessary skills and knowledge to perform the job well; continually strives to improve skill sets and assure total quality.
- *Team player:* Demonstrates good interpersonal skills; supports other team members.
- *Decision maker:* Provides input and makes decisions on issues that directly impact the work area.
- *Problem solver:* Understands and utilizes problem-solving techniques to regularly identify and solve problems.

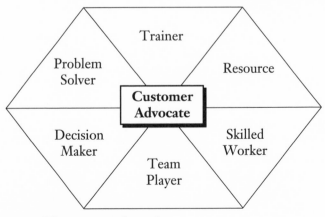

Figure 20.2 The team member role.
Team Tools training program by The Fisher Group, Inc. © 1989 The Fisher Group and BFR, Inc. All rights reserved. Used by permission.

SDWT Role Descriptions Differ Significantly
from Traditional Job Descriptions

It is important to help people understand how this kind of a role description differs from a traditional job description. Where a traditional job description is focused on separate individuals getting certain tasks done, this role description is focused on each team member sharing responsibility for getting the work of the team done. Team member responsibilities also include the planning, administration, and execution of tasks, instead of just the execution of tasks as in a traditional work system. A traditional job description is activity-driven (do cleanup, graphics, quality checks, and anything else required by your manager), whereas the team member role is purpose-driven (do what makes sense to satisfy customers).

SDWT Members Make Up Their Own "To Do" Lists

Traditional organizations write job descriptions that are organized like discrete "to do" lists. High-performance work systems, on the other hand, use more purpose-oriented words like *role* when describing responsibilities. Job descriptions, if they exist at all, are so generic that they are nearly meaningless.

One company charged new employees to "find things that need to be done and do them" in lieu of a specific job description. How can they do that? Because SDWT members take direction from the work to be done, not from job descriptions or supervision. They can figure out what to do themselves as long as the work processes are visible to them. It is like being a member of a family. When adults become parents, no one gives them a "mother job description" or a "father job description." They figure it out as they go. And they are more or less effective, of course, depending on their skills and their situations. Similarly, team member roles take on enhanced clarity not from job descriptions but from ongoing training and information if the role and organization structures are properly designed. For other ideas on helping team members change, see Table 20.1. Explaining the role in this way often reduces resistance.

Table 20.1 Helping Team Members Change

Clarity	Felt Need	Support	Self-Awareness
Demystify the role by visiting with other organizations.	Present a vivid organization case for change that outlines current business realities.	Allay job security fears.	Model behaviors such as recognizing and admitting mistakes.
Empower people to take on special project responsibilities that are exemplary of the new role.	Provide one-on-one coaching to focus a personal need to change.	Provide reinforcement through performance discussions, policies, practices, and pay systems.	Foster an environment that encourages honesty and self-disclosure.
Create opportunities to highlight good examples of the new role within the organization.	Through visits, speakers, conferences, or training, credibly demonstrate the personal benefits of the change.	Provide training and tools to support newly required expectations.	Add peer input to performance appraisal, promotion, and recognition processes.

Felt Need

The second facet of effective role change has been well documented. Gene Dalton's review of the personal change literature led him to conclude that change only occurs when individuals feel a personal need to make the change. This is often overlooked when SDWT transformation efforts begin. In a number of organizations where I have worked, for example, well-intentioned leaders have assumed that organizational sanction alone would compel role changes across the ranks of employees. On many occasions when this strategy has been used, however, I have observed people respond with "talk" changes but with little in the way of real "walk" changes. "This too will pass," they say, noting the common program-of-the-month focus in their organizations. They can often get by with imitating the form without the substance of the change. This is, of course, unhealthy for both the individual and the organization.

People Will Not Change Until They Feel They Need to Change

Until individuals are personally convinced that they need to change, they will not change. Thus, creating what Dalton called "felt need" is an essential part of the transformation process. For some people this is accomplished simply by being exposed to a change champion in the organization who has developed and articulated a compelling vision for the future. Ron, a management team leader, had this kind of influence on some of the members of his team in a division of a high-tech company on the West Coast. When he became convinced that high-performance work systems were essential to the operation of his division, Ron began to share that conviction with his management team. These discussions became eloquent dissertations on the necessity of creating partnerships throughout the organization, which Ron delivered with the quiet intensity of a thoughtful human rights advocate. "His passion for people involvement is like a virus," said one staff member. "It is hard to be around him for very long without catching it."

Present a Case for Change

Other leaders create the environment in which individuals can feel this need by presenting a compelling case for organizational change—a vivid description, often tied to the history of the organization, that illustrates the necessity of transforming the people in the group and includes the implications of not changing. Fred Hanson, then vice president of the Portables group at Tektronix, created a felt need by addressing the division soon after he had arrived from Hewlett-Packard. He showed them a Gary Larson cartoon of a group of dinosaurs standing in an auditorium listening to a stegosaurus speaking to them from behind a podium. The caption reads, "The picture looks pretty bleak, gentlemen. The world's climates are changing, the mammals are taking over, and we all have a brain about the size of a walnut." Hanson went on to explain that everyone, including himself as the senior stegosaurus, was going to have to change to meet the emerging realities of the business. He presented data about the new international competition and Tek's subsequent substantial revenue loss. Armed with the information from this case for change, people became convinced that a change was a business necessity, not just a style preference of the new leader.

In yet another example of a case for change, the senior management team at the Monsanto Pensacola plant created a series of short dramatic videos that emphasized the risks associated with not changing the organization. The first tape graphically demonstrated the negative aspects of not changing (that Monsanto would lose to increasing competition and become extinct). This was followed up with a tape one year later illustrating specific examples of where the plant had successfully changed. Plant management describes the videos as a sort of one-two punch that first got people's attention and then gave them confidence in their own ability to make the change.

Support

The third facet of successful role change is organizational support. Without it, the change will likely come undone over time. Change is like a rubber band. Through training, meetings, and even personal coaching sessions, team members are often motivated enough to stretch to the different role, much as one end of an extended rubber band stretches to a different position when pulled. When the tension is released, however, the rubber band springs back to its original position. Similarly, the team members spring back to the well-known and comfortable roles of the past when the organization does not sustain the pull for the change.

Make Employment (Not Job) Assurances

To sustain this change, people need help. This help comes in a variety of forms of support. The immediate support requested is usually organizational reassurance that team members will not be put out on the street as a result of transferring many of their skills and responsibilities to other employees. This applies as much to teams of mid-level managers as it does to teams of workers. We are all concerned with these basic security issues. Team members cannot be expected to put forth the effort to change when they fear that their reward for this effort will be elimination. Nor will they change for make-work positions of diminished responsibility and status. Job security (your job won't change) cannot be promised, because all jobs change significantly in the high-performance workplace. And people are smart enough to see through an ironclad guarantee that no one will ever lose employment during the time period of the transition. Performance issues and market swings will always affect organizational stability. But a reassurance that the purpose of the change is not to facilitate an elimination of employees is important to assure the buy-in of those affected.

Pay and Other Reinforcements Need to Be in Sync with SDWTs

Team members also need other kinds of formal organizational support. Unless reinforcement systems like performance appraisals, promotions, compensation, and other rewards support the emerging role, we send a confusing message about our expectations to the team members in the organization. In one company the effort stalled when people perceived the performance appraisal system as being inconsistent with the emerging direction. Though the SDWT required flexibility, cross-training, and information meetings, the employees were measured exclusively on individual productivity. The system discouraged teamwork and punished people for "nonproductive" time like meetings, which could not be billed back to a customer. Until appropriate changes were made to eliminate this double message, people obviously felt a lack of credible organizational support for the SDWT effort.

Organization Structures Need to Be Aligned with SDWTs

A perhaps even more important form of support is also required during these transitions. Gene Dalton, for example, found that new or modified social relationships were required to sustain personal change over time. Although a number of these transformations have been made with the same intact work groups and their managers, there is a higher probability of success when the role changes accompany organizational changes that modify the makeup and charter of a team.

In one change effort in a high-tech company, for example, the role change was supported through a production realignment in the organization, which required managers to shift from their assigned work groups to completely different teams. Though initially confusing, this personnel rotation created an opportunity for team leaders to work out a role change "contract" with a new team that was not encumbered with the habits and work history they had created together over time. In another example, a Digital facility staged the implementation process by moving team leaders to the next section of the organization to be transformed. These operations team leaders would overlap with the existing supervisors to learn the organization, allowing the existing supervisors to manage the business while the team leaders focused on managing the transition issues. After some period of time, the old supervisor group would turn over the work teams to the new team leaders, and the old supervisors would be transferred en masse to the next organization, where they would become the new operations team leaders.

While these illustrations of social change are rather dramatic examples of musical chairs, less significant structural support may be equally helpful. New technologies, new products, or new business programs may provide sufficient change in the organization to refocus the social system to be consistent with emerging role changes.

Financial Reports, Training, and Other Tools Need to Be Consistent

Still another form of organizational support is essential to the effective transition of the team member's role. This support is resources and tools. To encourage people to act and think differently without providing them some means to accomplish the change is futile. They need tools and training to work in a way that is consistent with the values of high involvement. A number of people, for example, have found that the financial tools used in traditional organizations are no longer useful for the SDWT. Teams need data that is pertinent to their area of influence and formatted in a way that is readily understandable. Much of the existing financial tooling is geared to reporting information up and out of the organization, and is of little use to teams trying to manage quality, cost, and schedule. Even when it is available, it is so abstruse that it is often unhelpful. Other resources, such as tools and resources for gathering, communicating, and coordinating general information, are needed as well.

Ongoing skill training is essential in these operations, as has been discussed in previous chapters. Institutionalizing methods and processes for this training is prudent. In one Chevron refinery, for example, when the organization was redesigned into high-performance work systems, a "school board" was established for the purpose of coordinating the massive amount of business, technical, and interpersonal training that would be required to help employees be successful. This team of representatives from each area of the newly designed operation was charged with developing plans and systems to coordinate the training efforts.

Self-Awareness

The final facet of successful role change is self-awareness. Team members who are aware of how they affect others are more likely to be effective than those who do not seek feedback about this. This is especially true of team members who have responsibilities for some type of team leadership (which at some point includes everybody on the team). The fact of the matter is that most of us think we are probably a little better than we really are. We judge ourselves on our intentions, while others judge us on our behaviors. Team members who think that they are acting appropriately may be surprised when they find that their peers perceive them differently. How do you get this information? Ask for it.

Peer Feedback

One of the most effective ways to help people complete the role change is to show them how they are perceived by others whom they care about. This is the reason that peer pressure can be such an effective motivator in SDWTs. Perceptions can be shared through a variety of means such as peer appraisals, but it requires extreme sensitivity and skill to do it properly. Many people, unaccustomed to giving and receiving feedback, can be harmed by ineffective processes.

I have worked with numerous team members who have believed that they were fulfilling their responsibilities when their peers thought they were not pulling their share of the load. Some team members are seen as lazy when they intend to be helpful, or uncooperative when they want to be honest. Devil's advocates, for example, who honestly believe they are representing the true views of their teammates when they raise issues or concerns on task forces or committees, are sometimes seen as working their own individual agendas that are contrary to the emerging group consensus on the particular issue. Blinded by their own good intentions, they do the wrong things for the right reasons.

Summary

Clarity, felt need, support, and self-awareness are required for a successful role change. Although some of the resistance to change manifested by team members early in the process of the transition arises simply from the normal tendency to dislike disruptions to established life patterns, most of it can be reduced by working through the suggestions listed in this chapter.

In the next chapter we will deal with the primary resistance and the most critical barrier to the transition to SDWTs: supervisors at all levels who don't want to change.

Helping Supervisors Become Team Leaders

"When I started this business of teams, I was anxious to get it done and get back to my real job. Then I realized that, hey, this is my real job."

Ralph Stayer, *CEO of Johnsonville Foods*

A NUMBER OF concerned team members and team leaders alike express skepticism about whether supervisors can change into team leaders. Says John Homan, a previous plant manager of one of the A.E. Staley SDWT plants: "One of the questions I have asked myself is, can all supervisors be successful in the 'new' systems, even with extensive training? My assessment right now is no. I have seen too many examples of people who would not or could not change." Pat D'Angelo, vice president of the Bakery, Confectionery and Tobacco Workers International agrees. He says that some of the Nabisco supervisors just flat didn't make it. "We had a lot of problems with supervisors. They either straightened up or they looked for other jobs." Some supervisors in this situation can be moved to less "damaging" positions where they don't manage others. These supervisors can be gainfully employed in technical projects or in other individual contributor roles. But that is neither appropriate nor practical for most cases.

We have already talked at length about why this is such a difficult transition for supervisors at all levels to make. But in this chapter I would like to suggest some more specific ways to help people change from supervisors into team leaders. While it is true that not all supervisors will necessarily choose to change, the experience of many companies is that people certainly can change if given the opportunity. Some, in fact, require only organizational sanction to do what they have already been practicing for years. What does it take to help the others?

In a Work in America national policy study, Jerome Rosow and Robert Zager make a number of suggestions for helping supervisors change into team leaders. These include:

1. Redefine supervisors' jobs.
2. Reorient and retrain them for the new role.
3. Give them employment security.
4. Provide them some relief from pressures that might compel them to fall back on the comfortable practices of the past.

I would like to elaborate on these suggestions by discussing the change model introduced in the last chapter.

Change Model Affects Team Leaders

All facets of the change model—clarity, felt need, support, and self-awareness—are just as important for the supervisor role change as they are for the team member role change. For example, what started out in one company looking like a successful team leader transition later backfired when only some of the facets were sustained over time. A mid-level manager, who had previously been nicknamed "Little Hitler" by the workers, was motivated by very frank feedback from his management team leader to change his role from sheep herding to shepherding. People were amazed at the transformation. Although this manager made remarkable changes during the first two years after the feedback, when his boss was replaced by someone who was not a champion of these concepts, the organizational support decreased, and he felt little need to continue with the difficult role. He consequently slipped back to old familiar ways even though he clearly understood the team leader role and was very aware of how others perceived him. He didn't care.

Clarity

Where does clarity, the first facet of the model, come from? From first redefining and then from communicating the new role. In one P&G plant undergoing a transition from a traditional system to SDWTs, supervisors were sent to a three-day session where they role-played some open-ended cases as team leaders and learned about the under-pinning philosophy of empowerment. The role plays were critiqued by a supportive panel of peers who gave supervisors individual feedback about how their behavior was perceived. Following this education session, the supervisors visited different SDWT plants where they inter-viewed team leaders and team members to determine for themselves how team leaders behaved. This demystified the role and allowed the supervisors to meet face to face with successful people who shared many of their concerns and objectives. By spending time with these people, supervisors saw how the roles were played out in another organization, and they could ask about the process of personal transition in a forum that was less threatening than their own organization.

Involve Supervisors in Defining the Team Leader Role

To the extent that supervisors participate in the development of the specifics of the team leader role, they feel not only increasing clarity about it, but ownership of it, as in the Kodak example. In the Kansas City division of Allied Signal, a representative supervisors' network has been established to clarify the role in that organization. As more of the organizations are moved to work teams, the supervisors use this net-work as a forum to understand what specific kinds of responsibilities they will pick up over time. Middle managers and general management also use the network meetings as an opportunity to empower those who become team leaders to assume business projects that were previously reserved for more senior managers. These kinds of activities help managers and supervisors understand more specifically what this transition will mean within the fabric of their own organizational culture.

At the American Cyanamid plant in Niagara Falls, Canada, three supervisors were driven off the original design committees by stinging criticism from their peers. Recognizing that something was terribly wrong, culture team leaders invited supervisors to nominate representatives for a new task force commissioned specifically to look at the traditional supervisory job and redesign it. After a slow start, the process worked. The supervisors became fully engaged in the change process. What started out to be a process that disenfranchised supervisors ended up being driven by them. If supervisors are not dealt with properly, they can undermine the entire transformation process.

Not Involving Supervisors Creates a Self-Fulfilling Prophecy

This brings us to another related point. Sometimes supervisors are excluded from the high-performance design and implementation process because teams, unions, or executives fear that they will resist the change. When companies assume that supervisors won't support these changes and exclude them, however, the supervisors become even more resistant because they are not included. It becomes a self-fulfilling prophecy. A better strategy is to include supervisors early.

Supervisors Need to See How Team Leaders Act

These types of clarifying activities are essential to understanding this emerging role. But they are not enough by themselves. Supervisors need to see examples of team leaders in action to fully comprehend this role. Remember the 13 Room experience at Kodak. Perhaps most important to the process of creating role clarity is the presence of viable role models. Not models for others to imitate, but models that clarify and illustrate the visible and invisible elements of effective team leadership.

In the early stages of the transition, tours to other facilities are a common and effective way to expose managers and supervisors to examples of such leaders. Ultimately, however, the organization needs to have its own role models. The "do as I say, not as I do" method of managing people does not work here. As one successful team leader at a high-performance Weyerhaeuser plant put it, "We are this way because our plant manager is this way." Managers at Corning echo the sentiment: "We follow his (the manager's) feet, not his mouth," a group of them told me about the good example of a management team leader who walked his talk. Conversely, another transformation effort just could not get off the ground. I was in the cafeteria one day having lunch with one of the second-level managers and I asked him why the effort was going so sluggishly. He put it succinctly: "We won't change until (the general management team) does. The reason we manage like this is because this is the way we are managed." For other change ideas for each of the four facets of the model, see Table 21.1.

Felt Need

The second facet of the model is felt need. One vice president at Procter & Gamble created a felt need with a thought-provoking letter he sent to several plants in the manufacturing company. The letter stated that the technician work systems had simply outperformed the more traditionally managed operations over the last 15 years. By suggesting that these organizations would replace the traditionally managed ones within the next five years and by requesting retrofit transition plans for traditional plants, the vice president created a felt need in a number of supervisors to transition themselves and their organizations to SDWTs.

For other supervisors, general attempts to create a felt need are not enough. These people need specific personal coaching to help them feel a need to change to the new role. One-on-one discussions with people they respect—a boss, a peer, or a friend—can help supervisors create a need for personal change and prepare an appropriate transition.

I have been told of skilled managers who have had real heart-to-heart discussions with supervisors that focused, for example, on basic assumptions. "Tell me the truth," they might say, "do you really think that your subordinates' ideas are as good as yours?" or, "Why did you say this morning that the team *works for you?* What did you mean by that?" or, "Why do you often say 'I did this' instead of 'We did this'?" Confronting gut-level values is a delicate but useful exercise for developing a felt need to change. Some people use survey data to create an opening for these discussions. We have often seen companies employ 360-degree assessments of team leader effectiveness to this end.

Table 21.1 Helping Supervisors Change into Team Leaders

Clarity	Felt Need	Support	Self Awareness
Set up a task team of managers to design the responsibilities included in the new role.	Have supervisors work closely with senior mentors who are champions of change.	Allay job security fears.	Model behaviors such as recognizing and admitting mistakes.
Establish forums for supervisory role discussions and debates.	Provide one-on-one coaching to focus a personal need to change.	Provide reinforcement through performance discussions, policies, practices, and pay systems.	Create mechanisms for supervisors to solicit feedback from others.
Demystify the role by visiting with other organizations.	Ask questions that allow supervisors to confront their own values and assumptions about other people.	Create mechanisms for peer support like brown-bag lunch sessions for supervisors.	Add team member and peer input to performance appraisal, promotion, and recognition processes.
Create opportunities to highlight good examples of the new role within the organization.	Use survey and interview data to share perceptions of management style and method.	Provide training and tools to support newly required expectations of leaders.	Create opportunities for senior managers to make their own role change progress (warts and all) visible.

Different Supervisors Require Different Approaches

The best way to work with these supervisors to create felt need differs according to their situation. Bill Belgard and Janice Klein have developed a useful management typology for understanding how to deal with different supervisors who are changing into team leaders. Belgard and Klein posit that there are five types of changing supervisors: trailblazers, pilots, intellectuals, late bloomers, and traditionalists. This deserves more discussion.

Trailblazers, Pilots, and Intellectuals

Trailblazers embrace the concept and have probably been practicing it all along. They don't need a lot of help, just a little permission. *Pilots* are the supervisors who know how to get somewhere but need to know where to go. They are cautious at first, and will not be won over without a lot of effort other than the normal vision-sharing and role clarification activities. *Intellectuals*, however, believe they support the concept and they say the right things. But they don't walk the talk. They need strong conversations with their own team leaders or consultants to provide a felt need to do anything different. Their mentors can show them the discrepancies in their behavior and language. "You say this, but do something else," might be the words used with intellectuals.

Late Bloomers and Traditionalists

Late bloomers resist for some time and then change. They require a lot of patience. Often their change comes only after they personally are convinced over a long period of time that there is a better way. Lots of felt need discussions are required here, but eventually they pay off. Late bloomers, in fact, sometimes turn into the strongest supporters later on, much as ex-smokers become more supportive of nonsmoking policies than people who have never smoked. *Traditionalists*, however, won't be won over. They feel the SDWT concept is fundamentally flawed. For traditionalists, discussions to create felt need are not helpful. It is better to find other jobs.

Support

The third facet of team leader role change is support. One important type of support is job reassurance. Companies won't get far with the supervisory role changes if they allow the perception that SDWTs put supervisors at any level out on the street. While it is true that SDWT operations typically require fewer management positions, it is important to create meaningful roles for those who will not have formal team leader assignments. Even if these roles are eliminated via attrition, they are an important way to demonstrate commitment to these people who have often served long and faithfully in traditional assignments. Other supports are needed as well. After team leaders are educated about the new role and their need to change, they need to be supported by their bosses and reinforced by all the policies, procedures, and processes of the organization.

Get Rewards and Recognition Systems in Sync with the New Role

In one unionized plant, several supervisors thought the transition to participative management would be a short-lived fad. When the next rare promotions from first- to second-level management occurred, however, both people promoted were individuals who had strong reputations and demonstrated ability as SDWT managers. Though a few managers still expressed skepticism about the longevity of the change, most acknowledged that demonstrated proficiency as a team leader would be rewarded and supported. Appropriate SDWT leader behaviors should be clearly identified and rewarded if they are to continue.

Supervisors need formal organizational support. Unless reinforcement systems like performance appraisals, promotions, compensation, and other rewards support the emerging role, we send a confusing message about our expectations to the supervisors in the organization. At least one expert's research clearly demonstrates that when support systems do not change, supervisors do not change into team leaders.

In the organization just mentioned, supervisors were told about the changing expectations for their role sometime earlier. Only a few weeks after that, some coincidental promotions were announced, which included two supervisors who had the reputation for being very strong technically, but who exhibited Theory X assumptions and values. Although the promotions were deserved and, in all fairness, had been in the works for a number of months prior to the work with the other supervisors, the juxtaposition of the promotions and the initial discussions with the supervisors was unfortunate and confusing. It wasn't until several months later that the situation was rectified by the new SDWT-consistent promotions.

As a contrasting example, in a number of the P&G facilities undergoing transformation, all team leaders are measured by what is called the "what counts" factors. These factors are performance requirements that are consistent with the expected practices of a high-performance manager. In Lima, part of my raise was determined by the same people who had helped to hire me: the team. This process allowed an institutionalized opportunity for team feedback to the team leader and helped to keep the reward system in sync with the requirements of the work system. A similar idea was recommended by an engineer I interviewed at Intel. Suggesting that numerous problems would be resolved by changing the performance review process typically used in the United States, he said, "Everyone should be reviewed by the customer(s) they support. Managers should get them from the team, and my team should get them from manufacturing. That would help everybody here to remember whom we work for."

Peer Networks Provide a Different Kind of Support

Peer networks are another kind of support that is very useful in team leader transition. In one organization, for example, a group of managers decided to meet once a week for lunch. They called themselves "AA," for Autocrats Anonymous, and used this lunch time to review challenges and share ideas with supportive colleagues. During times of transition, peer networks give people fresh ideas, renewed energy, and support. People come to realize that they are not in this thing alone.

Use Empowerment Schedules to Provide Transition Help

Another important support for transitioning team leaders is some sort of change structure that helps the supervisor track transition milestones. In General Electric's jet engine turbine blade plant in Bromont, Canada, for example, team leaders agree on a schedule of empowerment. This schedule has proven to be a very effective aid to transition. The traditional supervisory responsibilities were listed with a date for when each appropriate responsibility was to be assumed by the team. This provided a much-needed organization for the transition and helped team leaders put together training plans for the teams to prepare them to assume the new responsibilities. This same idea can be used to identify the new tasks and projects to be assumed by team leaders after the empowerment. This will give the leaders something to look forward to and plan for as they develop their teams to assume many of their former responsibilities.

Self-Awareness

The final facet of the role change diamond is self-awareness. As you might suspect, this is not resident in every changing supervisor. It is least common in senior managers who have been protected from personal constructive criticism for years. But it is a weakness that can occur at every level of supervision. Too many supervisors evaluate their own progress by their good intentions rather than by how they are perceived by team members and others (see Figure 21.1).

This facet of the change diamond is more critical than it may appear at first blush. I have worked with numerous supervisors (from lead technicians to vice presidents) who really believed they were effective team leaders even though others did not share that opinion. SDWT progress was halted until these people could recognize and react to others' perceptions. They walked around "naked," as it were, until they began to hear and believe the cries from the bystanders, "The emperor has no clothes!" Self-aware team leaders know that, even if the perceptions of others are incorrect, those perceptions drive behaviors. Thus, the only practical reality is perception. If team members as a whole think you are a traditional manager, for all intents and purposes you are a traditional manager.

This realization is uncommon. In a survey completed in preparation for a Supervisory Congress for all of the managers in Esso Resources, for example, were two interesting questions. One was, "Are you a participative manager?" and another was, "Is your boss a participative manager?" Ironically, only about 30 percent of the people in management

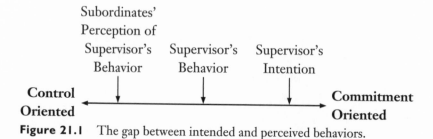

Figure 21.1 The gap between intended and perceived behaviors.

were perceived to be participative by their subordinates although about 70 percent of those same managers wrote that they considered themselves to be participative. Supervisors, like everyone else, are not always self-aware. I know this has been a challenge personally. When I have asked in the past for the consultants I lead to fill out an assessment on my leadership skills, I have been humbled to see that although I receive some very positive feedback, my self-assessment is almost always higher than my team's assessment of my behavior as a leader.

Effective leaders know the truth about how they are perceived and they are not defensive about it. They elicit feedback and take action on it. They also admit mistakes. We saw these behaviors when we visited with Ralph Olney at Kodak, as discussed in earlier chapters. Organizations need to create environments in which it is okay for managers to say they were wrong. In some operations that is career suicide. This must change. Until supervisors are rewarded for candidly admitting their own frailties, an environment of trust and self-awareness is unlikely.

Self-Aware Team Leaders Admit Mistakes Openly

We normally expect our leadership to act consistently with well-publicized elements of their values and vision. But when they act contrary to these and then acknowledge and modify their behavior accordingly, it leaves a lasting impression about the depth of their conviction. After all, even the most well-intentioned supervisor will sometimes fall off of the vision wagon. Those who openly confess and rectify actions that are perceived as incongruent with the stated vision are often actually seen as more authentic and committed to their vision than those who cover up or ignore these unintentional inconsistencies.

People in one company, for example, frequently reference what is now known as "the coffee incident." In this situation, Joe Burger, a management team leader who professed to support significant employee involvement, decreed (seemingly arbitrarily) that there would be no more food of any kind allowed at workstations. Some of the employees in the organization were outraged that Joe had created this policy without first discussing it with them. After they confronted him he acknowledged his error and rectified it. He publicly told this story about himself multiple times, and his team often used the example to demonstrate that he was now truly committed to increasing involvement.

Summary

The role change model applies to team leaders as well as team members. Leaders need role clarity, felt need, support, and self-awareness to change successfully from supervisors to team leaders. The way we work with transitioning supervisors is different depending on whether they are trailblazers, pilots, intellectuals, late bloomers, or traditionalists. But we must work with them even if we are skeptical about their ability to change.

There are a number of important aids to transitioning leaders. These include training programs, modeling, and visits to other sites to clarify the new role. Data and coaching discussions can create a felt need to change roles. Job reassurances let people know that while their responsibilities will change, they won't be laid off because of SDWTs. Delegation schedules help to organize the transition. Consistent reward and recognition systems send the message that this is the way we intend to manage. Peer networks provide emotional support. Mentors provide examples and a safe environment for self-awareness. Supervisors, of course, will be much more supportive of roles they help to define than those they are given by assignment. Early involvement of the supervisors in the implementation process is a key to generating their support of SDWTs. Without their involvement, supervisory resistance become a self-fulfilling prophecy.

Can supervisors change successfully into team leaders? The answer is yes. And organizations have a moral obligation to assist in the transition process even if some supervisors choose eventually not to change. Even though I have never seen this transition process proceed without some supervisory casualties (mostly by self-selection), it is incumbent on team leaders to assist supervisors in the process of their personal role change. Why? Because they are valuable resources. The stakes are high here. Simply put, if supervisors don't become team leaders, you can't have successful self-directed work teams.

In the next chapter we will review a particularly difficult issue relative to team leader transitions. What do you do if your boss is the one having problems changing from a supervisor into a team leader?

Managing Upward: When You Don't Have the Support of Senior Management

"We're creating a hierarchy of ideas. You say, 'This is the right thing to do here,' not 'We're going to do this because I'm boss.' "

Raymond Gilmartin, *CEO of Becton Dickinson*

NANCY IS A management team leader in a large financial services company. Before she came to this company, she worked with a corporation that had used SDWTs successfully for several years. Although she is firmly committed to the SDWT concept, she doubts that someone at her level in the corporation can make any significant dent in the autocratic culture of this place.

Walt is an operations team leader of an SDWT in an auto parts plant. When Maria, the new plant manager, tours the area, she listens to the accomplishments of the customer service team. Although she expresses admiration about the improvements in quality, cost, and speed, she confides in Walt that the team seems a little too independent for her liking.

Can people like Nancy and Walt make a significant difference? There is an old joke about the difference between involvement and commitment. It says that while a chicken is *involved* in producing breakfast, a pig is *committed*. While it is always easy to be involved as a team leader, managers and supervisors are often less enthusiastic about being strongly committed to SDWTs when senior management doesn't champion the concept. Most will opt for the path of the chicken—especially when the perceived outcome of commitment is career suicide.

Orderly Top-Down Change Is More Fiction than Fact

The fact of the matter is that the idealistic notion that championship of the high-performance work culture starts at the top of the corporation and then cascades through the organization in an orderly manner is much more fiction than fact. With the notable exceptions of senior leaders like Stayer at Johnsonville Foods, or Semler at Semco S/A, who launched full-scale transformation efforts from the executive suite, virtually every organization that has implemented SDWTs has done so because of early efforts from the management level of team leaders or from middle-management staff.

SDWTs Start with Champions in the Middle of the Operation

The work at Procter & Gamble, for example, which started in the late 1960s, didn't occur because senior management wanted to change the corporation. It started because plant managers and corporate internal consultants sought ways to reduce labor problems and to improve work flows and processes in the new plants. Union officials and middle-level staff members were key promoters of the SDWT concept at Corning before organization-wide efforts were sponsored from the office of CEO Jamie Houghton. Single facilities in General Foods and Digital Equipment Corporation used SDWTs primarily because facility managers like Lyman Ketchum of General Foods and Bruce Dillingham of DEC wanted to see it happen. The same stories have been repeated at General Electric, Cummins Engine, and elsewhere.

Generally speaking, there does need to be sponsorship of the idea at the culture team leader level for the particular unit to be changed. However, this is usually the plant manager or regional manager level of general management, not the vice president or other senior-level personnel. While it is true that the idea for this alternative management technology must eventually take root at a high enough level of formal authority (where culture-changing action can take place), the SDWT seeds are usually planted lower in the organization by people with limited hierarchical power.

Change Influencers Versus Change Drivers

A number of people play a significant role in the evolution of organizations who do not have the formal authority to personally drive a transformation of this magnitude. These individuals focus their energy on influencing rather than sponsoring the management change. As change influencers, they can affect the change process from almost any level of the organization regardless of their personal authority base.

Naturally the buck stops with the person in power. It would be unrealistic to suggest that change influencers can impact change efforts if those at the top of the organization refuse to accept their ideas. It is equally unrealistic, though, to suggest that top-level managers will never listen to or act upon the ideas brought to them by middle- and lower-level management. Unfortunately, it is often the perception of those in the middle that "their hands are tied"—that what they have to say cannot make a difference. This is simply not true.

How Do Change Influencers Act?

The manner in which the change influencer operates is difficult to characterize. To a casual outside observer it would appear that he or she initiates a series of loosely coupled activities that have little strategic or systematic orientation. Specific actions here might include conversations in the parking lot or local coffee shop, informal networking, making presentations, phone calls, lobbying, and occasional blank stares.

Although to all outward appearances change influencers may seem to be operating in a state of chaos, randomly thrashing about as they attempt to get their ideas heard, there is a method to their madness. They focus their time and energy on three activities:

1. They create a vision of the future state.
2. They take advantage of every opportunity to discuss their vision.
3. They tenaciously support processes that facilitate vision implementation and discourage processes that inhibit it.

It boils down to three things: vision, opportunity, and tenacity.

Vision, Opportunity, and Tenacity

Let's walk through how Nancy might influence change at her corporation. Once she is clear in her own mind about what self-directed work teams are and why they are needed in the organization, she then takes advantage of opportunities to make her case heard. Some of these opportunities to discuss the vision are planned, such as meetings in which she can influence the agenda; others are unplanned, such as meeting a key executive in the parking lot, in which cases she can "leverage serendipity."

If Nancy is prepared and sufficiently skilled, she will be able to take advantage of both kinds of opportunities. If you follow influential team leaders around, for example, you will find that they spend precious little time doing the activities that the leaders often use to describe their responsibilities, such as planning or formal training. Most of their time, as shown in studies by John Kotter and others, is spent taking advantage of chance occurrences to further their goals. Change influencers carry around their agendas in their heads, including a list of the people they need to talk to, ideas on how to approach these people in conversation, and a vision of a better future for the business. These unplanned opportunities are what makes the influencing process look so imprecise. The precision and rationale for the seemingly unrelated activities are integrated by the internal work agenda of the change influencer. While the process is certainly not linear or systematic, it is highly rational.

The final cluster of activities relates to simple tenacity. The vision communication process is fraught with frustration, resistance, and passive neglect because the change influencer does not have enough personal authority to make SDWTs happen on his or her own. But change influencers persist until critical mass is reached, and then they apply their creative tenacity fully to the implementation process. The path is described by most as frustrating and boring at the same time, but in the end, a clear, well-crafted vision with compelling business advantages often wins over skeptics.

Change Influencers Are Politically Astute

A note of caution is that change influencers must temper their persistence with politics. By behaving with tenacity, change influencers display their commitment to the vision they are advocating. But change influencers are politically astute and they are sensitive about what behaviors are appropriate in their organizations. They recognize that if they alienate the change drivers with the way they present the vision (pounding tables, demanding credit for the change, blaming people for doing things the way they do them now, etc.), they will strangle the initiative they are so passionate about implementing. They tend to operate with a kind of calculated audacity. When obstacles appear, they search for new paths. They seem to recognize intuitively that the path to cultural transformation is crooked and unpredictable. They adapt, change directions, and explore new alternatives with ease.

Case Study

Let's review how change influencers act by looking at a case study. The organization is a medium-size high-tech company located in the western United States, where managers and staff members with limited hierarchical power were able to influence the creation of SDWTs in significant parts of the corporation through vision, opportunity, and tenacity.

Change influencers realized early on that they would need to get the support of change drivers who had legitimate authority and could authorize the significant support system changes required for the effective implementation of SDWTs. Although the process of influencing the drivers was much more enigmatic and disorganized than it will appear in this account, the activities did fall into the three activity clusters.

Vision

For the vision activity cluster, the change influencers first had to clearly articulate a compelling, business-driven vision of an attractive future. They began by getting together in a network meeting open to anyone interested in the SDWT idea. The meetings soon filled with managers and staff members who had interest in the concept, but who had insufficient organizational clout to create the change on their own. As a collective, though, the group had access to several change drivers. The network served as a forum for coalescing the shared experience of the body into a collective vision, which was captured in a visioning tool with behavioral statements along a continuum of employee involvement from low involvement to semiautonomous work teams. The tool identified key SDWT characteristics and provided a vehicle for discussion of the concept that allowed the change drivers to participate in the creation and ownership of the emerging vision of greatness for several divisions of the corporation.

Opportunity

Once the vision was emerging, the change influencers looked for opportunities to make the vision salient. "People Involvement Network" meetings continued to provide a forum for discussion of the SDWT concepts and applications. A workshop was developed to share the emerging vision with people across the organization, and change drivers participated in the beginning and closing of the workshop. Change influencers also invited a consultant to make a presentation to the senior managers, and the presentation excited and focused the change drivers. In an unplanned leveraging of serendipity, the senior operations officer of the company introduced a four-pronged program to improve the company that included "People Involvement" as one of the four key initiatives. Change influencers lobbied heavily to be the ones to define the emerging initiative, and in so doing made an instant champion of the executive.

Tenacity

Even though the SDWT ideas began to take root in various parts of the organization, tenacity was required to institutionalize the fragile transformation. From time to time mid-level management made presentations to keep senior management up to speed, to ask senior managers to set certain examples, or to break down certain barriers to effective implementation. Reward systems, performance appraisals, and job descriptions were refocused, and each required a herculean effort in addition to the already vigorous demands of the workplace. As results started improving, the transition became easier.

The SDWTs never permeated the entire company. At the time of this writing, there are still no corporations of that size with self-direction across an entire operation. But what started out as the dream of a handful of mid-level change influencers became the preferred way of managing in major portions of the organization. Among other things, the SDWTs were credited with saving one of the divisions that had been incapable of competing. This division became the most profitable in the company, and hundreds of jobs were spared.

What If the New Boss Is Unsupportive of SDWTs?

While this case is helpful to the team leader who is trying to get SDWTs moving in an operation for the first time, what do you do if the teams are already established but your boss isn't a supporter? What could somebody like Walt, the customer service team leader, do if his new culture team leader was unsupportive of self-direction?

This is not a hypothetical question. At P&G, new plant and brand managers have been transferred into SDWT facilities for more than four decades. Team members and team leaders alike have experienced some trauma over these transitions, because the new transferees are often "high-potential" managers with track records as aggressive traditional supervisors. But in the vast majority of these cases, the new team leaders would leave the facilities as SDWT supporters even though they may have been skeptics when they arrived. What changed?

Being Results Oriented Versus Control Oriented

What usually changes is that team leaders personally experience results that are unobtainable in the traditional paradigm of management. The experience convinces them over time. They are smart and practical people. But this is still a difficult personal change process for most. As mentioned in an earlier chapter, while current wisdom suggests that most traditional supervisors are just too results oriented to mess around with this touchy-feely SDWT stuff, the truth is that most traditionalists are not results oriented enough. They value control more than results. When the senior team leaders come to understand that their own personal desire to control things gets in the way of better results, they have a choice to make. Results or control? A lot of them choose results. How can change influencers aid this process?

Typically, team leaders who are effective at managing upward display a few common characteristics. They:

1. Take risks.
2. Keep leaders informed.
3. Create heroes.

Each of these deserves some elaboration.

Dare Greatly

Traditional organizations have usually created supervisors who are risk averse. In operations dominated by hierarchical decision making and problem solving, supervisors are wary of doing anything that would potentially tarnish their relationship with superiors. Thus they conform. They don't challenge superiors and they pretty much espouse the party line. That is the safe approach. Effective change influencers, however, take personal career risks. They dare greatly. Although they are sensitive to the political realities of their situation, they are more apt to gently confront their superiors' doubts about SDWTs. Walt is unlikely to influence his new manager if he doesn't do this. Why should she change her opinion about SDWTs if she has no reason to?

Thus Walt might say to the new culture team leader:

> **Maria, if you're anything like I was when we first changed over to these SDWTs, you're thinking that this place is pretty weird. But these teams really seem to work. Why don't you come over to one of the customer service team meetings next week sometime, and we'll give you a presentation on what we're doing. I'd like you to meet the team. I think you'll be impressed.**

Change influencers don't normally use an in-your-face, highly argumentative approach to convince executives that SDWTs are the way to go. Nor do they spend time getting permission from senior officers to continue empowerment. Instead, they get on with the business of using SDWTs to accomplish extraordinary results. They demonstrate the effectiveness of the nontraditional management paradigm. They get results. And they don't back away from the SDWT way of doing things as an automatic reaction to the new leader's hesitations. Is it risky? Yes. But it has been done successfully in companies like P&G, Apple Computer, and Weyerhaeuser for years.

Working with Resistance from the Senior Levels

More difficult is the situation in which new leaders have been in the operation for a while, and you find that they are intellectuals, late bloomers, or traditionalists. Exposure and experience alone don't seem to be changing their feelings about SDWTs. How do you address this situation? Sometimes, of course, there isn't much you can do. If the person is a full-blown traditionalist, it is better to wait for the next new manager. But I have seen this situation dealt with very effectively where the senior manager was an intellectual or a late bloomer.

Commit to the Success of the Leader

One of my colleagues, for example, is very skilled at doing this. He normally opens up the conversion by asking something like, "Pierre, what is it that you want that you don't already have?" When Pierre says he wants this improvement or that improvement, my colleague commits to helping him get it through the SDWTs. I have seen him do this with equal effectiveness both as a team leader and as an external consultant. My colleague also tells his counterpart that he wants to do everything possible to ensure the success of the operation, including giving Pierre feedback about what the others in the operation need from him to accomplish the improvements. This is where "daring greatly" comes in. "Pierre," my colleague says, "I know that a lot of senior managers never get feedback about how they are perceived by subordinates. I would like to have a deal with you that I will give you that information straight. Are you interested?"

Make the Deal to Share Feedback

If Pierre takes the deal, you have an agreement to share personal observations and feedback from the teams with him. This kind of feedback can be very motivating to the senior manager if it is delivered skillfully. It can help him change. If he doesn't take the deal, however, the relationship with him may be very awkward and uncomfortable from this point on. That's the risk. Some fascinating psychology is at work here. The phenomenon, called *cognitive dissonance*, works something like this. If Pierre takes the deal he will think, "I'm a smart guy. I just agreed to let this team leader give me feedback. So this team leader must also be a smart guy. I'm going to listen to him." Taking the risk may actually raise your credibility with the more senior manager.

No Surprises

The second thing team leaders do to manage upward is share information. One of the important unwritten rules of management is, "Never surprise your boss." Effective change influencers are particularly sensitive about this. They are very good at keeping change drivers informed about the accomplishments and decisions of the teams. Whenever possible, they create firsthand interaction with the senior team leaders and the team members themselves. Something about this personal experience is much more powerful than the secondhand information that is typical in traditional operations (memos, staff meeting reports, etc.). One of the reasons P&G plant managers were usually won over to the SDWT concepts was that they regularly toured each team area to hear presentations about team accomplishments. These tours occurred at least once a month, often with a visiting dignitary from corporate headquarters. Nothing can replace the impact of hearing something with your own ears.

Keeping the boss informed of team decisions is especially important. In traditional operations senior managers always know the decisions because they always make them. But in an SDWT operation, where decisions are being made continuously at all levels, it is easy for managers to feel as though they are out of the loop. For traditional managers, this is the worst possible place to be. It makes them want to institutionalize controls that give them better visibility of things. To address this issue, many operations hold sitewide operations meetings every day. These meetings are collections of representatives from each work area who normally are appointed by their peers to represent them in the meeting. The job is rotated regularly (about every six months to a year) to give everyone who wants to serve in this capacity a chance to do so. While the primary purpose of the meetings is to coordinate issues affecting multiple teams, an ancillary benefit is that managers gain real-time access to the changing issues and problems of the workplace. This creates a higher degree of comfort and allows the managers to release control.

Make Heroes

Finally, the third thing change influencers are very good at is making their bosses heroes when things go right. They realize that credit for team accomplishments is shared by everyone who helps (including the team leaders). Recently I saw members of a Weyerhaeuser pulp mill team talk to another group of team leaders about how important their mill manager has been in the changeover to SDWT. They extolled his virtues fairly extensively. Even though he wasn't there at the time, I know that this message got back to him. And I suspect that this positive reinforcement makes him feel good about his role in the mill.

Some change influencers have obtained major speaking engagements at conferences or universities for their senior managers to talk about what the teams have done. Others set up benchmarking and customer visits to their sites and enlist the managers in appropriate hosting and presentation roles. Still others find ways to have the managers interviewed for the corporate or community press as appropriate. While care should be taken not to transfer the credit for the work accomplishments back to the managers and away from the teams (that is the same old traditional stuff again), appropriate exposure gives the managers positive reinforcement for being team leaders instead of supervisors. It does another thing as well. The more a senior manager tells other people about how great the teams are, the more he or she tends to believe it. It is that cognitive dissonance idea in action again.

Summary

Orderly top-down transitions from traditional workplaces to high-performance work systems are extremely rare. These transitions are usually the result of a middle-up effort, in which management-level team leaders or staff members plant SDWT seeds for some time before the official champion comes on board. Since these people have no formal authority to institute high-performance work systems, however, they are change influencers rather than change drivers. They influence change drivers like the culture team leader of a plant or hospital (some moderately autonomous site) to champion the changes. Their efforts seem to fall into three activity clusters. Change influencers work on creating a vision for a better future, they create planned and unplanned opportunities to communicate their vision to the change drivers, and they display the tenacity to stick with it until their objectives are achieved.

Once the change is under way, however, it is especially difficult when your own team leader is unsupportive of self-direction. In some cases, the only solution is to wait until someone else comes along. But in other circumstances, daring greatly, keeping the leader informed, and creating heroes can influence significant change in the organization.

In the next chapter we will look at another difficult problem in the team-based organization. What do you do when it seems like no one is accountable?

Creating Accountability Systems for Teams

"No leader can possibly have all the answers ... The actual solutions about how best to meet the challenges of the moment have to be made by the people closest to the action ... The leader has to find the way to empower these front line people, to challenge them, to provide them with the resources they need, and then to hold them accountable."

Steve Miller, *Group Managing Director of Royal Dutch/Shell*

"OUR DILEMMA IS that everyone, and, therefore, no one is responsible," said a manager who was struggling to make teams work in his operation. "The reason I don't believe in the team concept," confided another manager, "is that there is no accountability in teams. You always need a single manager to be accountable for getting results." Although a lot of us disagree that only managers can be accountable, my experience suggests that part of what these managers say is valid. Only individuals, not groups, can be accountable.

In far too many cases, well-intentioned leaders assume that achieving high performance simply means delegating the management accountability for the day-to-day business to the team as a whole (as in "the team is now responsible for this," or "the team will solve that problem"). That doesn't work. This problem is more complicated than the management abdication issue discussed in earlier chapters. Even if the team leader empowers people and trains them properly, inattention to accountability systems can cause confusion and reduced results. Without specific individual clarity on who is responsible for what by when, team members are unable to monitor and coordinate their efforts.

If Everyone Is Responsible, Then No One Is Responsible

For those who think this is contradictory to the primary message of this book, let me explain with some illustrations. Some time ago, I heard about some research that was done on tug-of-war contests. Apparently the study showed that people would exert less personal pull (up to 14 percent less) when pulling on the rope with other people than when pulling by themselves. Reduced personal effort in a group setting such as this is common enough that it actually has a name. The experts call it *social loafing* or *diffusion of responsibility*. What happens in these situations? In many group settings everyone assumes that someone else will pick up the slack for him or her. Conversely, if I am pulling alone, then I and I alone am clearly and visibly accountable for my own success or failure.

Social Loafing

This sounds true to me. What else would explain the odd and painful reality we often see when groups—sometimes even large groups—fail to respond to calls of help from a crime victim? Sometimes crowds will stand and observe a crime rather than intervene. Surely these groups know they could minimize personal injury to any one individual by combining their efforts against the attacker, but instead they too often wait for someone else—the police or a hero—to do the job. In these unfortunate situations no one accepts personal accountability to take action.

Fortunately this doesn't happen in all group settings. Effective sports and business teams somehow motivate people to increase rather than decrease individual effort. Studies of collective farms in Israel, for example, show that in some situations the collectives actually produce more than the total output when the farms were individually run. How do they do this? What allows individuals associated with large groups to feel personally accountable and overcome the tendency to social loafing? I believe that an important part of the answer to this question is that these operations have effective accountability systems.

Creating this sense of accountability requires a clear understanding of what each person is personally responsible for. Each individual must agree to accept those responsibilities. Then and only then is affiliation with a group a multiplier instead of a divider of personal effort.

Accountability Systems Shouldn't Be Used to Punish

Before we discuss the nuts and bolts of building team accountability systems, I would like to explain what I mean by accountability. There are two considerations to review. First, I am not as concerned as some people are about making distinctions between the words *responsibility* and *accountability*. While scholars may argue the differences, I will tend to use the words interchangeably. What is really important here, I think, is the *feeling* of being accountable. Whether people say, "I am accountable for this" or "I am responsible for this" is less important than whether their behavior indicates that they accept the ownership for ensuring results in a particular endeavor. Accountable people act like they have a mission, not a job.

Second (and more important), for purposes of our discussion I will not use *accountability* as a synonym for *culpability* (as in "Who is accountable for this mess?" or "Find the accountable party and sue them!"). Some organizations think of accountability systems as the method for determining who to blame when things go bad. This creates fear and makes people less willing to use the system. The most effective team leaders see the system instead as a process for clarifying responsibility and facilitating ownership. Although this clarification is a necessary prerequisite for coaching when people fail to accomplish the results for which they have responsibility, these systems are put in place to avoid failure and disciplinary action, not to facilitate it. If anything, a good accountability system should focus primarily on how to identify areas, individuals, and teams that warrant celebration and positive acknowledgement.

Accountability Systems

Teams use a variety of methods to identify areas of accountability for individual members. The best teams consider both task and business result accountabilities. First let's discuss specific task accountabilities.

Task Accountability

Task accountabilities clarify who is responsible for various projects or activities. Each person should know what he or she is responsible for and how his or her responsibilities fit with the assignments of others on the team. Some responsibilities may be common to all team members. Each person, for example, may be personally accountable for acting in a safe manner or for supporting team decisions. Other accountabilities may be very different from person to person. Bob, for example, may lead one project while Mary leads another one. Good teams put a system in place that helps people understand both the long-term task accountabilities and the short-term, day-to-day ones.

These accountability systems don't need to be elaborate. They can be as simple as a checklist or chart. But there are two criteria a system must meet to be effective: (1) it should be visible to all team members, and (2) it must be followed up on.

A Task Accountability System in a Consulting Firm

For example, in our consulting group we have an annual team strategy meeting to negotiate our roles and responsibilities for the year. Using a team tool we have developed to organize our discussions, we clarify accountabilities that are shared and post the key individual task accountabilities for each team member on chart pad sheets around the room. By the end of the meeting(s) everyone knows what the key assignments are, who is leading what projects, what the core responsibilities are for each individual, and what cross-training is projected to be completed during the year. These agreements are renegotiated during the year as necessitated by personnel changes, shifts in project priorities, or new business needs.

We also keep a notebook on the table of our team room for assigning and recording the short-term day-to-day accountabilities. There are sheets in the book divided into three columns. The first column is headed "Who," the second is headed "What," and the third is headed "When." Each time we make a team decision, we write down who will do what by when to implement that decision (see Figure 23.1). For example, if we decide to modify part of a training program, we would jointly determine who would call what customers, who would do what research, who would do what development work, who would do what graphics work, who would come up with marketing strategies, and so forth. This is duly noted in the notebook.

We review the notebook regularly as part of team meetings and each person gives a public accounting of his or her assignments due on that day. There is no intention to embarrass or to blame, although we are all reluctant to have to explain why a particular assignment went unfilled in front of our team members. Why? Because the system makes us feel accountable to do the things we said we would do.

Before we had the notebook, we discovered that lots of things were falling through the cracks. But now the notebook makes it unnecessary for hierarchical intervention to assign or follow up on our responsibilities. The process works as long as we retain the discipline to use it.

WHO	WHAT	BY WHEN

Figure 23.1 A simple task accountability system.

Results Accountability

Empowering leaders also share accountability for business success with team members. More than task delegation, shared accountability for results creates a feeling of real partnership. In traditional organizations, employees often feel that management is solely responsible for results. Conversely, many of the improvements that come from high-performance organizations stem from everyone feeling personally responsible for business outcomes.

The Star Point System

Some possible areas of business results accountability might include things like customer satisfaction, training, productivity, cost reduction, project velocity, quality improvement, and so forth. Although there are several nonauthoritarian methods for assigning business accountability, one of the most popular is the star system, which is based on a simple but powerful idea originated by Jay Galbraith. Galbraith suggested that the key elements of an organization are all interrelated but can be separately identified as points on a star (see example in Figure 23.2). This

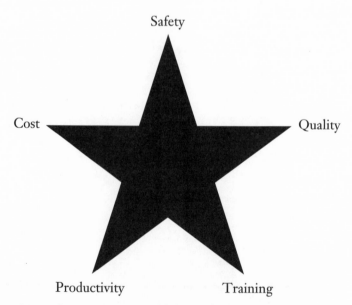

Figure 23.2 A star point accountability system.

system has been expanded and widely used by consultants like Michael Donovan and others.

Importantly, using a star as a way to graphically display these key areas of accountability forces the team to identify only a few important result areas (a star typically has five but no more than seven points). This keeps the focus on the most important results and minimizes the diffusion of effort that can hobble organizations.

A Star Point System at Cummins Engine

A Cummins Engine small truck engine plant in Indiana, for example, uses a star point system to create accountability for key business results areas like safety, quality, cost, efficiency of the production system, and so on. Each team determines who its star point representatives will be. Star point representatives meet weekly to solve problems, communicate new information, review the status of various projects related to their star points, and share best practices. They then take their information and assignments back to the production teams they represent.

Each star point meeting is built into the production schedule, with one meeting on Monday afternoon, another on Tuesday afternoon, and so forth. This ensures that coverage is always available for the star point activities.

Each team of star points has a star point advisor who is usually an expert in that particular area. These advisors are managers or engineers responsible for coordinating the activities of the star points. But, like all good team leaders, these advisors facilitate rather than direct the star point teams. It is the team of representatives and not management that is responsible for dealing with the issues associated with the star point areas. If, for example, corporate headquarters required a strategy for reducing operating expenses for this facility, the cost star point representatives would develop the strategy. To ensure maximum involvement and participation, star point assignments are rotated on a regular basis (about every one to two years, depending on the assignment and the team's ability to rotate). Thus, over time, every employee will serve as a star point representative and most will rotate through all star point assignments over their careers.

Goals and Measures Are Essential

For accountability systems to be effective, there is still one more thing to consider. Essential to both task and results accountability are (1) goals (What do we want to accomplish?) and (2) measures (How will we know we accomplished it? How will we track progress?). But simply saying, "We need to keep the customer satisfied," is not enough. Good goals are:

- Specific (e.g., 5 percent improvement in our customer satisfaction index)
- Measurable (i.e., based on real business results used throughout the organization)
- Challenging (i.e., difficult enough that people feel motivated to "stretch")
- Realistic (i.e., achievable enough that team members make an attempt)

Assuming that a good customer satisfaction survey process is in place, a better customer satisfaction goal would be, "We will improve our customer satisfaction survey numbers to 99 percent by year end."

Summary

For accountability systems to be effective, they must use goals and measures. The best teams have systems both for results accountabilities (for example, the star point accountability system) and for short- and long-term task accountabilities. These systems are used to teach, coordinate, and empower, not to punish people. Without these accountability systems, teams can be prone to social loafing and dilution of responsibilities, which will degrade organizational results.

In the next chapter we will focus on another common and significant barrier to high performance: what do you do when the organizational structure itself needs to be redesigned?

When the Problem Is the Organization: Redesigning for Teams

"If you always do what you always did you'll always get what you always got." .

Irish proverb

ALTHOUGH MANY OF the common problems team leaders run into can be resolved through better personal interaction with team members, there is a whole category of problems that can only be resolved through a fundamental restructuring of an organization. We have already talked about the importance of redesigning reward systems, job responsibilities and titles, management levels, performance appraisals, and other systems and processes to make them consistent with high-performance work systems. If governance systems don't require employee involvement, the jobs are inconsistent with self-directed work team principles, or important sitewide communication infrastructure is missing, the organization needs to be redesigned. In previous chapters we have discussed *what* needs to be redesigned to limit the inappropriate constraints of traditional hierarchy and bureaucracy. In this chapter I would like to review *how* to redesign in such a way that both the outcomes of the redesign process and the means used to obtain them are consistent with self-directed work teams.

Why Redesign?

Like the proverb that opens this chapter suggests, continuing to use traditional structures and processes will always give you traditional results. Hoping you'll get self-directed work team results without creating self-directed work teams and the reinforcement systems they need is like hoping corn will grow from carrot seeds. Please don't misinterpret what I'm saying here. Changing leadership behavior alone can create tremendous empowerment. Barrier busting and boundary management tasks can make a big difference even inside traditional work systems. We have all had leaders who, because of their personal style alone, have involved us in decisions and made us feel like true partners in the operation. But what happens when such a leader leaves and the replacement isn't so inclined? Empowerment based on management style is fragile and often temporary. Redesign puts an infrastructure into the operation that makes it less vulnerable to the style preferences of individual managers. It designs empowerment systems and processes that will be used as a substitution for hierarchy.

Consider some examples. One high-tech firm said it wanted a team-based organization, but its performance appraisal system forced managers to rank all team members in a numerical order. The order affected pay, with top-ranked team members receiving larger raises than lower-ranked employees. This broke down the collaborative team spirit and made the team members reluctant to help each other lest it affect their relative ranking. In another operation managers said they believed in empowerment, but employees were skeptical because the primary decisions continued to be made in staff meetings where there was no permanent employee representation.

Some organizations have traditional jobs that limit the contribution of the workforce. Other organizations have financial authorization policies based on rank rather than on work assignment. In one such organization, a project engineer was required to get a senior manager's signature on a large project expenditure. Although the expense was already budgeted and had been agreed on by everyone involved at the early stages of the project, it exceeded the engineer's signature authority. Engineering and operations leadership were out of the facility that day, and so the only person of the necessary rank available to sign was the director of human resources. I asked the director later what she knew about the project. "Nothing," she confided. "All that authorization policy accomplishes is reinforcing the hierarchy and slowing down project activity." It was clearly inconsistent with the self-directed work team philosophy espoused by leadership. Examples like this are legion. In these cases certain policies, systems, and structures of the organization need to be modified to support team-based operations. Sometimes minor tweaks aren't enough. The entire operation may need to be evaluated and changed.

Let's review some high-performance work system redesign methodologies and also introduce a new organizational structure that is sometimes a product of these redesigns. We call this structure a *learning lattice*.

Organization Redesign

Let's consider some redesign examples. The Santa Clara division of Hewlett-Packard designs and produces test and measurement devices such as oscilloscopes. The organizational structure the division used well into the nineties was very effective for a while, but it was inconsistent with the high-performance work system culture employees wanted to deploy in their operation. The functional silos that had helped them to develop their technical expertise eventually caused people to focus on what was best for the function instead on what was best for the customers. The level of true employee participation varied from manager to manager. And, at the same time the integration of various technical and production specialties was becoming more important for the successful introduction of new products or the resolution of thorny business problems, the structure made integration difficult. People had more allegiance to jobs and functions than to business effectiveness. They decided that they would have to redesign.

Another organization made a similar decision but for different reasons. A large Chevron oil refinery on the Gulf Coast used many of the behaviors of a high-performance work system already, but wanted to institutionalize them. A benchmarking survey confirmed that other refineries were moving to high-performance systems, and corporate leadership supported the effort. Partway through the redesign effort, a hurricane temporarily shut down the facility. This reinforced the resolve of refinery employees and management to create systems and structures that allowed them to work every day in the manner the storm teams did during the recovery effort. During that time, people flowed to the work instead of feeling limited by job description or level. Decisions were made by the people directly involved rather than by others up and out of the operation. Information flowed through the organization freely. Teams worked closely together on clear common goals without regard to rank, function, or other distinctions. The employees determined to change their organization to reflect this way of working with each other.

Both the refinery and the test and measurement division wanted to redesign. The division decided to use a redesign method known as the STS or socio-technical system approach. The original structure had traditional R&D, engineering, manufacturing, marketing, and support services organizations. Employees at the division put together a design team of employees and managers to evaluate the effectiveness of that structure. They did analysis, gathered data, and then came back with a recommendation to redesign the operation into something else. The refinery used a hybrid approach. There, employees used conferences to involve large numbers of people in the analysis phase of the redesign and then used smaller cross-representational teams for design and implementation work. Although a detailed discussion of these common redesign methods is far beyond the scope of this single chapter, a brief review will highlight some key points.

Redesign Methods

Unlike many of the reengineering efforts that have swept across North American organizations over the last several years, the methods we will discuss of redesigning organizations into high-performance work systems are participative and democratic. They also have a better track record. They have been used for several decades and proven in a variety of organizations ranging from mines to hospitals. Redesign is not done by senior management nor by external consultants, but rather by the workers themselves, who must implement the results of their efforts.

The STS Redesign Approach

The first method is called the socio-technical system (STS) approach. It is rooted in the early work of Eric Trist, Fred Emery, and others in the Tavistock Institute located near London, as already mentioned. There are two groups of people important to this approach. The first group is called the *steering team*. This team is composed of senior managers (and union officials in organized settings). Charged with leading the effort and authorizing the final design, this team provides boundary conditions, allocates resources, and commissions the design team. The *design team* is the second group. This team is composed of representatives from the operation to be designed. Normally numbering about 8 to 10 people, this group is set up in proportion to the people it represents, with fewer management representatives than employee representatives. The design team thus involves the actual people who will have to live with the final design of their work system.

The design team goes through a three-step analytical process. In another departure from the reengineering processes that tend to place the emphasis primarily on cost reduction and work process simplification, this analysis balances the needs of the business, the employees, and the technologies. The first step is to evaluate the business requirements for the design. Called the *environmental scan*, this step surfaces customer and corporate requirements, competitive information, and financial goals. In the second and third steps the design team completes the social and technical scans. The *social scan* identifies the employee issues that need to be considered and the *technical scan* evaluates the technical constraints, problems, and opportunities.

Armed with this analysis, the team recommends a new organization design, generally including new team compositions, reporting relationships, and support systems and processes. Special emphasis is given to balancing the requirements of the environmental, social, and technical systems. Adapting the work of Joyce Ranney, my colleague Lois Bruss and I have developed a sequence of redesign steps as a suggested approach for redesigning after the analysis is complete (see Figure 24.1).

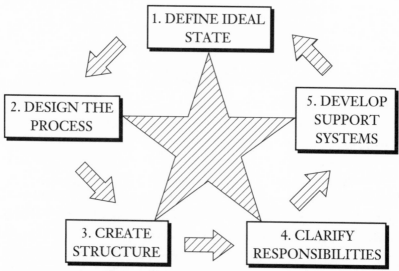

Figure 24.1 The Bruss-Fisher redesign process.
Adapted from the work of Joyce Ranney.

By using the STS method, the Santa Clara division of HP came up with a different organization that was more customer focused and team oriented. The design team's recommendation was to dissolve the functional silos and reorganize the division into two customer segments with workers in each segment now reporting to a business leader instead of a technical leader. A functional manager still exists in each business, but that leader's role is to maintain technical excellence, not to manage a specialty area.

Dennis McNulty, an organization development manager with the operation, reports that business improvements followed the redesign. But he also notes that simply putting people into the new structures doesn't work well. Employees need to be trained in how to operate in the newly designed high-performance work system. Leadership training is especially useful.

The Conference Method

The STS method is well established and has been used successfully for decades. But in the nineties several organizations found the method too lengthy and not participative enough. Another approach was developed. This second way to do work redesign is the Conference Method used by R.R. Donnelley & Sons, Weyerhaeuser, and numerous others. Although the Conference Method uses many of the tools developed for the STS approach, consultants Dick and Emily Axelrod have created it as a way to both involve more people and accelerate the effort. There are a number of other accelerated design methodologies, including those developed by Bill Pasmore and the Participative Design approach developed by Fred and Merrilyn Emery. For sake of brevity, however, we will focus primarily on the Conference Method.

This method uses a series of conferences with wide employee participation. The conferences are generally attended by up to 40 percent of the employee population. Every employee is encouraged to attend at least one conference.

In these conferences large numbers of employees see data and make decisions through the heavy use of small subgroups of about 10 people each. Highlights of the subgroup work are shared with the conference participants. The conferences are planned and facilitated by a logistics team composed of cross-representatives of employees from the organization to be redesigned.

The first conference focuses on vision and incorporates many of the social scan activities modified for use with large numbers of people. The second conference, called the *customer conference*, covers the environment scan analysis and allows a large group of employees to hear customer expectations directly from customers themselves. The third conference includes the technical scan activities. After these first three conferences are completed, the remaining conferences focus on redesign and implementation activities.

The Hybrid Method

The refinery discussed earlier in the chapter found the idea of the conferences very compelling as a way to shorten the analytical process and get more employee involvement. But employees were concerned that using a design conference would force the participants in the 1200-person refinery to come up with a design that would not be detailed enough to be implemented. They decided instead to use a hybrid of the STS and the Conference Method. Developed by Mareen Fisher and me, the hybrid approach includes a large group of employees in the first three conferences. But the actual design is completed by a small, cross-representational design team as in the STS approach. This allows the design team more time than a two- to three-day conference to develop a robust design alternative. Although the refinery decided to have the design team come up with the final design, this approach normally suggests that the design team come up with two to three design alternatives that can be shared at a special design review conference. In this conference, employees would debate the relative merits of the different designs and then select the final alternative.

Organizations that have used this approach at Weyerhaeuser, Chevron, and other locations report that this process facilitates widespread involvement and also allows for more progressive, detailed, and implementable designs.

The Learning Lattice Organization

Organizations that redesign themselves using methods like those just described typically create team-based operations with dramatically increased employee involvement. For example, some redesign teams create employee representative governance councils—decision-making bodies that substitute for traditional hierarchical structures such as general management staff groups. Others institutionalize information sharing or problem-solving activities that facilitate teams. Many companies now also create the types of accountability systems mentioned in the previous chapter as part of the redesign. It is common to change from structures that emphasize tasks—such as functional silos—to organizations that emphasize purpose—such as business teams, customer teams, cross-functional project teams, and so on.

In its redesign, the Chevron refinery created some special senior leadership jobs designated *strategic business managers*. Prior to redesign, the leaders managed technical, operations, or maintenance staff. Now, however, they focus on specific strategy accomplishments—like cost reduction or environmental safeguards—involving people from a variety of disciplines. The design calls for these business managers to have no direct reports. They facilitate and influence cross-functional groups rather than direct a single function. Those in a position called *area team leader* still provide leadership for the employee teams, but this design changes the focus from dealing with functional activities to meeting strategic objectives that are cross-functional in nature. It also takes out a level of management and reduces the emphasis on hierarchy.

Each of these redesign structures has benefits and drawbacks. To address some of the common drawbacks associated with cross-functional organization designs, some companies have come up with an interesting solution. Let me explain.

As a result of a redesign process, organizations like the Port of Seattle, Hewlett-Packard, and others have created what we call *learning lattice* organizations. When drawn on paper, these organizational structures look like the lattices used for garden supports or privacy screens (see Figure 24.2). Hence the name "learning lattice." Unlike the matrix-type organization popular in the 1980s, the lattice organization doesn't have the worker reporting to multiple organizations. In a matrix organization, for example, an engineer might have a direct reporting relationship to a manager of engineering with a secondary "dotted-line" reporting relationship to the division the engineer usually supports. The engineer would be expected to receive work direction and coaching from both managers.

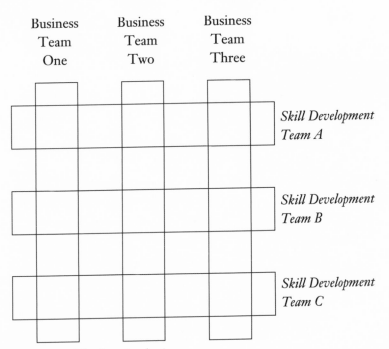

Figure 24.2 The learning lattice.

The learning lattice organization, on the other hand, has employees reporting to only one organization—normally a cross-functional team—for consistency of work direction. But the learning lattice organization provides a supplementary team of similar professionals that work together for developmental purposes.

The learning lattice organization was pioneered by Esso Petroleum, a Canadian petrochemical giant, in its early work redesigns in the 1980s. Esso was trying to balance the contradictory demands of full integration of technical specialists into the business without diluting the technical proficiency and professional development of these team members. Prior to redesign, geologists would report to a geology department, chemical engineers would report to chemical engineering, mechanical engineers to mechanical engineering, and so forth. Business divisions would call on the appropriate technical specialists as needed when, for example, they were evaluating a new geography for drilling. Integrating the specialists into business groups increased the coordination of various activities, focused everyone on what the business needs were, and improved communication between people.

But it had some downsides too. Although the functional silos caused some problems, one of the things that structure did very well was allow the people in it to communicate best practices and to advance their technical competence. Although Esso was eager to get away from the functional focus, it was reluctant to lose the technical strengths these silos encouraged. Could it have both? The redesigners came up with a clever way to balance the demands. They called it "Centres of Excellence."

During the redesign, most technical specialists were decentralized into the business teams they supported (this is represented by the vertical rectangles in the diagram in Figure 24.2). This made the business teams truly cross-functional teams with all of the skills necessary to run the businesses resident on the team. In order to maintain technical expertise when their new bosses were not members of their disciplines, share best practices, and learn about new developments in their respective fields, however, the designers came up with a simple but powerful design idea. They created Centres of Excellence, represented by the horizontal rectangles in the diagram seen in Figure 24.2. There would be a Geological Centre, for example, which allowed the geologists spread throughout the various business teams to gather together regularly to focus on learning and skill development for their discipline. These four- to eight-hour meetings every other week or so were built into the normal work schedule. The members of each Centre team would elect one of their peers to coordinate their activities, and this individual would be given work time to help the Centre do three things: (1) communicate best practices, (2) develop technical skills, and (3) create technical standardization across the organization when warranted. This position was not to be a hierarchical one. No one reported to a Centre manager or received assignments or performance reviews from a Centre manager. Instead, the Centres were intended to exist exclusively for the skill development of the team members.

Summary

The Esso design illustrates an organizational structure that is increasingly common. We call this structure a *learning lattice* because when the skill development teams are overlayed on the business teams the graphic looks like a garden lattice. In this chapter we have also reviewed three methods for redesign: STS, the Conference Method, and the hybrid method. Looking at examples like the Santa Clara division of HP and the Chevron refinery in Mississippi, we can get some sense of the complexity and the power of these efforts. Typically used in organizations that are trying to restructure themselves without incurring the disadvantages of reengineering, these methods provide a more participative and democratic way to reorganize. Redesign may be the only way to resolve particularly tenacious problems that are outside the control of individual team leaders.

In the next chapter we will discuss knowledge teams and review some of the special challenges associated with teams that work more with their minds than with their hands and backs.

CHAPTER

25

Overcoming the Special Challenges of Leading Knowledge Workers

"It is becoming increasingly difficult to differentiate between knowledge work and manual labor. There is a blurring of management and non-management work, for example, as we redistribute power and responsibility from managers to the workers in our plants and mills. The model we are using drives us in the direction of having manufacturing employees do much more non-routine, non-linear, knowledge type work that used to be done by managers or staff

professionals. That will continue. It has to continue for us to be competitive."

Bob Wroblewski, *Director of Human Resources for Weyerhaeuser*

IN THIS CHAPTER we will consider the shift from an industrial to a knowledge society and review how that change affects the work of team leaders. In particular, we will look at the transformation of the workplace focus from physical to mental work, discuss knowledge work and its implications on contemporary teams, and suggest some tips for leading knowledge workers and managing knowledge systems. If you work with engineers, salespeople, office workers, doctors, scientists, teachers, nurses, managers, insurance agents, or others who use their brains more than their brawn, then you work with knowledge workers. But chances are that if you work in a factory, farm, or forest, you work with knowledge workers too.

Shifting from Physical to Mental Labor

Peter Drucker, a management consultant and former economist, coined the term *knowledge worker* several decades ago to distinguish people who work more with their minds from those who work more with their hands and backs. Drucker predicted that knowledge workers would outnumber physical laborers by the year 2000. He was right. Knowledge workers now outnumber physical laborers as the fundamental working class of modern societies. Take the United States as an example. In the U.S., technical workers (medical technologists, technicians, paralegals, etc.) and professionals (accountants, scientists, engineers, doctors, etc.) are the largest single segment of the workforce, with over 23 million people. If you include all knowledge workers, the statistics are even more amazing. By 1990, service workers accounted for 75 per-cent of all jobs. Although not all service work is knowledge work, most of it is, with some of the fastest-growing businesses in this category including consulting services. The U.S. Bureau of Labor Statistics pro-jects that industries providing services will account for about four out of five jobs by the year 2005. Some estimates for overall knowledge work growth run even higher. According to economists such as Nuala Beck, roughly 97 percent of all employment growth is now coming from knowledge work.

The Industrial Legacy

This is a far cry from our industrial heritage. The vast majority of jobs in industrialized societies involved physical rather than mental labor. Workers were called "hands" to distinguish them from the foremen and managers who served as factory "heads." Henry Ford felt that the workers at his plant didn't want to put forth much physical effort and that they certainly didn't want to have to think. Whether Ford's assess-ment about workers' desires to be relieved of any mental responsibili-ties was accurate or not, it was commonly believed by the industrial leaders of the day. And while the employers of that time period were normally unable to accommodate workers' wishes to minimize physical exertion, they did a number of things to create jobs where most of the thinking was left to others.

Different Work Requires Different Forms of Organization

Part of this work transformation from physical to mental labor that has occurred since the days of Henry Ford is simply due to a shift in the predominant types of modern corporations. Traditional smokestack industries like automobile, steel, mining, and chemical operations have been in decline for years, while organizations in brainpower fields like software development, Internet, business, technology design, and con-sulting have been on the rise. The products and services of these new companies require more knowledge and less physical work from the vast majority of their employees. And these kinds of companies con-tinue to grow rapidly. The famous Fortune 500 list, once reserved for industrial giants dominated by physical work, now includes companies like Microsoft, the prototypical knowledge work monolith. Darlings of Wall Street include rapidly growing Internet companies that sell software, books, and stocks and conduct electronic auctions. I hesitate to even name them because the current merger and acquisition mania is changing their company names every day.

But knowledge work is not confined to organizations outside the heavy industrial sectors. Inside GM and Ford, for example, there is a shift away from physical labor to high-tech computer design and installation. New cars are a symbiosis of computers, metal, plastic, and electronics—a far cry from the steel frames, nuts, and bolts of a decade ago. The new components require more knowledge to assemble and test than was necessary on the old assembly line. Robotics commonly replaces heavy physical chores like welding, assembly, and painting operations. There are fewer assembly line jobs per vehicle than ever before, and the nature of those remaining jobs has changed dramatically to include more maintenance, troubleshooting, analysis, and decision making and less heavy lifting. There are a number of other changes affecting operations that have traditionally utilized physical work that also deserve some elaboration.

Knowledge Work in Factories

Once the bastions of manual labor, many manufacturing operations are introducing new technologies and work systems that have fundamentally changed their organizations. No longer the assembly line operations of the past that employed workers' hands and backs without fully utilizing their minds, these organizations are using technologies that often require very sophisticated expertise. Mindless jobs that were the norm during the days of Henry Ford are disappearing, even though they lingered in major parts of most companies up until very recently. As mentioned in earlier chapters, contemporary companies in developed societies often can't afford to pay people to do nonthinking work. With the exception of a few industries that will likely retain manual work for a number of years (e.g., clothing and textiles, etc.), most manufacturing operations find that competitive advantage is only found when employees use more than their backs and hands. Thus the use of *laborer* as a synonym for *employee* is now obsolete.

As evidence of this shift, consider training requirements. In one Cummins Engine plant in Indiana, employees now receive a minimum of 292 hours of training to do the basic job. This includes 72 hours in math, 36 hours in statistics, and 56 hours in process and product technology. These types of training requirements are becoming increasingly common in many production jobs. For example, almost one-third of the workers in the Saskatoon Chemical plant in Saskatoon, Canada are college graduates. In spite of this relatively well-educated production workforce, the plant added a fifth work shift to facilitate coverage for the several additional weeks of technical and business training required for each employee annually. These activities teach employees how to use the increasingly complicated computer systems that are necessary to monitor their equipment. The training also covers business issues like financial, quality, economic, and interpersonal skills. This is an expensive investment that the company believes is justified because of the requirements for everyone to do more knowledge work.

Saskatoon is not alone. An Imperial Oil refinery has added a fifth shift as well. Moreover, when employees of a Rohm and Haas plant in Kentucky redesigned their workplace, they created a number of positions that were taken by several former supervisors and foremen. Rather than being responsible for directing the workforce, these managers now coordinate technical, safety, health, environmental, and interpersonal training.

The training requirement extends to what employers want before someone is hired. In one Intel wafer production factory in Hillsboro, Oregon, all new manufacturing hires must be college graduates just to have the baseline education necessary to be effective production workers. Current employees are expected to complete classes toward a degree as well.

Although there is still some physical work to be done, factory workers now spend the majority of their time doing knowledge work. What does this mean for the team leader?

Responsibilities for Knowledge Management

Rather than being responsible for supporting physical labor, virtually all team leaders are now responsible for leading knowledge workers. An essential piece of this assignment includes facilitating the development of knowledge management systems. Knowledge workers need knowledge to be successful.

What is a knowledge management system? A comprehensive series of technical and social processes for helping team members acquire, share, and apply knowledge. Elements of this system include many of the training and information-sharing ideas already discussed earlier in the book. But it is much more. How can team members benefit from the learning of other teams? If one group creates important knowledge about a particular customer, technology, project, or piece of equipment, do all other teams have to go through the painful process of relearning that same lesson, or can they benefit from what others already know? Although it is only one component of a knowledge management system, the knowledge transfer process deserves some special attention.

Knowledge Transfer

What used to be the sole responsibility of a few types of high-tech companies, universities, or technical departments is now the purview of virtually every team leader. We must all learn how to transfer knowledge from one person to another and from one part of the operation to another. The need for this work, of course, increases even more as team members become empowered as business partners. We have already mentioned a number of ways to do this. Team meetings facilitate the flow of information inside of a team. Governance councils and the learning lattice structure help share learnings across an organization. Good information systems are crucial. But we must often add technological and cultural changes to facilitate this transfer process as well.

Knowledge Management at Andersen Consulting

Technologies aid this knowledge transfer. Andersen Consulting, for example, has a proprietary database that requires 300 servers and more than 100 full-time knowledge managers and is the equivalent of 1.5 million pages of documentation. Development, administration, and maintenance costs for the system are in the neighborhood of 500 million U.S. dollars annually.

The database includes research and learnings from the firm's consulting activities. The 65,000 employees are expected to contribute to the Lotus Notes–based system to keep it current and are rewarded for doing so (you can't be promoted without being perceived as someone who shares his or her stuff by writing and posting white papers on the intranet). The database automatically tallies requests for certain information to identify the most useful reports. It is indexed both by industry tracks and by skill tracks to facilitate effective knowledge transfer.

This is an impressive knowledge management system. But, as with any technology aid, it is the behavior of people (whether they actually search, share, and use the data) that is crucial to the effectiveness of the knowledge transfer process. I believe technology is only a tool. The culture at Andersen supports and encourages sharing. Without the culture in place, the technology is only a waste of money.

Low-Tech Solutions

Low-tech solutions to the knowledge transfer process may be just as effective (and much less expensive). Teams that debrief mistakes and victories, share tips, do project postmortems, and problem solve together regularly create a culture that fosters knowledge transfer. Like so many other things we have discussed in this book, effective knowledge transfer requires a process that the teams will actually use.

Internal consultants at Hewlett-Packard, for example, have created an intranet where basic templates for presentations and best practices can be posted. If an employee wants to see what other divisions have done to use statistical tools for gathering data on process equipment downtime, to learn about how parts of the company apply something called a network organization design, or to view a sample new product/project development plan, he or she can access and use these and other materials. Periodic company conferences on certain topics are held that employees of any level can attend in order to get and give information face to face. Both the successes and the failures of organizational improvement efforts are openly shared in an attempt to transfer this hard-won knowledge to others who can benefit from it. Thus, the practical learnings of one part of the operation are shared directly with the people who use the information without having to go through the time-consuming process of using the chain of command.

Weyerhaeuser uses some similar processes in the area of high-performance work system knowledge transfer. Through the first part of the new millennium, the company offered courses on the practical steps required to create a high-performance work system with self-directed work teams. The classes were attended by change leadership teams composed of general managers, union executives, operations leaders, and human resource consultants from each of the interested units. Members of the teams listened to external experts, did benchmark visits to successful sites, and shared their own plans and learnings with each other in the three one-week sessions spread over a six-month period. Importantly, these sessions created a common vocabulary and a learning network, and shared a six-phase change process that people could use to structure their future discussions inside their operations and between sites. People from interested sites were later invited to attend conferences where team members from sawmills, pulp plants, staff groups, box shops, and other operations made presentations and answered questions on topics such as creating change plans, developing new pay systems, training managers in their new roles, and so on.

These types of learning communities can be used for any topic. Some companies get people together to share learning about new product development, technologies, markets, or competitive changes. Some organizations have even changed the architecture of their buildings to facilitate knowledge transfer. Sun Microsystems, for example, built what it calls "Sun rooms" into a new facility at Menlo Park, California, in order to encourage the informal exchange of ideas. Each Sun room has comfortable couches, a whiteboard, and meeting supplies to allow the design engineers who work there to share ideas and talk more comfortably. Only 35 percent of the interior space is office space, but there are 225 meeting places within the complex. The reason, says William Agnello (Sun's vice president of real estate and the workplace) is to create an environment where engineers will talk to each other informally.

Many organizations are finding these forums for knowledge transfer to be very important. For team members who work independently on their computers all day, for example, the temptation to avoid interaction with other human beings is common. Stories are told in high-tech companies about how engineers will write e-mail messages to someone in the next cubicle rather than stand up, walk over, and talk openly about ideas and concerns. In one case we know about, an employee actually received his performance appraisal over e-mail. It is difficult to do good coaching when you aren't even in the same room as the player. Although technology is essential to learning transfer, by itself it is never as effective as face-to-face interactive activities where people can debate, disagree, support, amend, and question.

Learning in Public

Knowledge work expert Richard McDermott has found that effective knowledge transfer is frequently inhibited by the reluctance of people to "learn in public." Knowledge workers have often been educated in such a way that discussing incomplete ideas, admitting and learning from mistakes, and figuring things out as a team have been discouraged. But without these kinds of knowledge transfer activities, organizations suffer. What can leaders do? Encourage regular activities to learn in public. Set an example by offering incomplete ideas or admitting personal mistakes. Create an atmosphere of trust, and encourage and recognize people who take the risk to learn in public.

Summary

Team leaders can do much to overcome the special challenges associated with leading knowledge workers. Activities that enhance learning in public aid the knowledge management process that is becoming so critical to organizational competitiveness. Social and technical systems that foster knowledge transfer can range from intranets to modifications in the architecture of buildings to establishing ongoing learning communities to encourage more interaction. Perhaps the key learning about knowledge transfer is that the cultural norms must support it. But one thing is certain; the information age has permanently shifted the core work of developed societies from physical labor to mental labor. Learning to help teams capitalize on their intellectual assets will be essential in every type of operation.

In the next chapter we will review a particular challenge associated with team leadership. How do you lead virtual teams where people may be geographically dispersed all over the globe?

Leading Virtual Teams: How to Work with Teams That Are Geographically Dispersed

"The company of the future could have 50 people working in 10 different countries who are linked through inexpensive TV screens that can automatically translate words and voices into different languages."

Jack Kahl, *chairman and CEO of Manco Inc.*

A REGIONAL SALES director for AT&T has team members located throughout the U.S. He is in Denver, Colorado, but he has team members living in Minneapolis, Las Vegas, Salt Lake City, San Francisco, and Los Angeles. Some have offices at client sites, some at AT&T office complexes, and some just work out of their homes and cars. As you might imagine, this virtual team has special challenges. The members don't share a common office, they seldom see each other, and they normally work on their own. How can they be an effective team?

Several sales environments, including other parts of AT&T, IBM, and Compaq, use virtual teams. Why do these operations use teams if they are more difficult to operate? One answer is cost. At Compaq, virtual sales teams have resulted in revenues doubling while the sales force dropped by one-third. IBM spends about $8000 per sales rep to equip the workers in the areas where it uses virtual teams with ThinkPads, software, two home phone lines, faxes, remote printers, pagers, and cell phones. The company's real estate costs in these operations have been reduced by 50 percent. But cost isn't the only reason we see so many virtual sales teams. Another motivation is improved customer satisfaction. Customers in these situations often feel that the sales representatives are now on the customer team rather than representing a vendor. This increases sales and loyalty.

Virtual teams are on the rise, and they are not limited to sales and marketing environments. Levi Strauss uses them to ensure that people from around the world participate in setting strategy. HP uses them for product development to ensure that the right technical experts are included regardless of location. Hundreds of organizations have found that these teams are necessary in a global economy. Although it is unlikely that virtual teams will become the dominant type of high-performance work team, they probably are the fastest-growing type of SDWT for reasons we will discuss later in the chapter. In this chapter we'll also review the challenges associated with leading these unique teams and suggest some tips for helping them become more effective.

Characteristics of Virtual Teams

Virtual teams have three characteristics that distinguish them from other teams we have discussed in earlier chapters. First, their members are distributed across multiple locations. Team members may be spread across different time zones, countries, and even companies. Second, they are often considerably more diverse than other teams, representing not only different technical specialties but different cultures, languages, and organizational allegiances. Third, these teams do not typically have constant membership. Team members may float off of or onto the team throughout its existence. Some may participate in all team activities, while others may only work on some. Although some virtual teams, like the sales teams we reviewed at the beginning of the chapter, are long-standing teams, many are short-term or part-time project teams. For all these reasons, virtual teams are often more difficult to lead than other types of teams.

Virtual Teams on the Rise

Virtual teams have become more common for a number of reasons. Companies like Hewlett-Packard, Intel, Boeing, IBM, Delphi, Weyerhaeuser, and others are using virtual teams for product development. These teams are composed of people from multiple sites, often including people from outside of the company who have special expertise in critical hard or soft technologies. This is true whether the product is a new computer, an extensive new training program, or a new corporate financial or information system.

Virtual teams are showing up in other situations as well. Hospitals in certain parts of the United States, for example, are concerned about the surfeit of hospital beds. For the first time they find themselves competing for customers to survive. Many have active marketing programs under way to make potential patients aware of their services, and they may create unique new niche services—such as maternity suites that look more like bed and breakfast hotels than the stereotypical white and chrome hospital rooms—to attract customers. New services like these, and the marketing programs to support them, create new challenges that often require virtual teams composed of administrators, medical personnel, accounting personnel, members of the community, and insurance people to complete the various aspects of the project. A simple internal task force may not suffice.

Levi Strauss decided that the best way to develop a marketing strategy for Asia was to use a virtual team with representatives from the U.S. and multiple Asian countries. The meetings were held in Singapore and were conducted in English. The bulk of the work was done between meetings and was shared in real time on the server network created for this team. Although the virtual team process was very difficult (someone always had to participate in teleconferences during the middle of the night, translations weren't always perfect, the server capacity turned out to be too small, the travel for the meetings was hard on everyone, etc.), Levi Strauss believed it was the only way to create a workable strategy everyone could buy into.

Common Challenges for Virtual Teams

To further complicate matters, consider another common challenge. If working on one virtual team is difficult, what do you do when you have to work on multiple virtual teams at the same time?

Multiplexing Problems

Design engineers with Delphi Delco Electronics, for example, formed a virtual company with engineers from Hughes to create an electric automobile. In addition to the mammoth technical hurdles these engineers have had to overcome to accomplish the purpose of their organization, however, they have also faced a number of other extremely challenging problems.

One of the challenges is the dilemma of how to work on a number of different project teams at the same time—something the Delphi engineers call *multiplexing*. There are only so many people to go around, and they must be spread across many critical virtual project teams to complete the various systems in the car. Engineers may serve on a half-dozen product development teams simultaneously and thereby have to manage the inevitable resource conflicts this causes. How many virtual teams can one worker be on without diffusing his or her effectiveness? Is it possible to form cohesive, focused virtual teams under these types of circumstances? The Delphi-Hughes Team has shown it is possible to overcome these challenges, but not without a lot of hard work.

Working with Home-Office–Based Team Members

There is a trend, in many technical organizations in particular, to have people work out of their homes. The Strategic Alignment Services (SAS) team of internal consultants at Hewlett-Packard also uses virtual teams. Special projects (i.e., to create learning diffusion processes throughout the company) rely on virtual teams composed of managers and organizational development consultants. But these workers find it difficult to get together because they have no shared meeting place. The consultants travel so frequently that they have little need for a shared office location—called *collocation* by many companies. Some have no HP office at all. But when the team must work together on a short-term project, the lack of collocation creates special communication challenges.

In one Weyerhaeuser virtual team, problems arose because one team member worked from her home, while the others worked at the office. The office team members felt that the work-at-home member wasn't pulling her fair share because they had the same workload on projects that she did, plus additional responsibilities associated with maintaining the office (phone coverage, dealing with walk-ins, more meetings to attend, etc.). The homeworker, on the other hand, felt like she was often left out of the communication loop since the office team members had more opportunities to talk to each other between teleconferences.

It is much easier to coordinate activities with other team members when you see them frequently. Savvy managers have known for years that some of the most important coordination and information sharing occurs informally in hallways, breakrooms, and parking lots. One possible answer to this challenge, of course, is to move everybody into a common location during the duration of the virtual team work if the project at hand has a beginning and an end. But this is often impossible because of multiplexing requirements, cost constraints, or numerous other reasons. And even if it were possible, it isn't always desirable.

Use Operating Guidelines

There are a few things that help virtual teams become more effective. The first tool is a charter that produces a common vision. As we discussed earlier, having a clear and common purpose is central to any kind of teamwork. But it is especially critical for virtual teams. The second tool is operating guidelines. Although we have already discussed operating guidelines earlier in the book, allow me to describe why they are so important for virtual teams.

Like the U.S. Constitution, operating guidelines provide a common base of shared values and some processes for team governance. In much the same way that the autonomic nervous system takes care of breathing and other critical functions "automatically," having agreed-upon guidelines means that there are certain things you can take for granted—agreements about working relationships that can be assumed. This frees up the team(s) to focus on more pressing technical and business matters.

We have used these techniques in our own company. Our travel keeps consultants out of the office most of the time. But having these governance systems in place provides a common touchstone that helps us to transcend our minimal face-to-face interaction. Our operating guidelines are revisited regularly and posted in our team room. We have guidelines regarding communication frequency (we will call in from the road every day to pick up messages and update the team on client projects) and interaction agreements (we will assume that team members have good intent, and we won't talk behind people's backs when we have a problem with them, etc.). These help us work together more effectively even when we aren't together.

Other teams who spend even more of their time in a virtual team environment than we do have used this technique as well. One such team included as part of its guidelines a communication preference protocol. Members found that some of their colleagues preferred e-mail communication, others voicemail, and still others faxes. They identified these preferences and agreed to use the methods most helpful to each team member between their face-to-face meetings.

Software developers at Lotus have used a similar idea to develop some agreed-upon methods for managing their team. For example, they refer to unproductive discussions as *ratholes*. The first person who recognizes the problem shouts, "Rathole!" It causes the team to correct its course. Members also try to avoid what they have come to call *piling on*—the practice of spending a lot of time agreeing with one another. Having the discipline to adhere to these guidelines saves hundreds of hours per year, claims Jeffrey Beir, vice president of Lotus Development Corporation.

Operating guidelines can make a huge difference for virtual teams that cross organizational and cultural boundaries. It is important to devote sufficient time to this discussion to reach a true commitment without compromising understanding or offending other team members. This may require considerable sensitivity and listening skills.

Many virtual teams use a third-party facilitator to help them with this process.

Use Goals

All teams require a common purpose to be successful, but specific, measurable goals do even more—especially for virtual teams. Goals provide a clear focus for day-to-day activities and a practical arbitrator for the inevitable conflicts, trade-offs, and resource compromises that go with teamwork. Good goals provide at least one additional important benefit—they are another substitute for hierarchy, assisting the team to become a self-directed work team. Virtual teams must answer questions such as:

- What do we need to do to be successful?
- What are our key goals?
- How will we measure our goals/track our progress?
- What do our customers need from us?
- What do our stakeholders need from us?
- What are our priorities?
- What will we do if we get off track?
- How will we link our goal and reward systems?

Let's explore some other more specific tips for solving some of the virtual team challenges introduced earlier in the chapter.

Virtual Collocation

Research shows that linking workers together through networks and other communication devices as though they were located in the same office is critical to effectiveness. That is why the sales teams find it so important to provide cell phones, computers, and fax machines to virtual team members. In addition to providing a communication link to customers, this technology allows team members to share ideas, solve problems, and make group decisions even when they aren't together face to face. A Xerox service team, for example, struggled with how to be effective as a team that could only meet physically on occasion—until all the members started using headset radios. These radios allowed team members to be in constant communication with each other. In addition to facilitating communication, it helped with troubleshooting and problem solving as well. Although it wasn't cost-effective to send multiple service technicians to a single client site to repair equipment, the headsets allowed team members to talk to each other in real time and benefit from the experience of each member of the team. This was especially useful since the simultaneous increase in both the complexity and the reliability of equipment made it virtually impossible for each technician to person-ally experience many of the major problems they were expected to repair. With the headsets, the technicians could ask each of the other technicians if he or she had encountered a tricky problem, almost as if all the team members were working on the machine together.

HP takes the collocation concept further to include a type of psy-chological collocation as well. Some teams have a meeting place even if they will only use it periodically. Even though they seldom meet together in person, this gives team members a shared location that pro-vides a common identity. The virtual office is less important for its physical presence than for its symbolic significance. It shows people that they are part of a certain important community even when they are not physically there.

Many teams have their virtual office locations established through technology. They have a common cyberspace locale like a server or a web page for e-mail messages and announcements. To make it more human, some virtual teams scan in their photographs on their e-mail locations. Others use team names, slogans, or symbols, like the famous Macintosh development team at Apple Computer that flew the skull and crossbones over its team location to reinforce the members' image of themselves as pirates operating on the edge of the corporation. While these symbols are helpful for any team, they are especially useful for virtual teams, which often struggle for a clear team identity.

Virtual Team Start-ups

Perhaps the most useful thing team leaders can do for virtual teams is to ensure that they meet face to face periodically. This is important for a number of reasons. Mark Bluemling, a vice president at SNET Mobil-ity Inc., a regional telecommunications company, suggests that work-ers—even those on virtual teams—have to get together once in a while to meet their own social needs. Even if the work doesn't require inter-action to pass along information or make team decisions face to face, members need the periodic reminder that they belong to a team.

This appears to be especially important at the start-up of a virtual team. The start-up meeting allows the virtual team to build the neces-sary foundation to be successful. HP and Levi Strauss have found that an effective face-to-face start-up can dramatically accelerate the effec-tiveness of the team. With this start-up, team members get to know each other, reach agreement on a common purpose and direction, develop guidelines on how they will work together, and put together a schedule for interactions. Many use this meeting to determine how they will communicate with others and solve problems. This early face-to-face start-up meeting provides an important personalizing touch for team members and serves to facilitate later online or non–real time communication.

Similarly, ongoing virtual teams benefit from these interventions to establish or revisit operating guidelines. Without these periodic face-to-face meetings, most virtual teams succumb to the overwhelming challenges associated with this type of team.

Summary

One of the most difficult types of teams to support is the virtual team. But team leaders can help virtual teams be more effective by doing a number of things. One of the most important is to ensure that the vir-tual team has a face-to-face start-up with all team members in atten-dance. This meeting allows the team members to get to know each other and to create the foundation for effectiveness by developing their charter, common goals, operating guidelines, accountability systems, and so forth. Comprehensive communication systems and virtual collo-cation also help to ensure the effectiveness of virtual teams. Virtual teams face a number of special challenges above and beyond those of regular teams. But team leaders will need to find ways to meet these challenges as the numbers of virtual teams continue to increase in mod-ern organizations.

In the final section of the book we will review a number of practical tools to aid team leaders in a variety of circumstances.

PART VII

Team Leader Evaluation Tools

The Team Leader Litmus Test: Do I Fit as a Team Leader?

Instructions

Choose the selection that best describes your own thoughts or behaviors on the following.

1. The primary role of the supervisor is to:
   - ☐ a. Get the work of the organization done through other people.
   - ☐ b. Meet agreed-upon goals and objectives.
   - ☐ c. Satisfy customers.
   - ☐ d. Make employees' work lives more enjoyable.
2. How would the employees you manage describe the primary role you have played over the last two work weeks?
   - ☐ a. Making employees' work lives more enjoyable.
   - ☐ b. Satisfying customers.
   - ☐ c. Getting the work done through other people.
   - ☐ d. Working to accomplish goals and objectives.
3. You have four phone calls that come in simultaneously. One can be taken while the others must remain on hold. Whose call do you take?
   - ☐ a. The president of your corporation.

    ☐ b. An irate customer.

    ☐ c. An employee you have been counseling.

    ☐ d. A city council member.

4. You find out that someone in the organization two levels below you has requested a meeting with you to discuss a problem in the organization. Do you:

    ☐ a. Recommend that he or she first resolve the issue with his or her own manager?

    ☐ b. Refer the request to the human resources people?

    ☐ c. Try to find the employee and talk to him or her?

5. The primary responsibilities of management are to:

    ☐ a. Develop, inspire, coach, teach.

    ☐ b. Plan, organize, direct, control.

    ☐ c. Motivate, regulate, discipline, reward.

    ☐ d. Solve problems, make decisions, go to meetings.

6. How would the employees you manage describe the way you have used your time over the last two work weeks?

    ☐ a. Planning, organizing, directing, controlling.

    ☐ b. Motivating, regulating, disciplining, rewarding.

    ☐ c. Developing, inspiring, coaching, teaching.

    ☐ d. Solving problems, making decisions, going to meetings.

7. Your boss comes into your area to tell you that you should stop working on a project that you and your group are very excited about. You disagree with the reasons. Do you:

    ☐ a. Tell members of the group that you are being pressured to shut down the project and you can't do anything about it?

    ☐ b. Confront your boss and disagree?

    ☐ c. Bring your boss into the group to discuss his/her concerns?

    ☐ d. Quietly shut down the project as requested?

8. A member of the group you manage has a promising improvement idea. Do you:

    ☐ a. Suggest that the member write a memo?

    ☐ b. Put it on an agenda for discussion with the rest of the group?

    ☐ c. Talk to the member and then present the idea personally to senior management?

    ☐ d. Help the member develop the idea and a justification for it more fully?

9. Members of your group complain that a corporate policy is inhibiting their ability to get their work done. Do you:
   - ☐ a. Ignore the policy and do what you feel is best for the group?
   - ☐ b. Do the work the best you can within a broad interpretation of the policy?
   - ☐ c. Work to change the policy?
   - ☐ d. Ensure compliance to the policy?

10. You are at a social gathering when the name of someone who reports to you comes up. Which of the following would you be most likely to say?
    - ☐ a. He or she works for me.
    - ☐ b. We work together.
    - ☐ c. He or she is in my organization.
    - ☐ d. I don't really know him or her very well.

11. When someone in the company asks you to describe your organization, how do you do it?
    - ☐ a. Talk about how your customers use your products or services.
    - ☐ b. Explain the tasks your group performs on a daily basis.
    - ☐ c. Draw an organization chart.
    - ☐ d. Describe your equipment/technology or work process.

12. Rank the following in order of importance to you from 1 (high) to 5 (low):
    - _____ a. Promotions (career growth and increased responsibilities).
    - _____ b. Meaningful work (doing the kind of work you find interesting and important).
    - _____ c. Accomplishment (making worthwhile things happen).
    - _____ d. Being liked (having the people you work with like you).
    - _____ e. Status (being more important than other people).

13. Which of the following best describes the way you usually think about subordinates when they have performance problems?
    - ☐ a. If I don't stay on them all the time they screw up.
    - ☐ b. They are well intentioned but not very capable.
    - ☐ c. They are lazy and need to be motivated.
    - ☐ d. They need better information, training, and tools.
    - ☐ e. They are devious and need to be controlled.

14. When a group of people are having difficulty coming to a decision at work, do you usually:

    ☐ a. Come to their rescue and make the decision for them?

    ☐ b. Express your opinion but avoid taking over?

    ☐ c. Observe and wait until it resolves itself?

    ☐ d. Help them come to a decision?

15. Which of the following best describes the way you are most comfortable working with your group?

    ☐ a. Staying out of the day-to-day operations until there are problems.

    ☐ b. Having all important decisions and information go through you.

    ☐ c. Allowing the group to do whatever it feels is best.

    ☐ d. Providing resources and support to the group.

16. What would the people who report to you say is the way you are most comfortable working with them?

    ☐ a. Providing resources and support to the group.

    ☐ b. Having all important decisions and information go through you.

    ☐ c. Staying out of the day-to-day operations until there are problems.

    ☐ d. Allowing the group to do whatever it feels is best.

To what extent do you agree with the following statements? (Circle a number from 1 to 5)

	Strongly Disagree 1	Disagree 2	Neutral 3	Agree 4	Strongly Agree 5
17. People want to do a good job.	1	2	3	4	5
18. Mistakes are caused by bad processes or information, not by employee errors.	1	2	3	4	5
19. I would rather satisfy the customer than satisfy my boss.	1	2	3	4	5
20. People can be trusted to do their best.	1	2	3	4	5

	Strongly Disagree 1	Disagree 2	Neutral 3	Agree 4	Strongly Agree 5
21. Managers need to be teachers, not directors.	1	2	3	4	5
22. I know what people think about my management style and skills.	1	2	3	4	5
23. I know when I am getting in the way.	1	2	3	4	5
24. Business results are more important to me than the status that comes with being the boss.	1	2	3	4	5
25. I like to see team members perform my responsibilities.	1	2	3	4	5
26. I get a real kick out of watching people grow and develop.	1	2	3	4	5
27. A primary job of management is to share information.	1	2	3	4	5

Scoring: Add your selections.

1. a. 1 point
   b. 2 points
   c. 3 points
   d. 0 points
2. a. 0 points
   b. 3 points
   c. 1 point
   d. 2 points
3. a. 1 point
   b. 3 points
   c. 1 point
   d. 2 points
4. a. 2 points
   b. 0 points
   c. 3 points
5. a. 3 points
   b. 1 point
   c. 0 points
   d. 2 points
6. a. 1 point
   b. 0 points
   c. 2 points
   d. 3 points
7. a. 0 points
   b. 2 points
   c. 3 points
   d. 1 point
8. a. 0 points
   b. 2 points
   c. 1 point
   d. 3 points

9. a. 1 point
   b. 2 points
   c. 3 points
   d. 0 points
10. a. 1 point
    b. 3 points
    c. 2 points
    d. 0 points
11. a. 3 points
    b. 1 point
    c. 0 points
    d. 2 points
12. 3 points for
    b,c,d,a,c or
    c,b,d,a,e (high
    to low)

    2 points for
    b,c,a,d,e or
    c,b,a,d,e (high
    to low)
    1 point for
    b,d,c,a,e,
    c,d,b,a,e,
    b,c,d,e,a, or
    c,b,d,e,a (high
    to low)
    0 points for
    others
13. a. 0 points
    b. 1 point
    c. 0 points
    d. 3 points

    e. 0 points
14. a. 1 point
    b. 2 points
    c. 1 point
    d. 3 points
15. a. 2 points
    b. 0 points
    c. 1 point
    d. 3 points
16. a. 3 points
    b. 0 points
    c. 2 points
    d. 1 point
17–27. Add the cir-
    cled numbers

Scoring Interpretation:

90–103	Good fit.
80–89	Minor change required.
70–79	Major change required.
60–69	Poor fit.
0–59	Consider opening a bait and tackle shop in the Alaskan wilderness.

CHAPTER

28

Assessing Team Leader Effectiveness Sampler*

Instructions: Think back over the last six months and determine how frequently you demonstrated the behaviors described in each statement. Place a check mark in the appropriate circle for each statement.

To what extent is this an accurate description of you as a team leader? (Check one box for each statement.)

	Never 1	Infrequently 2	Sometimes 3	Frequently 4	Always 5
Leader					
1. Is obsessed with a clear, future-oriented vision for the team.	☐	☐	☐	☐	☐
2. Creates commitment and energy in the team.	☐	☐	☐	☐	☐
3. Manages by sharing information/data, not by asking people to conform to unnecessary rules and regulations.	☐	☐	☐	☐	☐

	Never 1	Infrequently 2	Sometimes 3	Frequently 4	Always 5
Living Example					
4. Provides a personal example of the way people act in a team setting.	☐	☐	☐	☐	☐
5. Admits mistakes freely and openly.	☐	☐	☐	☐	☐
6. Has clear values about right and wrong.	☐	☐	☐	☐	☐
Coach					
7. Makes sure the team has the training needed to work effectively.	☐	☐	☐	☐	☐
8. Deals appropriately with poor performance.	☐	☐	☐	☐	☐
9. Develops the team so that it can manage the day-to-day operation without him or her.	☐	☐	☐	☐	☐
Business Analyzer					
10. Discusses specific data about product/ service performance with the team on a frequent basis.	☐	☐	☐	☐	☐
11. Helps the team decide how to be responsive to marketplace information.	☐	☐	☐	☐	☐
12. Acts like serving the customer is the most important priority.	☐	☐	☐	☐	☐

	Never 1	Infrequently 2	Sometimes 3	Frequently 4	Always 5
Barrier Buster					
13. Works actively to remove unnecessary policies, procedures, or work practices that hinder team performance.	☐	☐	☐	☐	☐
14. Helps the team understand the difference between real and perceived barriers.	☐	☐	☐	☐	☐
15. Recognizes when he/she is a barrier to the team and takes necessary improve-ment actions.	☐	☐	☐	☐	☐
Facilitator					
16. Works to procure necessary tools and equipment for the team.	☐	☐	☐	☐	☐
17. Helps the team solve problems.	☐	☐	☐	☐	☐
18. Encourages the sharing of stories and experiences among team members.	☐	☐	☐	☐	☐
Results Catalyst					
19. Focuses on results.	☐	☐	☐	☐	☐
20. Clearly states the limits (boundary conditions) within which the team can make decisions.	☐	☐	☐	☐	☐

	Never 1	Infrequently 2	Sometimes 3	Frequently 4	Always 5
21. Strives to manage by a set of guiding principles rather than by policy.	☐	☐	☐	☐	☐

Assessment interpretation

The most effective team leaders tend to have all responses in the 4 or 5 range as perceived by the work team members reporting to them.

The Team Leader Survival Guide

HIGH-PERFORMANCE WORK teams, also known by some as self-directed work teams (SDWTs), cannot be implemented successfully as another management or corporate program. This is not just an organizational structure; it is a fundamental culture change. Operations that treat it as anything less are doomed to fail.

Things to Remember

HPWTs are inevitable. We need to learn how to make them work. This means that supervisors and managers at every level of an organization need to change their roles. (Chapters 1 and 3)

All else being equal, teams outperform traditional operations. High-performance work teams are a response to a need for faster, more flexible, and more committed operations. The fact that most people like them better is a nice by-product, but it is not the reason businesses are using them. Bureaucracy and hierarchy don't work well in today's competitive world. (Chapters 1 through 4)

SDWTs apply all over the organization, not just to workers. Management teams should also be self-directed. (Chapter 1)

High-performance work teams are a journey, not a destination. They are not a thing to do; they are a way to do things. Team leaders who forget this have serious (sometimes terminal) problems. Don't get caught up in a means-ends inversion. Don't measure things like training time and numbers of teams; measure the true business results like quality, cost, and speed to determine the effectiveness of the teams. Don't focus on individual teams to the detriment of the whole organization either. These are common but avoidable mistakes. (Chapter 2)

SDWTs take their direction from the work to be done and not from the supervisor. A better name for these teams would be work-centered or high-performance work teams. (Chapter 2)

SDWTs need management even though their name doesn't sound like they do. They need a different kind of management. They need team leaders, not supervisors. They don't need planning, organizing, directing, and controlling. They do that themselves. They also don't need bosses, directors, or police. They do that themselves. They do need trainers, coaches, and leaders. (Chapter 5)

The role of team leader is a different way of thinking. It is a shift from thinking that the role of the leader is to control (the control paradigm) to thinking that this role is to elicit commitment (the commitment paradigm). The inability to make this shift is probably the single greatest reason for the failure of individual team leaders. (Chapter 9)

Certain values and assumptions can inhibit a person's ability to be a successful team leader. Assuming that people are lazy, or that their ideas are not as good as yours, for example, limits your ability to manage an SDWT. (Chapter 9)

Supervisors work in *the system, team leaders work* on *the system.* Team leaders are boundary managers with responsibilities for managing the impact of the business environment on the team. This includes many non-traditional responsibilities such as market analysis, technology forecasting, and working on community and government issues of importance. (Chapter 11)

Formal performance appraisals are a lousy coaching tool. Give ongoing feedback. (Chapter 12)

The team leader role changes with the maturity level of the team. As team maturity expands, team responsibilities increase. (Chapters 15 through 17)

Role changes require clarity of the new role, a personal need to change, organizational support, and self-awareness. Keep this in mind when working with either team members or other team leaders. (Chapters 20 and 21)

Managing upward requires influencing skills like vision, taking opportunities, and being tenacious. Try to "leverage serendipity" to meet your objectives. (Chapter 22)

Only individuals, not teams, can be accountable. It is a mistake to assume that a team as a whole can be accountable. (Chapter 23)

Sometimes the only way to make teams effective is to redesign the organization. Structures like reporting relationships, organizational groupings, team size, pay systems, and so forth can help or hinder teams. Most of these cannot be controlled by individual team leaders and require major organizational intervention for a lasting solution. (Chapter 24)

The workers should perform redesign functions themselves. Don't have managers or consultants dominate a redesign activity. (Chapter 24)

Most teams are becoming knowledge work teams. Leading knowledge workers requires good knowledge management processes to help people acquire, transfer, and apply knowledge. (Chapter 25)

Even virtual teams require periodic face-to-face meetings. Some things can't be done in cyberspace. (Chapter 26)

Things to Do

Give team members authority, resources, information, and accountability. Empowerment requires all four of these things. Anything less is a sham. (Chapter 2)

Make job assurances and avoid the wingwalker problem of telling people what not to do. The transition to SDWTs is tough on team members and team leaders alike. But it is most difficult on supervisors. Some don't make it. Organizations need to help reduce the anxiety. (Chapter 5)

Involve team leaders in designing their own jobs. Leaders, like other team members, should help design their own jobs. (Chapters 6 and 7)

Develop the capability of team members. Remember that blaming shuts down learning and development. (Chapter 7)

Focus on purpose, not problems. Help the team focus on accomplishing its purpose, not just on problem-solving activities. Focusing too much on problems can result in teams becoming bogged down in blaming or becoming depressed. (Chapter 7)

Act more like a shepherd than a sheep herder. Team leaders lead by example, not by driving the flock in front of them. Shepherds develop other shepherds, not passive sheep. (Chapter 10)

Manage by vision and values. This includes the ability to manage joint visioning processes, which align groups toward common goals. (Chapter 11)

Use substitutes for hierarchy. Team leaders don't rely on the power of position to get things done. They use information, education, and other substitutes. They create an infrastructure that substitutes for hierarchy. (Chapter 11)

Develop competencies in leadership, setting an example, coaching, business analysis, barrier busting, facilitating, and getting results. These competencies are key to leadership effectiveness. (Chapters 11 through 13)

Manage by principle, not by policy. This is a way to provide autonomy without bureaucratic restrictions. (Chapter 12)

Ask questions to develop team members. Don't just give answers. Socratic coaching helps you teach without lecturing. People remember their learnings better if they have to work through things themselves. (Chapter 12)

Walk the talk. People don't care what you say. They care what you do. (Chapter 12)

Keep the team riveted on meeting external customer needs. Too much focus on internal customers, or too much emphasis on day-to-day operational issues, makes team members spend too much energy on activity that adds little value. (Chapter 13)

Plan for a lot of training time. Teams typically need from 15 to 20 percent of their time for ongoing training in business, technical, and interpersonal skills. Only a portion of this is classroom training. Most of it is used for meetings, cross-training, and real-time problem-solving activities. This training must be reinforced in the workplace to be useful. (Chapter 13)

Actively eliminate restrictive policies and procedures. If you aren't changing some big things, you won't get big improvement. (Chapter 13)

Institutionalize effective processes for gathering and communicating information. Without facts and data, high-performance work teams are dead in the water. Good decision making and problem solving requires good information. People also need regular forums to discuss the information. (Chapter 13)

Don't be a marshmallow manager. Team leaders share accountability with the teams, but they do not abdicate their responsibility. They are still responsible for good results. (Chapter 14)

Set boundary conditions. Boundaries allow autonomy while providing needed clarity and direction. (Chapter 14)

Put good accountability systems in place. Accountability should be pushed down to the individual level so that each team member clearly understands both task and result accountabilities. (Chapter 23)

Put knowledge management systems in place. But remember that creating a culture for knowledge transfer is more important than the technology to support it. (Chapter 25)

Use face-to-face start-ups for virtual teams. There are some things, even in geographically dispersed teams, that require personal interaction. (Chapter 26)

Summary

Remember: "If you think you are already there you haven't started. But if you think you have a long way to go, you are already on the way." (This is a quote from a team leader who understands this messy and uncomfortable change process.)

Endnotes

Introduction

xxxi Mercer Management Consulting Report, April 1, 1996. Data from 179 large companies.

xxxii "Is conscientiousness always positively related to job performance?" Robert P. Tett, The Society for Industrial and Organizational Psychology, as posted on www.siop.org/tip/back issues/TIPjuly98/TETT.HTM.

Chapter 1

1. "The teams at Goodyear . . . ," "Is Mr. Nice Guy Back?" John Greenwald, *Time*, January 27, 1992, p. 43.

4. . . . the second industrial revolution . . . , "The Second Industrial Revolution," R. L. Ackoff, unpublished white paper, date unknown; "The Evolution of Socio-technical Systems: A Conceptual Framework and an Action Research Program," Eric Trist, Issues in the Quality of Working Life, a series of occasional papers No. 2, *Ontario Ministry of Labour and Ontario Quality of Working Life Centre*, June 1981, p. 24.

4. "The idea of liberation . . . ," *New Traditions in Business*, John Renesch (ed.), Sterling and Stone, 1991, p. 42.

Chapter 2

11. "The great revolution . . . ," "On Leadership," Arthur Schlesinger, in *Abraham Lincoln*, Roger Burns, Broomall, PA, Chelsea House, 1986, p. 9. Used by permission.

12. "There are too many . . . ," John Stepp, speech presented at the Ecology of Work Conference sponsored by the Organization Development Network and National Training Laboratories, Washington, DC, June 24–26, 1987.

14. "We found that if . . . ," "Sharpening Minds for a Competitive Edge," John Hoerr, *Business Week*, December 17, 1990, p. 78. Used by permission.

14. "Everybody that works here . . . ," Ibid., p. 72. Used by permission.

15. Blacksburg turned . . . , Ibid., p. 72. Used by permission.

15. "It's no longer . . . ," Ibid., p. 78. Used by permission.

18. "At P&G . . . ," Charles Eberle, "Competitiveness, commitment and leadership," speech delivered at the Ecology of Work Conference sponsored by the Organization Development Network and National Training Laboratories, Washington, DC, June 24–26, 1987.

20. In the 1950s . . . , Eric Trist, "The Relations of Social and Technical Systems in Coal Mining," paper presented to the British Psychological Society, Industrial Section, 1950.

Chapter 3

25. "No matter what . . . ," "Who Needs a Boss?" Brian Dumaine, *Fortune*, May 7, 1990, p. 52. © 1990 The Time Inc. Magazine Company. All rights reserved. Used by permission.

26. Ninety-three percent . . . , "Designing Organizations that Work: An Open Sociotechnical Systems Perspective," John Cotter, La Jolla, CA, John J. Cotter and Associates, Inc., 1983.

26. . . . the single highest "lever" . . . , Mercer Management Consulting Report, April 1, 1996.

27. " . . . 30–40 percent more productive . . . ," "Management Discovers the Human Side of Automation," John Hoerr and Michael Pollock, *Business Week*, September 29, 1986, p. 74. Used by permission.

27. "This is the most cost-effective . . . ," Ibid., p. 74. Used by permission.

28. Federal Express claims . . . , "Who Needs a Boss?" Used by permission.

28. It was retained when . . . , As reported on *Morning Edition*, a news report program on National Public Radio, May 15, 1995.

28. Customer service and . . . , *The Distributed Mind: Achieving High Performance Through the Collective Intelligence of Knowledge Work Teams*, Kimball Fisher and Mareen Duncan Fisher, New York, AMACOM, 1998, pp. 60–63.

29. After less than one year . . . , Ibid., pp. 73–75.

29. "As a result . . . ," "Multi-skilled teams replace old work systems," K. Denton, *HRMagazine*, vol. 37, September 1992, p. 49.

29. Software giant Bill Gates . . . , "Bill Gates' New Rules," Bill Gates, *Time*, March 22, 1999, pp. 72–82.

29. Amdahl credits teams . . . , *The Distributed Mind*, pp. 106–108.

29. "The senior people . . . ," Ibid., pp. 125–128.

29. A Welch's team . . . , Ibid., pp. 219–221.

30. At the Mayo Clinic . . . , Ibid., pp. 45–46.

30. " . . . dramatic improvement in safety . . . ," Executive presentations to company representatives in "Course for Champions and Change Agents," 1997.

30. At Microsoft . . . , *The Distributed Mind*, pp. 46–48.

30. In steel industry . . . , "Effects of Human Resource Management Practices on Productivity," Casey Ichniowski, Kathryn Shaw, and Giovanna Prennushi, mimeograph, Columbia University, June 10, 1993.

30. In the automobile industry . . . , "Integrating Technology and Human Resources for High Performance Manufacturing," J. MacDuffie and J.

Krafcik, in *Transforming Organizations*, T. Kochan and M. Useem (eds.), New York, Oxford University Press, 1992.

33. Among 700 firms . . . , "Human Resource Management Practices and Firm Performance," M. Huselid, mimeograph, IMLR, Rutgers University, 1992.

33. In the Forbes 500 . . . , *The Human Resources Revolution*, D. Kravetz, San Francisco, Jossey-Bass, 1988.

33. Among 6000 work groups . . . , *Corporate Culture and Effectiveness*, D. Denison, New York, John Wiley & Sons, 1990.

34. . . . 70 percent of . . . , "Getting to Work," L. Bassi, mimeograph, Georgetown University, February 1993.

34. . . . 60 percent reported . . . , *Employee Involvement and Total Quality Management*, E. Lawler et al., San Francisco, Jossey-Bass, 1992.

34. A long-term review . . . , "Organizational Change, Design, and Work Innovation: A Meta-analysis of 131 North American Field Studies— 1961–1991," B. Macy and H. Izumi, in *Research in Organizational Change and Development*, R. Woodman and W. Pasmore (eds.), Greenwich, CT, JAI Press, 1992.

34. ". . . existing evidence suggests . . . ," "High Performance Work Practices and Firm Performance," U.S. Department of Labor, 1993, p. ii.

34. . . . within a year . . . , "The Impact of Human Resource Management Practices on Turnover, Productivity, and Corporate Financial Performance," M. Huselid, *Academy of Management Journal*, July 1995.

34. A study of 179 . . . , Mercer Management Consulting Report, April 1, 1996.

35. The financial improvement index . . . , "Benchmarking the Best Practices: Results from 102 North American High Performance Organizations," B. Macy, preliminary report published June 1998. The full report of this research is forthcoming in *Successful Strategic Change*, B. Macy, San Francisco, Berrett-Koehler.

35. . . . a strong positive correlation between . . . , *Strategies for High Performance Organizations: Employee Involvement, TQM, and Reengineering Programs in Fortune 1000 Corporations*, E. Lawler III with S. Mohrmann and G. Ledford Jr., San Francisco, Jossey-Bass, 1998.

35. A *Business Week* cover story . . . , "The Payoff from Teamwork," John Hoerr and Wendy Zellner, *Business Week*, July 10, 1989. Used by permission. Noted in the table Example of SDWT Results.

35. . . . a report in *Fortune* . . . , "Who Needs a Boss?" Used by permission.

35. In a study done in 1988 . . . , "High Involvement Organization Study," R. Wright and G. Ledford, the Center for Effective Organizations, Graduate School of Business Administration, University of Southern California, Los Angeles, November 1988.

35. In a related . . . , "Self-Directed Teams: A Study of Current Practice," Richard Wellins et al., *Industry Week*, the Association of Quality and Participation, and Development Dimensions International Study, 1990.

36. ". . . become habit-forming . . . ," "Management Discovers the Human Side of Automation," p. 72. Used by permission.

Chapter 4

39. "It can be argued . . . ," "Twilight of the First Line Supervisor?" Peter Drucker, *The Wall Street Journal*, June 7, 1983.
40. "Our prevailing system . . . ," Edwards Deming, quoted by Peter Senge in a presentation at the Association of Quality and Participation annual conference in Seattle Washington, April 7, 1992.
48. In a front-page story . . . , "Boeing's Switch Toward Japanese-style Work Teams: 777 Is Focal Point of Move to Put System into Effect Company-Wide," Byron Acohido, *Seattle Times*, Sunday, April 7, 1991.
48. " . . . a linchpin tool . . . ," Ibid., p. A8.
49. Other human technologies . . . , *Productive Workplaces: Organizing and Managing for Dignity, Meaning, and Community*, Marvin Weisbord, San Francisco, Jossey-Bass, 1987.
52. . . . advances in information technology . . . , *Teams and Technology: Fulfilling the Promise of the New Organization*, Donald Mankin et al., Cambridge, MA, Harvard Business School Press, 1996.
54. "We hold these truths . . . ," adapted from the Declaration of Independence, Thomas Jefferson, 1776.

Chapter 5

57. "Working through the corporation . . . ," "The Painful Reeducation of a Company Man," *Business Month*, October 1989, p. 78. © 1989 Goldhirsh Group Inc., 38 Commercial Wharf, Boston MA 02110. Reprinted with permission of *Business Month* magazine.
58. "Self-managed work teams are not . . . ," "Self-Managed Work Teams," Alan Cheney, *Executive Excellence*, February 1991, p. 12.
59. "For me it was . . . ," *The Leadership Role*, Belgard·Fisher·Rayner, Inc., videotape, © 1991. All rights reserved.
60. Prominent researchers . . . , "Dilemmas of Managing Participation," Rosabeth Moss Kanter, *Organizational Dynamics*, Summer 1982, pp. 5–26.
60. "Why Supervisors Resist . . . ," "Why Supervisors Resist Employee Involvement," Janice Klein, *Harvard Business Review*, September-October 1984."
60. "Work Restructuring and . . . ," "Work Restructuring and the Supervisor: Some Role Difficulties," Richard Walton and Leonard Schlesinger, *Report to the Harvard Business School*, March 1978.
60. "Do Supervisors Thrive . . . ," "Do Supervisors Thrive in Participative Work Systems?" Richard Walton and Leonard Schlesinger, *Organizational Dynamics*, Winter 1979.
61. At Honeywell . . . , "Wrestling with Jellyfish," R. J. Boyle, *Harvard Business Review*, January-February 1984, pp. 74–83.
61. Based on research . . . , the sobering graph on management transition difficulty is based on the writing of Janice Klein, especially "Good Supervisors Are Good Supervisors—Anywhere," *Harvard Business Review*, November-December 1986 (with Pamela Posey), and "Why Supervisors Resist

Employee Involvement," along with the observations and research of William Westley, "Quality of Working Life: The Role of the Supervisor," in *Employment Relations and Conditions of Work*, Labour Canada, 1981; Richard Walton and Leonard Schlesinger, "Work Restructuring and the Supervisor: Some Role Difficulties," and "Do Supervisors Thrive in Participative Work Systems?"; and K. Fisher, "Management Roles in the Implementation of Participative Management Systems."

63. "I miss the prestige . . . ," "From Manager into Coach," Beverly Geber, *Training*, February 1992, p. 28.

Chapter 6

73. "The signal benefit . . . ," "On Leadership," Arthur Schlesinger, in *Abraham Lincoln*, pp. 9–10. Used by permission.

Chapter 7

81. "The worst thing . . . ," "Who Needs a Boss?" Used by permission.

Chapter 8

91. "The most difficult thing . . . ," Bob Condella, from a presentation to the Corning Information Systems Group, Corning, NY, January 14, 1992.

92. "I would say a lot more clearly . . . ," Peter Vaill, personal correspondence, 1986.

94. "We had to get over . . . ," "The Bureaucracy Busters," Brian Dumaine, *Fortune*, June 17, 1991, p. 34. © 1991 Time Inc. Magazine Company. All rights reserved. Used by permission.

Chapter 9

97. "In warfare . . . ," *More Like Us: Making America Great Again*, James Fallow, Boston, Houghton Mifflin, 1989, p. 13. Used by permission.

98. "The regulars . . . ," *The Great War and Modern Memory*, Paul Fussell, New York, Oxford University Press, 1975, p. 13. Used by permission.

99. "For as he thinketh . . . ," Proverbs 23:7.

99. ". . . the drastic changes we made . . . ," "Managing without Managers," Ricardo Semler, *Harvard Business Review*, September-October 1989, p. 77. Italics added.

100. "Employee involvement . . . ," Ibid., p. 79.

103. . . . a similar argument . . . , *Managing in the New Team Environment*, Larry Hirschhorn, Reading, MA, Addison-Wesley O.D. Series, 1991.

105. Our paradigms are . . . , *The Structure of Scientific Revolutions*, Thomas S. Kuhn, Chicago, University of Chicago Press, 1970.

105. . . . calls this phenomenon . . . , *Discovering the Future: The Business of Para-digms*, Joel Barker, Burnsville, MN, Charthouse, videocassette, © 1990.
106. . . . identifies the primary difference . . . , "From Control to Commitment in the Workplace," Richard Walton, *Harvard Business Review*, March-April 1985.
110. "We tried to remove . . . ," "Is Mr. Nice Guy Back?" John Greenwald, *Time*, January 27, 1992, p. 43.

Chapter 10

118. . . . shepherds actually create. . . . See "Superleadership: Beyond the Myth of Heroic Leadership," Charles Manz and Henry Sims, *Organizational Dynamics*, Spring 1991, p. 18, for more information on this important topic of developing team members into leaders.
119. "[I] believe that many . . . ," Janice Klein, personal correspondence, 1987.
119. Klein's research with . . . , "Excellence in First Line Supervision," Pamela Posey, Harvard Business School doctoral dissertation, 1985; "Good Super-visors Are Good Supervisors—Anywhere."

Chapter 11

122. The ability to create . . . , "Traditional versus New Work System Supervi-sion: Is There a Difference?" Pamela Posey and Janice Klein, in *Revitalizing Manufacturing: Text and Cases*, Janice Klein, Homewood, IL, Irwin, 1990.
124. Social scientists call . . . , *Designing Organizations for High Performance*, David Hanna, Reading, MA, Addison-Wesley O.D. Series, 1988. Dave does a nice job of explaining open systems theory in this book. The original con-cept is usually attributed to Ludwig von Bertalanffy ("The Theory of Open Systems in Physics and Biology," *Science*, 111, 1950, pp. 23–28).
127. Rejects dropped . . . , "How I Learned to Let My Workers Lead," Ralph Stayer, *Harvard Business Review*, November-December 1990.
129. "I provided feedback . . . ," "The First-Line Manager in Innovating Organi-zation," William Snyder, unpublished paper, University of Southern Cali-fornia, pp. 16–17. Used by permission of the author.
130. ". . . a timely information system . . . ," Ibid., p. 39.
131. . . .calls them . . . , "Substitutes for Hierarchy," Edward Lawler, *Organiza-tional Dynamics*, Summer 1988.
131. . . . describes this new role . . . , "The New Managerial Work," Rosabeth Moss Kanter, *Harvard Business Review*, November-December 1989.

Chapter 12

137. "The greatest people . . . ," *In Search of Excellence*, J. Natham and S. Tyler, film based on the book by Thomas Peters and Robert Waterman, New York, Warner, 1984.

138. . . . this unique bag of skills . . . , "The Leadership Challenge—A Call for the Transformational Leader," Noel Tichy and David Ulrich, *Sloan Management Review*, Fall 1984, pp. 59–68.
145. . . . when R. J. Boyle of Honeywell . . . , "Designing the Energetic Organization: How a Honeywell Unit Stimulated Change and Innovation," R. J. Boyle, *Management Review*, August 1983, pp. 20–25.
148. Motorola spends . . . , "Motorola's Workers Go Back to School," Barbara Jean Gray, *Human Resource Executive*, November-December 1988, p. 33.
148. But plants that . . . , Ibid., p. 75.

Chapter 13

154. "I am a firm believer . . . ," Abraham Lincoln, in *Abraham Lincoln*, Roger Burns, Broomall, PA, Chelsea House, 1986, p. 51.
157. "You can't get people . . . ," "The Bureaucracy Busters," p. 2. © 1991 Time Inc. Magazine Company. All rights reserved. Used by permission.
162. Alexander the Great . . . , *The Life of Greece*, Will Durant, New York, Simon & Schuster, 1939, p. 541.
162. On one occasion . . . , Ibid., 550.

Chapter 15

173. "When we were . . . ," from a personal interview with the late Ross Silberstein, former plant manager of the Sherwin-Williams facility in Richmond.
176. ". . . calls incompleteness . . . ," "The Principles of Sociotechnical Design," Albert Cherns, *Human Relations*, vol. 37, no. 8, 1977, pp. 783–792.
179. The concern of a senior . . . , "Wrestling with Jellyfish," pp. 74–83.

Chapter 16

183. "The decisions take longer . . . ," "The Painful Reeducation of a Company Man," p. 78. © 1989 Goldhirsh Group Inc., 38 Commercial Wharf, Boston MA 02110. Reprinted with permission of *Business Month* magazine.

Chapter 17

193. "Forget structures . . . ," "The Bureaucracy Busters," p. 26. © 1991 Time Inc. Magazine Company. All rights reserved. Used by permission.

Chapter 18

201."You cannot do . . . ," "The Bureaucracy Busters," p. 34. © 1991 Time Inc. Magazine Company. All rights reserved. Used by permission.

Chapter 19

215. "To win, we need . . . ," "The Bureaucracy Busters," p. 34. © 1991 Time Inc. Magazine Company. All rights reserved. Used by permission.

Chapter 20

227. "The economy is . . . ," *Managing by the Numbers: Absentee Owners and the Decline of American Industry*, Christopher Meek, Warner Woodworth, and W. Gibb Dyer Jr., Reading, MA, Addison-Wesley, 1988, p. 283.
230. Consider the following . . . , This model and the team member descriptions are used with the permission of The Fisher Group, Inc. © 1989–1999 The Fisher Group, Inc. and BFR, Inc. All rights reserved.
233. Gene Dalton's review . . . , "Influence and Organizational Change," Gene Dalton, in *Organizational Change and Development*, Gene Dalton, Paul Lawrence, and Larry Greiner (eds.), Homewood, IL, Richard D. Irwin, Inc. and Dorsey Press, 1970.

Chapter 21

241. "When I started . . . ," "Who Needs a Boss?" p. 60. © 1990 The Time Inc. Magazine Company. All rights reserved. Used by permission.
241. "One of the questions . . . ," John Homan, personal correspondence.
241. "We had a lot of . . . ," Pat D'Angelo, *Ecology of Work*, presentation about Nabisco change efforts, June 1991.
241. . . . make a number of suggestions . . . , "New Roles for Managers, Part 1: Employee Involvement and the Supervisor's Job," a Work in America Institute National Policy Study, 1989. Directed by Jerome M. Rosow and Robert Zager. Case studies edited by Jill Casner-Lotto.
245. One-on-one discussions . . . , "Influence and Organizational Change."
246. . . . a useful management typology . . . , "Helping Supervisors to Change: The Missing Link," Janice Klein and Bill Belgard, unpublished discussion paper commissioned for *New Roles for Managers: The Manager as Trainer, Coach, and Leader,* issued by the Work in America Institute, June 1989.
248. At least one expert's . . . , Dr. Pam Posey's ongoing research at the University of Vermont confirms that performance appraisals and other management reward systems must support the new requirements for team leaders if these behaviors are to continue over time.

Chapter 22

253. "We're creating a hierarchy . . . ," "The Bureaucracy Busters," p. 30. © 1991 Time Inc. Magazine Company. All rights reserved. Used by permission.
256. Most of their time . . . , "What Effective General Managers Really Do," John Kotter, *Harvard Business Review*, vol. 60, no. 6, 1982, pp. 156–167.

Chapter 23

265. "No leader can . . . ," "Make Yourself a Leader," insert in *Fast Company*, June 1999.

Chapter 25

285. "It is becoming . . . ," Bob Wroblewski, personal correspondence, 1997. This quote also appears in *The Distributed Mind*, pp. 34–35.

286. . . . coined the term . . . , *Post-Capitalist Society*, Peter Drucker, New York, HarperCollins, 1993, p. 5. © 1993 Peter F. Drucker.

286. In the U.S. . . . , "How We Will Work in the Year 2000," Walter Kiechel III, *Fortune*, vol. 127, no. 10, May 17, 1993, p. 44. © 1993 *Fortune* magazine.

287. By 1900 . . . , "Working in Public; Learning-In-Action: Designing Collaborative Knowledge Work Teams," Richard McDermott, in *Advances in Interdisciplinary Studies of Work Teams. Knowledge Work in Teams* (vol. 2), Michael M. Beyerlein, Douglas A. Johnson, and Susan T. Beyerlein (eds.), Greenwich, CT, JAI, 1995, p. 36.

287. The U.S. Bureau of Labor Statistics . . . , *Occupational Outlook Handbook*, 1992–93 ed., U.S. Department of Labor, Bureau of Labor Statistics, Bulletin 2400, May 1992.

287. According to economists . . . , "Managing in an Information Highway Age," Nuala Beck, *Business Quarterly*, vol. 58, no. 73, Spring 1994.

287. Henry Ford felt . . . , *My Life and Work*, Henry Ford, Garden City, NY, Doubleday, Page and Co., 1926, p. 103.

292. The reason . . . , "The Idea Is to Talk," Michael A. Verespej, *Industry Week*, vol. 245, no. 8, April 15, 1996, p. 28.

293. . . . transfer is frequently inhibited . . . , "Working in Public; Learning-In-Action."

Chapter 26

295. "The company of the future . . . ," "A Workforce Revolution?" Michael A. Verespej, *Industry Week*, August 21, 1996, p. 21.

296. At Compaq . . . , "The Rise of the Knowledge Entrepreneur," William E. Halal, *The Futurist*, November-December 1996, p. 15.

296. The company's real estate costs . . . , "Welcome to the New Workspace," Michael A. Verespej, *Industry Week*, vol. 245, no. 8, April 15, 1996, p. 27.

300. Having the discipline . . . , "Managing Creatives: Our Creative Workers Will Excel—If We Let Them," Jeffrey Beir, *Vital Speeches of the Day*, vol. LXI, no. 16, June 1, 1995, p. 505.

301. Research shows that linking . . . , "Organizing for Concurrent Engineering," Robert Mills, Beverly Beckert, Lisa Kempfer, Barbara Schmitz, and Michelle Dibble, *Industry Week*, July 20, 1993, p. CC8.

Index

Accountability, 267–272
  result, 270
  task, 268
Adamoli, John, 163
A.E. Staley, 241
Aetna, 28, 158
Aid Association for Lutherans, 15,
  33
Air Products and Chemical Polymers,
  50
Alexander the Great, 162
Allaire, Paul, 157, 201, 215
Allied Signal, 243
Amdahl, 29
American Cyanamid, 244
American Transtech, 22, 28, 32, 129
Andersen Consulting, 155, 290
AOL, 139
Apple Computer, 32, 45, 139
ARIA (authority, resources, informa-
  tion, accountability) formula,
  16
AT&T, 22, 29, 52, 295, 296
  Credit Corp., 31
Autocrats Anonymous, 249
Axelrod, Dick, 279
Axelrod, Emily, 279

Barker, Joel, 105
Barrier Busters, 134, 152–153
Beir, Jeffery, 300
Belgard, Bill, 246

Bestfoods, 32
Bikson, Tora, 52
Bilodeau, Jimmy, 45
Bluemling, Mark, 302
Boeing:
  777 design team, 28, 44, 48
Boundary conditions, 169–171,
  223
Boundary managers, 123–134
Boyle, R. J., 61, 145
Bruss, Lois, 277
Bruss-Fisher redesign process, 278
Burger, Joe, 251
Burger King, 159
Business Analyzers, 134, 153–159

Case for change, 234
Center for Effective Organizations,
  34, 35
Centres of Excellence, 282
Champion Paper, 22
Change influencers versus change
  drivers, 255
Change model:
  clarity, 228, 229–233, 243–245
  felt need, 229, 233–235, 245–247
  self-awareness, 229, 238–239,
    250–252
  support, 229, 235–238, 247–250
Cherns, Albert, 176
Chevron, 49, 238, 275
Clark, Tom, 67

Coaches, 135, 159–161
Cognitive dissonance, 262, 263
Cohen, Susan, 52
Collocation, 299
  virtual, 301
Commitment paradigm, 106–107
Compaq, 296
Competencies of team leaders, 134
  Barrier Buster, 134, 152–153
  Business Analyzer, 134, 153–159
  Coach, 135, 159–161
  Facilitator, 134, 146–149
  Leader, 134, 138–144
  Living Example, 135, 161–163
  Results Catalyst, 134, 144–146
Condella, Bob, 40, 91
Control language, 108
Control paradigm, 106–107
Corning, 14, 140, 154, 245, 254
  Administrative Center, 28
  Blackburg, VA, plant, 14–15
  Oneonta, NY, plant, 44
Cotter, John, 26
Cummins Engine, 50, 255, 271, 289
  early adopter of teams, 21, 25
  Jamestown, NY, plant, 21, 31
Customer advocacy, 157
  misuse of, 158
Cypress Semiconductor, 52

Dade County, FL, schools, 22
Dalton, Gene, 233, 234, 236
Delphi Delco Electronics, 298
Deming, Edwards, 40
Digital Equipment Corporation, 237, 254
  closure of team operations, 27
Dillingham, Bruce, 255
Discretionary effort, 15
Donovan, Mike, 271
Drucker, Peter, 39, 40, 286
Duke Power, 63
Dyer, W. Gibb Jr., 227

Eberle, Charles, 19
Eintracht, Fred, 58
Emery, Fred, 277, 279

Emery, Merrilyn, 279
Empowerment:
  definition of, 15
  introduction to, 3
  schedules for, 249
Esso Resources, 250, 282
Evaluation tools, 305–321
  Assessing Team Leader Effectiveness, 313–316
  Team Leader Litmus Test, 307–312
  Team Leader Survival Guide, 317–321

Facilitators, 134, 146–149
Federal Express, 28, 31, 51
Fisher, Mareen, 279
Fisher Group, The, 134
Ford, Henry, 20, 287
Ford Motor Co., 32, 288

Galbraith, Jay, 270
Gandhi, Mohandas K., 140
Garrity, Norman, 14
Gates, Bill, 29, 52, 139, 156
Gault, Stanley, 3
General Electric, 4, 148, 249, 255
  Salisbury, MD, plant, 31
General Foods, 254
  early adoption of teams, 21, 25
  Topeka, KS, plant, 21
General Mills, 32
General Motors, 27, 288
Gilmartin, Raymond, 193, 253
Goodyear, 3

Hanna, Dave, 103
Hanson, Fred, 234
Hendrickson, Gene, 167
Hewlett-Packard, 14, 50, 281, 291, 296, 303
  Santa Clara, CA, plant, 32, 275
  Strategic Alignment Services (SAS), 298
High-performance work systems, 3, 25
  better term than *self-directed work teams*, 19
Hirschhorn, Larry, 103

Homan, John, 241
Honeywell, 32, 61
Houghton, Jamie, 254

IBM, 52, 296
Imperial Oil, 289
Implementation stages, 183–198
Information overload, 50
Intel, 249, 289
Invisible and visible elements of team
    leader role, 93–95
Iowa Public Service, 46

Jefferson, Thomas, 54
Jobs, Steve, 137, 139
Johnsonville Foods, 28, 127, 254
Junkins, Jerry, 25

Kahl, Jack, 295
Kanter, Rosabeth Moss, 60, 131
Ketchum, Lyman, 255
King, Doug, 15
King, Martin Luther Jr., 140
Klein, Janice, 60, 119, 122, 123, 246
Knowledge management, 154–155,
    290
Knowledge workers, 286
Kodak 13 Room, 69, 73–88, 147, 161,
    244, 251
Kotter, John, 256
Kuhn, Thomas, 105

Lawler, Edward, 34, 131
Leaders, 134, 138–144
Learning in public, 293
Learning lattice organizations,
    280–283
Leonard, Stew, 157
Leveraging serendipity, 256
Levi Strauss, 296, 297, 303
Lincoln, Abraham, 154
Living examples, 135, 161–163
Lockheed Martin, 45
Lotus, 300

Macy, Barry, 34
Majure, Miles, 63

Managing by principle, 144
Mankin, Donald, 52
Marsten, Ted, 27
Mayo Clinic, 22, 30
McDermott, Richard, 293
McGregor, Douglas, 101
McNulty, Dennis, 278
Meek, Christopher, 227
Meeting topics, 219
Mercer management study, 26, 34
Merlotti, Frank, 110
Microsoft, 14, 30, 49, 139
Middle schools, 22
Miller, Steve, 265
Monsanto, 39, 46, 235
Motorola, 49, 148
Multiplexing, 298
Myers, John, 36
Myth of the marshmallow manager,
    167–169

Nabisco, 241
NASA, 49
NBA, 161
NBTel, 29
NEC, 50
Netscape, 139
New York City Sanitation Depart-
    ment, 152
Nicholson, Rick, 60
Northern Telecom, 32, 51

Olney, Ralph, 74, 76, 77, 82–88, 251
Open systems theory, 124
Operating guidelines, 146, 299

Pasmore, Bill, 279
Peer feedback, 238
People's Express Airlines, 27
Pioneer Hi-bred, 140
Port of Seattle, 32, 281
Posey, Pam, 119, 122, 123
Procter & Gamble, 31, 153, 160, 243,
    245, 248–249, 254, 262
    Chicago plant, 39
    closure of team operations, 27
    early adoption of teams, 21, 25

Procter & Gamble (*Cont.*):
Lima, OH, plant, 5, 18, 67, 145, 177, 195, 219
results with teams, 19

Quality of work life, 152

Ranney, Joyce, 277
Rayner, Steve, 74
Redesign methods:
conference, 278
hybrid, 276, 279
participative design, 279
socio-technical system (STS) approach, 276
Reengineering, 13, 276
Results catalyst, 134, 144–146
Rittenhouse, Phil, 140
Rodgers, T.J., 52
Rohm and Haas, 31, 67, 289
Rosow, Jerome, 242
R.R. Donnelley & Sons, 47
Runge, Larry, 121
Rutgers university study, 34

San Diego Zoo, 22
Saskatoon Chemical, 289
Saturn, 27
Schlesinger, Len, 60
School-based management, 22
Scientific management, 20
strengths and weaknesses, 20
Search conferences, 49
Seattle Metro, 22, 47
Second industrial revolution, 4
Self-directed work teams:
definition, 17
differences from traditional organizations, 18
implementing, 176–182
introduction to, 3
management teams, 83
maturity of, 174–175
problems with term, 19
Semco S/A, 99, 254
Semiautonomous work teams, 21
Semler, Ricardo, 99–100, 254

Sheep herding vs. shepherding management, 117–119
Shell, 217, 218
Shenandoah Life Insurance, 22, 28, 31
Sherwin-Williams, 31
Sherwood, Jack, 16
Silberstein, Ross, 173
Situational leadership, 92
Skill vs. will, 224
Smith, Roger, 58, 61, 183
Snyder, Bill, 129
Social loafing, 266
Socio-technical systems (STS):
description, 21
history, 20
origin of self-directed work team concept, 20
Socratic coaching, 160
Star point system, 270
Stayer, Ralph, 99, 127, 241, 254
Steelcase, 110
Stepp, John, 12
Substitutes for hierarchy, 51, 131, 218
Sun Microsystems, 292
Supervisors, 7–9
network, 243, 249
Swanson, David, 27

Tavistock coal mine, 31
Tavistock Institute, 23, 277
Taylor, Frederick, 20
Team leaders:
culture, 9
different than supervisors, 8
litmus test for, 307–312
management, 9
operations, 8
role of, 134
Team member roles, 231
Technician systems, 21
Tektronix, 31, 43, 148, 153, 158, 168, 234
Tennessee Eastman, 67
Texas Instruments, 25, 45
Theory X, 101–102

Theory Y, 101–102
Tichy, Noel, 138
Toyota, 29
Training, 86, 134, 148
  amount required, 148
  simulations, 230
Trist, Eric, 20, 23, 277
Turner, Ernie, 197

Ulrich, Dave, 138
U.S. Department of Labor study,
  30

Vaill, Peter, 47, 92
Virtual teams, 295–303
Vision:
  nested, 141
  shared, 141
Volpe, Terri, 59
Volvo, 32

Walton, Richard, 60, 106
Watson, James, 81
Weekly activity guide, 215–224
Welch, John (Jack), 4
Welch's, 29
Wessel, Jim, 94
Westinghouse, 31
Weyerhaeuser, 15, 30, 45, 245, 263,
  291, 299
Whitesides, Paul, 59
Wiggenhorn, William, 148
Wingwalker problem, 65, 82
Woodworth, Warner, 227
Work in America, 242
Wroblewski, Bob, 286

Xerox, 32, 157, 301

Zager, Robert, 242
Zelleck, Stan, 44

About the Author

KIMBALL FISHER IS a cofounder of the Fisher Group, Inc. (www.thefishergroup.com), and has worked with many companies implementing high-performance management practices across North America, Western Europe, Asia, and Africa. These include Amoco, Apple Computer, Chevron, Corning, Hewlett-Packard, Monsanto, Motorola, NBC, Shell, Weyerhaeuser, and more. Fisher is a popular speaker at conferences on teams, leadership, and organization design and has addressed audiences all over the world.